D1301798

STERLING
Its Meaning in World Finance

SOME PUBLICATIONS OF THE

COUNCIL ON FOREIGN RELATIONS

FOREIGN AFFAIRS (quarterly), edited by Hamilton Fish Armstrong.

THE UNITED STATES IN WORLD AFFAIRS (annual). Volumes for 1931, 1932, and 1933, by Walter Lippmann and William O. Scroggs; for 1934-1935, 1936, 1937, 1938, 1939 and 1940, by Whitney H. Shepardson and William O. Scroggs; for 1945-1947, 1947-1948 and 1948-1949, by John C. Campbell; for 1949, 1950, 1951, 1952, and 1953, by Richard P. Stebbins.

DOCUMENTS ON AMERICAN FOREIGN RELATIONS (annual). Volume for 1952 edited by Clarence W. Baier and Richard P. Stebbins; for 1953, and 1954, edited by Peter V. Curl.

POLITICAL HANDBOOK OF THE WORLD (annual), edited by Walter H. Mallory.

RUSSIA AND AMERICA: Dangers and Prospects, by Henry L. Roberts.

FOREIGN AFFAIRS BIBLIOGRAPHY, 1942-1952, by Henry L. Roberts.

AMERICAN AGENCIES INTERESTED IN INTERNATIONAL AFFAIRS, compiled by Ruth Savord and Donald Wasson.

JAPANESE AND AMERICANS: A Century of Cultural Relations, by Robert S. Schwantes.

THE FUTURE OF UNDERDEVELOPED COUNTRIES: Political Implications of Economic Development, by Eugene Staley.

THE UNDECLARED WAR, 1940-1941, by William L. Langer and S. Everett Gleason.

THE CHALLENGE TO ISOLATION, 1937-1940, by William L. Langer and S. Everett Gleason.

MIDDLE EAST DILEMMAS: The Background of United States Policy, by J. C. Hurewitz.

BRITAIN AND THE UNITED STATES: Problems in Cooperation, a joint report prepared by Henry L. Roberts and Paul A. Wilson.

TRADE AND PAYMENTS IN WESTERN EUROPE: A Study in Economic Cooperation, 1947-1951, by William Diebold, Jr.

THE ECONOMICS OF FREEDOM: The Progress and Future of Aid to Europe, by Howard S. Ellis.

WAR AND THE MINDS OF MEN, by Frederick S. Dunn.

PUBLIC OPINION AND FOREIGN POLICY, by Lester Markel and Others.

THE PRICE OF POWER, by Hanson W. Baldwin.

OUR FARM PROGRAM AND FOREIGN TRADE, by C. Addison Hickman.

THE FOREIGN AFFAIRS READER, edited by Hamilton Fish Armstrong.

THE STUDY OF INTERNATIONAL RELATIONS IN AMERICAN COLLEGES AND UNIVERSITIES, by Grayson Kirk.

THE PROBLEM OF GERMANY, by Hoyt Price and Carl E. Schorske.

FOREIGN AFFAIRS BIBLIOGRAPHY, 1932-1942, by Robert Gale Woolbert.

THE UNITED STATES IN A MULTI-NATIONAL ECONOMY, by Jacob Viner and Others.

THE FAR EASTERN CRISIS, by Henry L. Stimson.

THE STRUGGLE FOR AIRWAYS IN LATIN AMERICA, by William A. M. Burden.

LIMITS OF LAND SETTLEMENT, prepared under the direction of Isaiah Bowman.

SURVEY OF AMERICAN FOREIGN RELATIONS (in four volumes, 1928-1931), prepared under the direction of Charles P. Howland.

DOLLARS IN LATIN AMERICA, by Willy Feuerlein and Elizabeth Hannan.

NEW DIRECTIONS IN OUR TRADE POLICY, by William Diebold, Jr.

INTERNATIONAL AIR TRANSPORT AND NATIONAL POLICY, by Oliver J. Lissitzyn.

STERLING
ITS MEANING IN WORLD FINANCE

By Judd Polk

Published for the
COUNCIL ON FOREIGN RELATIONS
by
HARPER & BROTHERS
New York

1956

The Council on Foreign Relations is a non-profit institution devoted to study of the international aspects of American political, economic and strategic problems. It takes no stand, expressed or implied, on American policy.

The authors of books published under the auspices of the Council are responsible for their statements of fact and expressions of opinion. The Council is responsible only for determining that they should be presented to the public.

STERLING: ITS MEANING IN WORLD FINANCE

For information address Council on Foreign Relations, 58 East 68th Street, New York 21

FIRST EDITION

American Book-Stratford Press, Inc., New York

Library of Congress catalog card number: LC 55-8030

There is scarce truth enough alive to make societies secure; but security enough to make fellowships accurst. Much upon this riddle runs the wisdom of the world. This news is old enough, yet it is every day's news.

MEASURE FOR MEASURE

FOREWORD

THIS study grew out of a suggestion by Lord Salter to Mr. Russell Leffingwell and me that it would be highly desirable to have an American examination of the sterling area. When Mr. Leffingwell presented Lord Salter's proposal to the Council, the first question raised in the discussion of it by the Committee on Studies, and also by the Rockefeller Foundation when a request was made for a grant to finance the study, was whether the literature on the area was not already so extensive as to raise a serious question whether a fresh major contribution could be made. At the time, the study by the Bank for International Settlements was in preparation, but it was felt that this study had much more of a financial, central banking approach than a Council study would have. For the rest, it was felt that most sterling area studies had been written from within, by the British and other residents of the area. Though there is also a fairly extensive Western European literature on the subject, this, too, is written largely from the standpoint of the relation of the European countries to the area. In this country, though our writing on international trade and finance in the postwar period has made numerous references to the sterling area, the major work on the subject is the ECA report by John Cassels and others of the staff of our London mission, published in 1952. This report, however, as an official document, does not pretend to be critical or analytical, but statistical and descriptive—and, as such, it has proved abundantly worthwhile and a mine of information for others.

The Committee on Studies came to the conclusion that Lord Salter's suggestion had much merit, and provided the opportunity for a book, written from the outside, which would attempt to analyze the sterling area in the light of the world economy. The Council was particularly receptive to this idea because it had repeatedly encountered sterling area problems in its other work, such as the study of Anglo-American relations carried on jointly with Chatham House (*Britain and the United States,* by Henry L. Roberts and Paul A. Wilson); Howard Ellis's work on the Marshall Plan (*The Economics of Freedom*); William Diebold's study on European cooperation, especially in connection with the European Payments Union (*Trade and Payments in Western Europe*); and Eugene Staley's study on economic development (*The Future of Underdeveloped Countries*).

In the present volume, Mr. Polk has been primarily interested in trends rather than in the often bewildering short-term fluctuations which might divert attention from the longer-run factors. For this reason, less attention is given to the events of 1954 and 1955 than to the postwar period seen as a whole, though the immediate past is by no means neglected. In setting the sterling area in a larger framework, Mr. Polk has tried to deal with the broad political and social problems of economic development within the area, to discuss the relation of the sterling area to the Commonwealth, and to analyze the significance in the functioning of the sterling area of Britain's traditional role as the center country, and the problems arising out of the growing economic importance and the increased political autonomy of the outer sterling area countries. He has also discussed the problems connected with the forthcoming independence of the British colonies.

The present book makes no pretense to being encyclopedic, or to being the definitive work, or even to superseding much of the excellent work that has gone before it. It is, inevitably, an interpretation, given shape by Mr. Polk's conclusions which are based on his analysis and his experience. Some are bound to disagree with his interpretation; but even they, I think, will find the study useful, in that he has given them the essential facts from which they could make an alternative interpretation. While not debating them at length, he takes note of interpretations contradictory to his own. No doubt everyone will wish that this or that subject had been discussed at greater length, but I think one of the virtues of the book is its brevity. On so complex and so controversial a subject, it is much harder to write a short book, which nevertheless conveys an impression of the writer's grasp, than a long one. Perhaps the key to the book is given by a remark made at the beginning of our study group meetings: "When you have a financial mechanism, the important thing is to know not only what it does but why you have it."

The meetings of the study group took place between October and May, 1953-54. The procedure was for Mr. Polk to prepare a memorandum for each meeting which was circulated to the members of the group in advance. This proved an excellent means of keeping the discussion on the track and helping it progress. While Mr. Polk took account of suggestions and criticisms, it was understood from the beginning that it was to be his study, and not that of the group. Indeed, I think it should be emphasized that there was a diversity of views on various aspects of the general problem. But this seems to me inevitable, and the purpose of the meetings will have been served if the author feels, as I am sure he does, that he benefited by the discussions. I have never had much use for group studies based on a few roundtable discussions, at which the actual writer pretends to be merely the rapporteur for the group. Such a book, to be of any value, would have to reproduce the discussions verbatim; and even then would be a very different kind of study.

The members of the study group were:

John H. Williams, *Chairman*
Emilio G. Collado, *Deputy Chairman*

Arthur M. Anderson
James W. Angell
John Cassels
Imrie de Vegh
William Diebold, Jr.
Albert E. Ernst
Wytze Gorter
Walter J. Levy
Franklin A. Lindsay
Thomas H. McKittrick
August Maffry
Raymond F. Mikesell
Ben T. Moore
Gardner Patterson
Lowell M. Pumphrey
Winfield W. Riefler
Robert V. Roosa
Thomas Schelling
Frank A. Southard, Jr.
Allan Sproul
George H. Willis
Neal Dow Becker
Robert Triffin

Sir Dennis Robertson and Lionel Robbins attended the last meeting of the group.

The Council feels very fortunate in having secured the services of Judd Polk for this book. Before coming to the Council to make this study, he had a long acquaintance with the problems of the sterling area. He had been, in his earlier career, a Rockefeller Research Fellow at the Council, a member of the Research Department of the Federal Reserve Bank of New York, and for eight years an official of the Treasury Department. In that capacity he served in Cairo and Brussels and then returned to Washington as Chief of the British Commonwealth and Middle East Division. Following the meetings of the study group, Mr. Polk made a trip around the world in the summer of 1954, visiting most of the sterling area countries.

That the sterling area is of great importance for the world economy we can all agree. The relationship between the dollar and the pound is one of the major, continuing economic issues of concern to the free world. But the real significance of the sterling area, for its member countries as well as for the rest of the world, is hard to determine in any fashion that will evoke general assent. The evidence is complex and its real import is often obscure or ambiguous. When the Council first undertook this study, one of our memoranda called attention to some of these problems. "Looked at from the outside," it said, "the sterling area is a 'closed' economic system, resting on trade and exchange controls that limit transactions with the rest of the world and discriminate against countries that are not members. From the inside, the sterling area appears as an 'open' economic system within which trade and payments are subject to fewer controls than most international exchanges. . . . To some American observers, the sterling area has appeared to impede progress toward a larger world trading system; to others it has seemed a helpful step on the way. Some Americans urge support for the sterling area because it is a source of strength to Britain; others see it as a shelter that hinders Britain from adapting its economy to the requirements of its new position in the world." Mr. Polk would be the last one to claim that his book settles these issues once and for all, or even that objective analysis of the evidence is capable of producing clear solutions to the policy problems involved. But I think there can be no doubt that his book deepens our understanding of sterling area relationships and gives us a fuller appreciation of what is involved in formulating policy toward this unique and complex economic system.

JOHN H. WILLIAMS

PREFACE

A STUDY of sterling problems from an American point of view should help dispel a few of the parochial shadows in a crucial and controversial area of the Western world's relations. That was part of the thought of the Council on Foreign Relations in undertaking the study which has resulted in this book. The Rockefeller Foundation generously financed the entire project. Their grant made it possible to discuss sterling problems in periodic meetings at the Council with informed people professionally interested in sterling problems. It also made it possible to discuss these problems with government officials, businessmen and students throughout much of the far-flung sterling world.

The nature of the Council's sponsorship has been active, not nominal. Here I feel the dilemma of trying to express as best I can the thanks due to the Council's staff and to the study group who met with me at the Council, without implicating them in the shortcomings of the work. Perhaps the best way out of this dilemma is to describe briefly the Council's procedure in this project. After careful discussion with George Franklin, Percy Bidwell, and William Diebold, Jr., of the Council staff, a group of twenty-five men with special knowledge, experience, and interest in the broad range of sterling problems were invited to meet periodically at the Council. John H. Williams, of Harvard University and the Federal Reserve Bank of New York, agreed to serve as chairman, and Emilio G. Collado, of the Standard Oil Company (N. J.), as deputy chairman of the group. In four meetings, each lasting four or five hours, we exchanged views on key aspects of sterling's place in world finance. At the last of our meetings, two distinguished British economists, Sir Dennis Robertson and Professor Lionel Robbins joined us.

Beyond the helpfulness of the discussions, the members of the group gave freely of their time in extracurricular meetings with me and in commenting on parts of the text. I am grateful to the group for a helpful and stimulating association. I owe special thanks to John Williams for the guidance I have derived not only from the meetings but also from his writings.

The topics discussed in our meetings were for the most part ones with an established reputation of controversy, and the views expressed had many shades of difference. This book is in no sense a catalog of these views. Had the members of the group the time and the occasion to set out their own views fully, their essays would differ greatly from mine. Had I not had the benefit of learning their views, mine would have differed greatly from what it is.

Walter J. Sedwitz and Verna D. Hink were my full-time assistants throughout much of the project. They know the thanks I owe them and can record only cryptically here.

The Council's excellent staff was helpful in innumerable ways. In particular I owe thanks to Percy Bidwell for his help in setting the project in motion and for his advice in the course of it. I am happy to join the long list of people who have benefited from the generous help of Ruth Savord and her library staff. Marguerite Hatcher and Alice Yoakum spent many hours in getting the manuscript in shape for the printer, and I am very grateful to them.

I would like to record warm thanks to John Williams, Emilio Collado, Percy Bidwell, Gardner Patterson, and Leroy Stinebower for their sympathetic reading of the final draft. I hope they will feel that the changes resulting from their efforts justify the time they gave to the task.

In early stages of the work, Professor Jacob Viner was generous in giving ill-spared time to suggestions and guidance.

Most of all, I owe thanks to William Diebold. He gave constructive help at every stage of the project. He offered definitive and workable suggestions in the initial planning stages and in the subsequent study stages. He gave many weeks to the editing of the final manuscript, always managing to make criticism a matter of encouragement.

I must acknowledge—though perhaps it goes without saying—my debt to other students of sterling and their works. This debt I have tried to indicate specifically in occasional footnotes and more fully in the bibliography. It is a large debt, and has grown rapidly in the last few years as the literature on sterling has grown. I hope this book is not an unhappy garbling of this excellent body of literature. Or, as my favorite author said:

> —With rough and all unable pen
> Our bending author has pursued the story,
> In little room confining mighty men,
> Mangling by starts the full course of their glory.

This study ran over a period of two years. In the course of it I had the stimulating and humbling experience of travelling some 40,000 miles in visits to sterling countries all over the world. In short visits in twenty-five cities I discussed sterling problems both with government officials and with private citizens. The visits included London and several European capitals, Britain's dependencies and near-independencies in Africa, the Federation of Malaya, and a number of the independent members of the sterling area—the Union of South Africa, Pakistan, India, Ceylon, and Australia. The visits were regrettably brief, and I became aware on occasion of a politely concealed concern on the part of my hosts that their courtesies would merely give birth to another whirlwind-tour expert. Those of them who are able to read this work will feel, I hope, that they managed to take some of the edge off my inexpertness. Everywhere I went I received hospitalities and help that would require a separate volume to record. I hope I have been able to express my gratitude in personal messages. I was struck in a heartening way by the frankness and even enthusiasm with which everyone met the inquiries of an outsider into the running of the sterling household. However restricted the financial lines of communication may get to be from time to time between the sterling and dollar worlds, there are no effective barriers to human communication and friendliness.

In any writing on problems touching British-American relations, a reader is likely to wonder whether the author is *pro* or *anti* the other country. Both Britons and Americans have learned to recognize a strange complexity and often a stranger acerbity in their relations. All speak the same language, though with elusive differences in meaning. They practice a democratic form of government, but differently. They have an avowed close identity of aims, nationally and internationally, yet Britons and Americans often appear arrayed along opposite sides of their line of agreement. Even to refer to the difficulties in sterling-dollar relations as *sterling* problems has a vindictive overtone for students who would prefer to describe the same difficulties as *dollar* problems, as indeed they might be.

But this is a book about sterling written by an outsider, so "sterling problems" it must be. I have tried as best I could to resist an outsider's bias, other than the bias of sympathy that comes in the course of long-sustained interest in Britain and the Commonwealth. The sterling world is not just another country, but an association of peoples almost as varied in their colors and races and institutions as the world itself. The effort here to look into how and why they handle their financial problems as they do has been made with the richness of this association in mind.

J.P.

CONTENTS

Chapter 1

ABOUT THIS BOOK AND ITS THEME

Indeed, it is a strange-disposed time:
But men may construe things after their fashion,
Clean from the purpose of the things themselves.

JULIUS CAESAR

THE STORY of sterling is a complex one and could be told in many ways. It could be told as the story of a small silver coin a thousand years ago, and how the coin was gradually transformed into the broadest system of international credit ever developed in the world. It could be told as the story of deep and recurring international financial crises which have frequently ruined banks, bankrupted businesses and frightened nations. It could be told as the story of high financial argument between nations or between factions in a nation over the nature of steps which national governments should take to stabilize their currencies and promote general prosperity. It could be told as the story of "high finance" and political maneuver as Britain has vied with other nations to gain advantage in the development of the world's economic resources. It could be told as the story of the costs of modern warfare. And doubtless in many other ways.

The telling of the story could have various designs—an essay in monetary theory, a statistical treatise, a history of political economy, a record of international negotiations and treaties, a catalog of commercial rules, a psychological investigation, or even a tale of adventure or mystery. The style could be polemic, satiric, epic, narrative, laudatory, obitual, prescient, wistful.

It is difficult to decide which aspects of the story should be selected for treatment in the small compass of a book, or which manner of telling would best suit the aspects selected.

Here the choice was strongly affected by the conclusions reached in the course of the study that preceded the book. As the conclusions are mixed, so is the method of exposition. These first pages describe the way subsequent chapters deal with sterling problems and set forth briefly the general nature of the conclusions reached. Three chapters follow that trace the history of sterling and the development of the present system as it grew out of the controls of the second world war. After that there are separate chapters devoted to the roles played by Britain as the center of the system, by the politically independent countries which are members of the sterling area, and by the dependent territories for which Britain is responsible. The last two chapters attempt to deal with the key problems of finance as seen both within the sterling system and outside of it, and to assess their significance for the sterling countries, for the United States, and for the financing of world trade in general.

It is important particularly to the United States to achieve as good an understanding as possible of the reasons, or lack of reasons, underlying the financial policies of the sterling world. The international stability of sterling is accepted by all but a few Americans as an essential supporting girder in the whole superstructure of international finance. Next to the dollar, the pound is the currency with which postwar American policy has been most concerned. Britain, as the center of the sterling world, has received more postwar dollar aid than any other country or monetary area. When serious financial problems have confronted Britain, as they have on several occasions since the war, they have become the subject of urgent discussion at the highest levels between Britain and the United States and sometimes Canada.

A sound and strong international status for sterling is a continuing concern of the many United States businesses which sell products and services in the sterling area, and must reach with their sterling customers some sort of understanding about how far sterling rather than dollars should be accepted in payment and how far the subsequent restrictions on their use of these sterling receipts should go. For firms with large volumes of business in the sterling world, this problem of reestablishing a satisfactory relationship between sterling and dollars has persisted throughout the post-war period. It is a major preoccupation of, to mention a few, the oil industry, the motion picture industry, international airlines, automobile exporters, drug houses, dealers in electrical equipment, and makers of soft drinks.

Opinions about the meaning of sterling in world finance are many. This is not surprising. Sterling, though the national money of a country less than a third the size of the United States in population and much less than that in production, is used as widely internationally as it is in the United Kingdom. Britons claim that half of the international exchange of goods and services of about $100 billion a year is financed in sterling. Sterling is the exclusive basis for the issue of currency in some countries and is their only, or, at least, main international reserve. In many other countries it is one of the major props of local currency issues and of the government's international credit rating. There is no part of the world of international trade to which sterling is not important in one way or another. It is of interest to importers, exporters, domestic producers, national treasuries, international policy makers, international organizations, and, of course, to students of world finance.

Any view of sterling is conditioned by the nature of the interest involved. The resulting differences are inevitably great and all people who have followed sterling problems in our own times know the amount of controversy which this variety of views has generated. More than any other issue, the "sterling problem" brings together and sets at odds all who are interested in international finance. The structure of the elephantine sterling system will appear differently to the observer of one facet than to the observer of another, just as the blind men, one by one, found the elephant's trunk made him a snake, or his side a wall, or his tusk a spear.

And so these men of Indostan
Disputed loud and long,
Each in his own opinion
Exceeding stiff and strong,
Though each was partly in the right,
And all were in the wrong.

One possible approach to the sterling elephant would be to examine the fences that enclose his movements. This is the aspect of sterling that international traders must be concerned with in their daily commerce. Exactly what are the rules and regulations that determine how sterling may be used? Can they be gotten around? Should they be abided by? These questions will be treated here only in a general way. To deal with them in adequate detail would involve a very lengthy and specialized treatise which would soon be obsolete because of continued changing of the rules. Moreover, it is doubtful that the resulting picture of sterling would come close to the characteristics that make sterling loom so large in present world financial problems.

An almost opposite approach would be to deal with the theory by which a financial association such as the sterling area might be regarded as economically advantageous or disadvantageous. Does the association improve its members' gains in trade with one another and with the rest of the world? Does it yield to the world as a whole a dividend in the form of gains from more highly specialized production? Or is it a barrier to the best use of the world's resources? The intellectual problems raised in the course of trying to answer these questions are formidable. Many of them have been dealt with definitively in Jacob Viner's book, *The Customs Union Issue*. Even more formidable are the difficulties of an effort to marshal the limited statistics now available in such a way as to yield a persuasive answer to the questions which the theory poses.

If this book cannot *answer* the questions which concern, in turn, the businessman, the banker, the trader, the theoretician, and the man of politics, it can at least bring together some of the information which bears on why the sterling area has become both a practical and an intellectual problem for these different kinds of men. The sterling area includes a wide assortment of people, and a very large number of people, four times as numerous as the people of the United States, more varied in race, religion and customs. In trying to deal with the whole area we have to face the complexity of its make-up, and in making the picture it has been necessary frequently to sacrifice the sharpness of a narrow focus for the sake of the breadth of wide-angle vision. It cannot be assumed that the behavior of this broad association of human beings is exclusively or even primarily economic, and our concern with the question whether their behavior results in the most productive use of their material resources is relevant to only one aspect of their association. The way in which this variegated association uses its material resources takes up many of the pages of this book. But the analysis of the financial and—more broadly—the economic activities of the area illustrates only a part of their reason for hanging together. The broadest problem, and the one motivating this American study of the sterling area, is whether the continued existence of the sterling area is on balance good or bad for the members, for the United States, and for the world in general.

Broadly, the argument of this book is that the sterling association, taken in relation to the Commonwealth of Nations (once called the British Commonwealth), is good. But the argument is made without benefit of complete facts or the comfort of final theoretical sanction. To accept these limitations is to accept only what the officials of the sterling world and the officials of the rest of the world face in reaching for the answers to the problems of policy which cross their desks. Often these problems become perplexing because of the immediate discrepancy between commercial and political objectives. This discrepancy is likely to be acute at a given moment, and then a little later forgotten. The aim of this book is to review the problems of sterling in the setting of its long history and its wide use all over the world.

Many broad questions of policy are involved in such an inquiry; many of the specific questions can be handled only cursorily—is this or that restriction good, are the mechanics of the system effective, does the coordination of economic policy yield material gain to each of the various members? The broader questions, which are the main concern in this book, have to do with the picture of sterling as a worldwide but restrictive monetary system, as the financial profile of the Commonwealth of Nations, as a "going concern" heavily supported by United States financial assistance and often heavily attacked on questions of international commercial policy. Are the restrictions which bind the sterling area together inconsistent with the emergence of a global monetary system that would facilitate world trade and world production?

Obviously these questions cannot be answered categorically; they have to be lived out, while the various points of view based on varying kinds of interests are brought to bear on the formation of policy. Is the sterling area a good thing compared to the real alternatives? The United States has to ask this question continuously as a matter of deciding how much support should be given it, and how much help may be expected from it in the drift of international changes. In this book the effort is directed at drawing a broad picture which may, if fair, provide a better background for the many people who must wrestle with sterling problems.

About Terms Used Broadly

Words are words, not numbers. Presumably authors would be mathematicians if their gift or yearning for intellectual precision were great enough and if the subject for expression and communication were susceptible of such precision. But there is something to be said for the roominess of words. They have the quality of covering up human situations comfortably (if ambiguously) like clothes, rather than barely (if exactly) like equations. The loose fit of words may not necessarily be a disadvantage to a thought, even though it makes for sloppy appearance.

There are a number of loose-fitting general words or terms that recur throughout this book. *Sterling* is a familiar adjective with a number of meanings. It is commonly used to describe favorably the quality of a metal, the perfection of a performance, and the character of a man. This use of the word as a kind of stamp of approval came from the widely recognized excellence of sterling as a money, which is, of course, the sense in which sterling is used in this work. But what is sterling as a money? It is now a fairly mysterious promise which the British Treasury makes through the Bank of England on a printed slip of paper known as the pound sterling. One side of this slip of paper says that the Bank of England promises to pay to the bearer on demand the sum of one pound. That is all. The obligation has the printed signature of the chief cashier of the Bank of England. On the other side there is a picture of the Bank. The many implications of this promise and even its relationship to the homely use of "sterling" as an adjective meaning "genuine" are what we have to pursue here in the effort to get at an understanding of sterling.

Sterling area is used to describe the group of countries which under British exchange control regulations are official members of the club. (They are listed in Chapters 6 and 7.) There are many differences among members, and many similarities among some members and some non-members. So the term describes a club in which it is often hard to distinguish insiders and outsiders. The term is loose fitting in another sense: the roster of membership changes from time to time, although so far only slightly—Egypt resigned, Palestine disappeared as a country, then Israel spent its way out. The connotation of "sterling area" derives not only from the basic official designation in British exchange controls, but also from the related controls over trade and payments used by the members designated. The term itself is the familiar equivalent of the official British exchange control phrase, "scheduled territories."

Sterling area members include both dependent territories and independent countries. For convenience, the term *sterling countries* is used here to cover both. The sterling area includes some countries not associated with the Commonwealth; since political and economic cooperation is closer among Commonwealth members of the sterling area, the term *Commonwealth sterling area* has recently come into use when there is occasion to distinguish countries which belong to both. All the Commonwealth countries except Canada belong to the area. A satisfactory short definition of the *Commonwealth* is not possible; in the last chapter an effort is made to suggest some of its implications. For the present we can take it to mean the informal political association between Britain, Britain's dependencies, and former dependencies which have achieved independence as dominions—in short, the British Empire, with independence permitted. The Commonwealth reflects the political aspect of Britain's closest international associations and most direct influence, as the sterling area reflects the commercial and financial aspects, even though there are slight differences in the geographic areas covered by the two types of association.

Sterling system as used in this book is meant to refer to the entire complex of rules and regulations imposed by any country (not necessarily Britain or other sterling area members) on the use of sterling. The most important rules and regulations are those imposed by Britain, and except for these rules there would not be a distinguishable sterling system. The sterling system differs from the sterling area; the latter is a geographic area distinguished in British exchange controls as an area in which a high degree of freedom in the use of sterling is permitted and in which such control as may be necessary is accomplished largely through coordinated but mostly informal arrangements. The sterling system is a broader concept, including not just the monetary arrangements among members of the area, but the rules governing the use of sterling anywhere in the world.

Sterling world is geographically the same as the sterling area, but connotes the more concrete association that goes beyond the technical exchange-control concept of the sterling area. In most literature on sterling, the term sterling area is used to have both the broad and the narrow meaning. But it seems convenient to have a separate term to describe the sterling association in which the members stand as countries rather than as exchange control entities, as societies rather than as bank accounts.

The term *sterling region* is frequently used and there are many references to the *regionality* of sterling. The term may not be a happy one, since it may suggest geographical propinquity while the far-flung character of the sterling area is one of its salient features. Lacking more exact terms, *region, regionalism,* and *regionality,* are used in this book to connote the sense in which the sterling system is more than national but less than global. As a currency, sterling is based on the more or less coordinated activities of a group of countries, instead of being a solely national currency like, say, the Swiss franc. Yet sterling is not a fully international currency in the sense that it was in the days of the gold standard. As a set of financial and commercial relations, the sterling system is regional in the sense that its members have a relation to one another that is different from their relation with countries outside the sterling system and that is also different from the relation between two countries outside the sterling system. Within the sterling area, trade and payments are freer than they usually are among countries with inconvertible national currencies. Between the area and the dollar world there are barriers of varying intensity that draw a line between the sterling system and a completely international system of multilateral trade and payments. Sterling is neither exclusively national nor completely international. It is somewhere in between the two. "Regional" occurs as the handiest word to describe this in-between position, which other writers might identify as the limbo of inconvertibility. In the context of the argument of this book, the broader and less decisive notion of regionality seems to make a better fit.

There are great difficulties in the use of a number of terms which have become conventional in discussions of international transactions—for example, world trade, international trade, multilateralism, convertibility, discrimination, liquidity, and international reserves. These difficulties are partly the semantic ones arising from the repeated use of the same term in different contexts or by writers with different notions of what the terms should mean. It is partly a matter of the difficulty of the basic concepts involved in the terms. It would not be very helpful to try to invent new terms, so the usual ones are used, with a warning against semantic difficulties and occasional inconsistencies.

About the Use of Statistics

It is almost standard procedure in economic essays to discredit available statistics, and then employ them at length in the course of the argument. This is understandable, and the growing numbers of highly competent statisticians who are bringing together a constantly broader and more accurate numerical portrait of sterling transactions are themselves the most insistent critics of the shortcomings of present statistics as a trustworthy basis for answers to broad economic problems. They also deplore the misuse of statistics by the rest of us.

It is hard to get around this difficulty. For example, in this work considerable use is made of balance of payments figures in interpreting the behavior of the various members of the sterling world. Such use should be based on a complete understanding of all the procedures and definitions used in their collection. Lacking this, I have tried to avoid major difficulties by using statistics only for illustration of broad trends.

A further difficulty arises because of the need to decree a cut-off date for the illustrative figures used. In the case of the tables in this book, that date is the end of 1953. Later figures have been published in a number of cases but to incorporate them in the tables proved impracticable because of the revisions and computations entailed. The events of 1954 and 1955 are discussed in the text. Although these two years are important, they probably are not critical to grasping the meaning of sterling in world finance. At least so the argument runs in a book that is concerned with the essential nature of the sterling area, rather than its immediate vicissitudes.

Another general problem is the sparseness of statistics relating to the commercial and financial activities of the sterling world taken as a whole. Statistics for any single part of that world are superior to anything available for the entirety. This difficulty is gradually being overcome. The almost annual meeting of the Commonwealth countries to discuss financial and economic problems is having a favorable effect on the adoption of uniform techniques, but has not yet produced general statistics that are publicly available. The activities of the International Monetary Fund in compiling financial statistics on a uniform basis are producing practical results in the form of published statistics available to all. They do not permit systematic analysis of sterling area accounts, but they are more than a mere beginning.

The Point of View and the Conclusions of This Book

Sterling was and still is a uniquely international currency. A very substantial proportion of the existing supply of sterling is held by people living outside the United Kingdom. To state an exact proportion would involve a very arduous series of definitions as to what should be considered as the supply of sterling. But whether the supply of sterling is considered as the total obligations of the British Treasury, or merely as that part of the obligations which conceivably would have to be met in some fashion on the demand of the holder at any moment, it would still be true that people living outside the United Kingdom have a large claim against the British Treasury, larger by far than the comparable proportion in the case of the United States.

Most of these outside holders of sterling live in the dependent and independent countries of the Commonwealth of Nations. For the most part their local currencies are bound to sterling by very close ties. Ordinarily, financial relations between any pair of nations in the world involve the periodic settlement of accounts in something other than the currency of either one. Not so with the sterling world. The members have a mutual line of credit with one another through the linkage of their credit structures. The line of credit is not unlimited, but the limits are flexible and large. The general effect of this lack of defined limits of credits is to create an international monetary area with some important characteristics of a national monetary area. The area has centralized reserves, more or less automatically related credit structures, and more or less coordinated policies for handling balance of payments problems and for accommodating economic development. The area lacks, however, a very vital characteristic of a national monetary system: centralized political authority coextensive with the monetary area. This division of political authority invites differences in policy which are the familiar accompaniments of independence.

It is a slight misnomer to call sterling international in the foregoing sense if nationality is understood to be a quality of a sovereign country. British *dependencies* are even more closely linked to the British monetary structure than are the independent ("national") sterling countries. A literal, but perhaps unnecessarily literal, designation of the unique quality of sterling would be its *extra*nationality. In any case, this international or extranational quality developed over a long period of time in the wake of Britain's rising influence in markets outside of England. During the nineteenth century peak of this influence, outsiders had a high degree of freedom in using their sterling for any purpose that suited them. Their freedom perhaps should be considered as greater than that accorded by Britons to themselves, since the outsiders were far less subject to the details of British legal jurisdiction.

Since that time of peak influence, the political and economic orientation of Britain has been altered by important changes in the contours of market structures in the rest of the world. Although trade among nations has continued to grow, domestic markets predominate in size and importance. The international market for goods and services now involves annual transactions of about $100 billion, but transactions within the United States market alone are estimated at over $350 billion. The shift from an extranational to an intranational market has occurred, though to a far less striking degree, in the case of Britain, too; the domestic market for British producers now is about three times as large as their international market.

The emergence of large national markets and large national powers has entailed major changes in Britain's position. The major trading nations, without exception, find that priority in policy must be given to their national markets. Policy is focused on the problems of economic expansion and the maintenance of employment, which is far from identical with a focus on the smooth operation of international markets and stability in the balance of payments of a nation with the rest of the world.

Beyond this general shift in the world's market contours, the emergence of the United States as the biggest trader in international markets has brought about an important change. The United States' interest in foreign trade is peripheral. Though the United States is very important to other countries as a supplier and buyer of goods and services, other countries are only moderately important to the United States in comparison with its national market. The significance of this fact for international finance is that the dominance in the international market of a nation whose basic economic orientation is inward has impeded the development of an international credit structure suitable to meet the fluctuations of international trade.

Since the peak days of Britain's influence and sterling's free regime in a world far less developed economically than Britain itself, the trend has been toward the consolidation of sterling regionality. The region has scattered and shifting geographical contours, and scattered and shifting relations with outsiders. This trend toward regionality has not reflected a deliberate belief in the monetary virtue of a regional system but rather an understandable effort to resist the shrinkage of sterling's once worldwide scope. In short, the trend has been a defensive one against the disintegration of the international position of sterling, rather than an intentional effort to construct a less-than-worldwide monetary region. For all that, a sterling region has developed, characterized by distinctively regional methods of handling transactions both inside and outside the region.

Some of the shortcomings of the regional sterling system have arrested attention since the war because of the recurrent "reserve crises" resulting from making payments out of central reserves to cover the sterling area's deficits with the rest of the world. The "rest of the world" by definition includes all places in which deficits cannot be settled in sterling. The region's deficits with the rest of the world have evinced a tendency to build up over a short period of time, and hence to make relatively large calls on reserves suddenly. The sterling system has not adjusted readily to trends in the international market. This insensitivity is not completely undesirable or undesired; the defensive aspect of sterling area policy implies a deliberate resistance to adjustments which otherwise would be forced by factors external to the region. For example, British industry could not be maintained in full production if the volume of needed raw material imports were automatically cut from time to time in response to a rise in international prices.

The sterling structure has exhibited certain weaknesses in the handling of financial relations within the region, although frequently these weaknesses are obscured by simultaneous difficulties in extraregional finance. The former do not directly affect reserves since they can be covered, at least for some time, by the use of sterling, but extraregional difficulties cause reserve drains, which in turn impair confidence in the stability of sterling everywhere. The intraregional difficulties have arisen partly because of the peculiar legacies of war finance (mainly the vast "sterling balances"), and partly because the postwar sterling system grew gradually on the basis of *ad hoc* policies designed to meet immediate problems quickly. Import policy was deliberately controlled, reserves were pooled, and regional meetings held. The building of a coherent regional system, which in the event actually developed, was never the overriding policy of the members of the sterling area, as perhaps it could not be in view of the discrepancy between the political and financial jurisdictions in the sterling world and the many conflicts of interest among member countries. It was the effect, rather than the intention, of these *ad hoc* policies to create a regional system. There seems to have been little official recognition that the evolving system was essentially a regional one and as such would have peculiar problems. Official statistics relating to the external operations of sterling countries are still cast largely in terms of the national positions of the various members and not in terms of the position of the area as a whole vis-à-vis the rest of the world. It seems likely that if in the early postwar days there had been greater recognition of the regional nature of financial problems, some of the difficulties in the actual operation of the system could have been moderated.

This description of the trend of policy involves an assumption which will have to be considered carefully later. That assumption is that measures appropriate to a satisfactory *regional* system might come in conflict with measures designed to bring about a satisfactory *global* orientation of sterling. Whether such an assumption is justified is difficult to determine and it goes to the heart of present debates on sterling policies. Will worldwide freedom of payments and high levels of production best be promoted by strengthening or dissolving the regional sterling system? A closely related and equally difficult problem has to do with how far in fact policies directed at the stabilization of production in any large market, whether national like the United States or regional like the sterling world, are likely to involve a choice over policies aimed at maintaining financial balance between such markets and the rest of the world.

As far as I know there has never been an official British pronouncement that there is any conflict between the regional strengthening of sterling and the frequently expressed aim of bringing about a greater freedom of payments on a worldwide basis. In fact, a familiar argument by Britain and other sterling area members is that the regional concert of policy has been in the direction of worldwide freedom of payments and that the real barrier is a matter of the dollar world's policy. Nevertheless, an underlying problem for Britain and its sterling associates has been to decide, step by step, whether the reestablishment of a greater freedom in the use of sterling by persons living outside the sterling world should have priority over the consolidation of its regional strength. It has been an added complication that opinions differ greatly as to whether a choice between these priorities must in fact be made.

The view in this book is that the choice does have to be made, and that it is in fact being made, implicitly or intentionally, in favor of consolidating the regional character of the sterling system. It is argued that this trend may be expected to continue, involving such clear-cut regional manifestations as the use of regionally coordinated import restrictions as a means of controlling the sterling world's relations with the rest of the world, and the coordination of development policy on the basis of greater regional self-sufficiency. To what extent such regionality involves or may come to involve continued choices between the regional and the international status of sterling is a complicated question, and later attention will be addressed to its critical aspects. The answer seems to depend most importantly on, first, the practicability of harmonizing the internal credit structure of the region with the exigencies of relations with the rest of the world. Second, and perhaps alternatively, the answer depends on how far the non-sterling world's demand for goods and services in the sterling world, or the rest of the world's willingness to grant credit to the sterling world in order to sell goods and services there, may increase so as to bring about a ready balance in the external accounts of sterling countries without resort to regional measures.

It will be argued that financial policy in sterling countries, and probably in all countries, will be motivated mainly by the desire to maintain steady and near-full employment and at the same time achieve an expanding structure of production; that this priority in policy is likely to lead to a continued regional approach in the sterling world; that continued regionalism will be reinforced by the lack of a volume of international credit anything like large enough to make regionalism appear unattractive to sterling countries.

If these judgments prove sound, the final question is whether a regional approach in the economic and financial policies of the sterling world jibes with the political well being, now and in the future, of the sterling world, and whether, since this study is made from an American point of view, it jibes with the interests of the United States. It is possible that the regional trend in the sterling world has taken place less out of the conviction of the authorities of sterling governments that such a trend represents good economics and finance as out of a conviction that such a trend is a natural reflection and necessary counterpart of political, military, and traditional Commonwealth ties. This in turn raises a question: Even though sterling regionalism may be judged to be bad economics, is it the necessary price to pay for a large, friendly, and relatively stable international community?

Chapter 2

THE PAST OF STERLING

What's past is prologue; what to come,
In yours and my discharge.

THE TEMPEST

STERLING, like so many British things, boasts a thousand years of tradition. Some students of its ups and downs since the last war argue that the roots of present sterling problems do not go any further back than 1939-40 when Britain instituted a rigorous system of import and exchange controls to meet the exigencies of war finance. This argument may be well taken; certainly the most debated sterling problems in recent years have had to do with these restrictions. Are they necessary? Are they fair? Do they help Britain, or Britain and the associated sterling countries? On balance do they hurt the rest of the world? Are they the cause of or the remedy for Britain's financial "crises" since the war?

These questions will be considered in a variety of contexts throughout this book, but the consideration may be helped by a brief review of what sterling has been like before our own day. A century ago sterling connoted *the* system of international finance. What has happened to change that identification? Can we expect that sterling will again be a relatively free international currency? And in any case, does the past throw any light on what sort of correctives we can expect sterling countries to take when they run into international difficulties in their accounts? What are the alternatives and what are the likely choices? For that matter, what constitutes a difficulty calling for corrective action? The three postwar crises of 1947, 1949, and 1951, and the more moderate drain on reserves in 1955, have all stimulated worldwide interest and concern in sterling policies. Have they really been crises? Or have they been more or less run-of-the-mill moments of adjustment?

How it is and *how it is likely to be* are elusive without reference to something, and as good a something as any is *how it used to be*. Even the logically preliminary question,—What is the sterling area?—carries us back immediately to decisions made more than fifteen years ago, and a search for the significance of those decisions carries us back much further.[1]

Apart from the help it may provide in threading a way through more recent complications, a synopsis of the history of sterling will suggest something of what Roy Harrod calls the "personality" of the currency. He says: [2]

> Rightly understood, every great currency has a vitality and a character, and, one may say, a personality of its own. If one wants to consider problems of the balance of payments of a currency, one will not get far unless one has a good conception of this personality. The personality may be due to characteristics of the nation concerned; it may also reflect the personalities of great men (or women) who have had in the past a decisive influence in shaping the currency. . . . I would say that one should not be able to fix one's thoughts on the pound sterling without getting a whiff of the personalities who were responsible for its essential historic characteristics.

The monetary authorities of Britain and the other sterling countries are aware of sterling traditions and are influenced by them in their current decisions. This suggests that an understanding of their decisions will be helped by attention to historical factors that are still active in their deliberations.

Early Problems and Policies

The early days of sterling's history are murky, and careful students of the origins disagree on many details. The following account is an attempt to piece together a consensus where no consensus really exists, but the general portrait of sterling's infancy probably errs only in minor details.

[1] In this summary of sterling's history I am greatly indebted to Walter J. Sedwitz for his unpublished paper, "The History of British Crises," prepared in the course of this study. His debts, and my other debts, are indicated in the critical bibliography, rather than in footnotes throughout the book.

[2] Roy Harrod, *The Dollar* (New York: Harcourt, Brace, 1954), p. 3.

To begin at the beginning, the basic unit of sterling, the pound, originated from the English penny, which was probably first issued in the eighth century and probably was copied from coins issued by the French under Pepin. At first both the pound and the penny, as money, were identified with the corresponding measures of weight. By the ninth century the pennies had found their way into all the Saxon kingdoms and by convention came to be accepted by count ("tale") rather than by weight, although the intention behind their issue was to make a pound of money the same as a poundweight of silver. In the eleventh century William the Conqueror issued a penny bearing the imprint of a star, called *steorra* in Anglo-Saxon. The penny itself was called a *sterling,* and though the coin has long since disappeared, its name has lasted as the distinctive designation of all British money. The word "shilling" comes from the Anglo-Saxon word *scilling,* meaning a piece cut off. William established the pound as 20 scillings, and the scilling as 12 pennies, making 240 pennies to the pound. Although there have been occasional changes in the cutting up of the pound, William's division is the one followed today.

The inheritance of nomenclature may be the most direct link between sterling as we know it today and as it was in its early centuries. Basic characteristics of sterling then and now could hardly be more disparate. Then, sterling meant coins, stamped usually out of silver, and later to some extent out of gold. Now, sterling means an obligation of the British Treasury to exchange one piece of paper for another just like it, and an undefined obligation of the British government to maintain such conditions in trade and production and finance as to leave such a sterile swap not worth testing. Silver, which is still widely identified with the meaning of sterling, actually no longer plays any part in the currency, not even in the coins. Gold, in terms of which the value of the pound sterling is defined, plays only an indirect part, and that largely in making payments to foreign countries. Between the early days and now, sterling's "silver cord" was indeed loosed, and the "golden bowl" broken.

For all that, the early centuries of sterling's history have their fascination, even from the standpoint of the complicated problems underlying the widespread current interest in sterling. In these early centuries the needs of the state, especially in financing wars, persistently raised money problems and caused more or less chronic monetary instability. The tendency of precious metals to flow out of the country from time to time was worrisome to the government and to the market, just as postwar drains have been. The problem of providing a suitable money to accommodate a growing domestic and international market was there, as now. Perhaps the greatest similarity between early years and now was the chronic problem of inability to out-guess the trend of financial problems, particularly international currency movements; and as now, in lieu of the hoped-for perfect answer, the makeshift answer was an arbitrary fabric of exchange controls, import controls, and protection of domestic enterprises against foreign competition.

Even before the industrial revolution Britain's economy had largely changed (1200-1500) from the subsistence farming of a feudal system to the interdependence of a market system; in short, from manors to money. The growth of the market and the number of producers dependent on it necessarily brought about a reduction in the self-sufficiency of the small producing unit, and concomitantly brought about an increase in the possibilities—associated with interdependence—of economic instability, as people came to depend on the market value rather than the volume of their produce. The growth of a market could not occur without a growth in the convenience of the means of exchange—money. The growth of the early British market was facilitated by the return of the Crusaders with their hoards of looted treasure, and by the discovery of the silver mines in the Harz mountains of Germany. Money became the link, as now, by which the prosperity or distress of one area was transmitted to another.

In those early days sterling started a five-century fall in value. This downward drift was punctuated by frequent crises, often involving great suffering by one part of the population as another part benefited.

Sterling crises in our day are associated with large drains of gold or gold-equated dollars from central reserves. The immediate object of actions taken to combat the crises has been to arrest the drain of reserves before international confidence in the ability of the sterling countries to settle their accounts with the rest of the world was destroyed. The national preoccupation with reserve drains has a long, and not always honorable, history.

When Edward I returned to England from the Crusades in 1274, he found the state of the coinage deplorable. Since the beginning of the century, the value of money had continually fallen because of the activities of the "clipper." Goldsmiths, money-lenders, and just ordinary owners of coins, filed off edges of coins before passing them on. This was a comparatively easy procedure, since the milled edge had not yet been invented. The result was a gradual reduction in the precious-metal content of coins. By the middle of the thirteenth century British coins circulated at a discount of about 5 per cent. Edward took stern measures. The death penalty was imposed on many money changers. In 1279, it was ordered that all clipped coins be returned to the mint, where they were purchased on the basis of their reduced metallic weight and then replaced, at an appropriate price differential, with full-weight coins. The substitution of the new coins for the more numerous old coins involved some deflation of prices but there is no evidence that the hardships were out of the ordinary.

This monetary therapy did not last long. As soon as the recoinage was completed, the clipper and the counterfeiter went back to work, despite the severe penalties aimed at discouraging them. Deflation, never a popular remedy for financial difficulties, was short-lived. Prices rose and the market value of precious metals rose above the mint value. Precious metals were sold in the market rather than at the mint. Just twenty years after Edward's first recoinage he ordered a second one. This, too, was a deflationary measure but for three hundred years after it deflation was out of style as a method of arresting reserve drains. As in the case of Britain's postwar policy, the favored technique in dealing with the loss of money which could be used abroad came to be administrative curtailment of imports and devaluation of the currency. Some of the causes of the continuing fall in the value of sterling also have a familiar ring; the almost uncontrollable expenses of war, the growth of imports at a rate suggesting the physical parallel of a glandular ailment, and the unpredictable droughts and infestations furnished by nature.

A succeeding king, Edward III, went even farther down the path of restrictions. In 1335 he decreed that coin and precious metals could be exported only under specific license from the crown; violations were made punishable by death. Official searchers were appointed by the king to enforce the act. The prohibition remained in force until 1666, although enforcement, difficult at best, was lax. The tendency for the pound to depreciate continued, and in 1351 the mint recognized the trend by again raising its official price for silver. The mint's action did not stop the nation's loss of silver, however, probably because of the intractable talents of the clippers and counterfeiters.

The Black Death (1348-1349), which halved the population of Western Europe, and the Hundred Years War (1338-1453) brought intense financial pressure. The government attempted to fix prices and wages, and manorial lords continued to demand the traditional forced services from an outraged peasantry. The Peasant Revolt was brutally crushed in 1381 but feelings about the state of the currency were bitter, and an official inquiry was conducted the next year. The inquiry blamed the devaluation of 1351 for the unpopular upward surge of prices and advised against further devaluation. As an alternative the inquiry made a recommendation which has a familiar ring in our own times: international trade should be governmentally regulated so that exports and imports would always be equal in value. This was virtually a prescription for international barter rather than for an international market. International payment through the use of bills of exchange, still rare, was forbidden on the specific grounds that this credit instrument discouraged the direct balancing of trade. As a result of the inquiry, restrictions were imposed on the wearing of "luxury" apparel by anyone making less than £40 a year and a tax on the export of luxury apparel was introduced. But basically the inquiry was less concerned with the causes of rising prices than with the loss of reserves occasioned by them.

The inquiry revealed a basic difference in ideas about the

make-up of a suitable monetary policy. The "bullionists," with their overriding concern to prevent the outflow of precious metals from the nation, pressed for direct governmental control of foreign trade as the only reliable method of assuring a satisfactory balance in external accounts. The other school of thought, typically that of foreign traders, opposed such controls. They believed that the successful operation of an automatic metallic standard and the maintenance of stable price levels depended on freedom to export and import precious metals and coins. The bullionist advocates of control prevailed.

In the fifteenth century sterling was twice more devalued; the mint raised the price of silver in 1411 and again in 1461. The former occasion was in the nature of an official clipping to provide the crown with funds for war on the European continent and for other royal expenses described as "affairs of state." The later rise in the price of silver—producing a substantial depreciation of 20 per cent in the value of money—was aimed at reversing the outflow of silver from the mint, and it succeeded. Prices did not rise, and there was no widespread popular complaint. In fact, from such accounts as are available, prices remained stable for the next hundred years, partly at least because the rise in the market price of gold and silver offset the official reduction in the quantity of metal used in the coins. Lesser amounts of silver became as greater amounts had been before.

1500-1700: A Market Emerges

The next two centuries are notable for the rapid extension of the "market" economy and the use of credit instruments. The way was paved for the later rapid and intensive industrialization of Britain, and so for the specialized and dominant role Britain eventually achieved in international markets during the nineteenth century. Most of the developments of this dynamic period must be passed by here, where our interest is in the growth of sterling as an international currency rather than in the growth of the British economy, close though that relationship is.

This period of growth started, strangely, with fifty years in which depression was the usual state of economic affairs and recurrent debasement was the usual monetary policy. It ended with fifty years of prosperity in an inflationary atmosphere, punctuated by speculative booms, financial panics, and temporary deflations. In both national and international transactions, monetary practices began vaguely to resemble modern ones. Coins became less important than credit. Needs of the state were covered by national borrowing (and, therefore, the birth of national debt) rather than by debasement of the coinage. Commercial banking based on paper currency and bank credit developed. The great convenience of credit arrangements in contrast to continuous shipments of precious metals in the handling of international trade was recognized, as was—somewhat paradoxically—the usefulness of periodic shipments of precious metals as a desirable means of settling international accounts.

In the course of these two centuries Britain was politically unified, first under absolute rule and ultimately under a parliamentary government in which Whig businessmen played the leading role. The economic aspect of the unification was reflected in the rapid growth of commerce and industry and in the further gradual transformation of the subsistence-farming peasant into a commercial farmer producing for others, or into an urban worker. Through most of the period the trend of prices was upward, and the trend of real wages was downward. In fact, the policies of the government often were designed to keep labor cheap, sometimes through harshly repressive measures. Men might be forbidden to loaf, or they might be enjoined to work for a maximum rather than, as today, a minimum wage. They might find it illegal to change their employment if their motive was merely to take advantage of higher wages offered elsewhere. The combination of high prices and low wages offered continuous hardship for most of the people, but it also made for a high rate of savings and investment and a correspondingly high rate of growth in national production.

The commercialization of British production brought the instabilities of production and employment we have come to identify as the main problem of modern market economies. As the market grew more rapidly than sophistication in monetary techniques, a general feeling developed that there was a dearth of money. The widespread feeling today that difficulties in international finance stem from a general shortage of dollars is parallel. The notion of money-dearth stimulated great interest in monetary theory, and the acceptance of a more flexible and complicated monetary structure. Paper money and credit instruments in both domestic and international trade became important for the first time and something like a modern credit system for an expanding national production emerged. With the accompanying expansion of international trade a basis was formed for the later international significance of sterling. The British economy was being rapidly, if painfully, released from dependence on a metallic coin system into an era in which monetary policy would be geared to the changeable needs of a rapidly growing trade at home and abroad.

The moral of these developments for the greatly changed conditions of our own times is hard to derive, but it is interesting to speculate about what we know of the earlier problems and practices in the light of our more detailed knowledge of present problems and practices. In the early days of sterling, the value of money was closely tied to the market value of the gold or silver contained in coins. But the value of the precious metals varied widely in different markets because of the high cost of shipment and because of poor communication between markets. The English mint set an official price on silver, but it had no monopoly on purchases and when the mint price fell below prices obtainable in the national market or in other markets it garnered no silver. The mint had to vie with the market as best it could. There were two major ways of doing this when the market price was higher than the mint price. The flow of metal from the mint could be stopped either by raising the mint's price or by taking measures to lower the market price. The former we now think of as official depreciation, the latter as deflation. The relative advantages of these two methods are still at the center of controversy over what measures should be taken in the effort to maintain a country's balance in international transactions, and are closely related to modern controveries over whether inflationary or deflationary measures are better suited to maintain or regain internal financial stability without arresting the expansion of production. During these early centuries deflation seems to have been the common approach to financial difficulties, but probably more as the result of governmental acquiescence in market reactions than as a matter of conscious policy.

In the narrative of sterling developments in the remaining sections of this chapter, the focus of attention will be almost exclusively on the sort of crises that developed and the methods, if any, which were pursued in trying to solve them.

Because economic developments are based on relations among human beings, they tend to match the fits and starts by which human beings develop. Economic crises, like critical times in human life, are hard to define. Historically, crises have been endured, handled, or mishandled, and it is not clear which word applies to any given one. The persistent tendency, however, among human beings in their arrangements with one another as nations has been to resist the cumulative insecurities which an unregulated market can produce.

The postwar "crises" in Britain and in sterling transactions have attracted great attention and have been the source of much international debate, largely because, as in the early days of sterling, precious metal flowed from the mint, and not because there was any serious reversal in the economic life of the nation. The latter would constitute a real economic crisis, but difficulties in reserves, when not accompanied by impairment of production, are only technical. Technical difficulties can be very difficult to resolve, but they do not suggest the collapse of a society.

The word "crisis" has a number of meanings. In the case of postwar sterling affairs it ordinarily has been used to suggest a state of financial affairs threatening bankruptcy for the entire association of sterling countries. The main dictionary definition is more moderate and more descriptive of what has happened: "The point of time when it is decided whether any affair or course of action must go on, or be modified or terminate." "Crisis" in this sense is a fairly continuous state in public affairs, and in this sense the decisions taken in the course of earlier sterling crises contribute perspective, if not understanding, to the study of the postwar ones.

1700-1800: The Drift toward Modern Currency Problems

The keynote of the eighteenth century was the industrialization of Britain, in contrast to its commercialization in the preceding century. Production expanded six- or eight-fold and although demographic figures are controversial, population is thought to have grown by from 50 to 100 per cent. The economy was integrated by a vast development of roads and canals, making the expansion of industry possible and agriculture more productive. Foreign trade expanded almost as rapidly as production. The feverish economic activity of this century brought Britain to a position of decisive world power and economic supremacy as the next century opened. The eighteenth century was dominated by Whig businessmen, who in their enterprising spirit managed to change most English institutions and, with the consolidation of farms, even the appearance of the countryside. It may be anticlimactic to add that there were many changes in finance.

But finance is our point of departure, and first should be mentioned the establishment of a gold standard. Given the crude state of overseas communication and the long delays involved in getting news of one market to another, considerable differences existed in the price of gold and silver in different markets and in the gold-silver ratio. In Europe gold was some 16 to 18 times more valuable than silver; in the Far East only some 9 or 10 times higher. Variations in the market price of gold, and the tendency for silver to be shipped to the Orient where it was more valuable, caused continuous difficulty for the smooth operation of England's virtually automatic silver standard. The hero in tackling the confusion was Sir Isaac Newton. Roy Harrod says: [3]

> Newton, the astronomer, brought to the currency question not so much those gifts that made him the father of modern physics as that insatiable appetite for particular detail that he displayed in the study of biblical chronology. Delving into the curious lore of gold and silver parities, degrees of fineness, mint charges and the like, he established the gold and silver values of British currency after a long period of considerable disorder and confusion, and his gold rating of the pound sterling showed its merit by surviving unaltered until 1931.

[3] Same, pp. 3, 4.

Other aspects of modern finance emerged in the eighteenth century. The use of paper money grew rapidly, and commercial credit became important. The Bank of England, which had been established in 1694 as a kind of fiscal agent for the government, gradually took over some responsibility for the stability of credit and thus began its transformation into a full-fledged central bank. A stock market was established, as was a market for short-term government securities. With these modern developments, there came too the problem of learning to operate this more flexible monetary structure so as to protect the value of sterling both in home trade and in foreign trade. There was a lot of learning to be done.

When the outbreak of the War of Spanish Succession (1701-14) led to a run on banks resulting in a number of failures, nothing was done officially to intervene. Six years later, the opponents of the new Bank of England organized a run on it. This time there was help from private financiers and the government, in recognition that the failure of the Bank would have more than ordinary consequences for the whole financial community. In 1720 came the famous bursting of the "South Sea Bubble," a remarkable story of a good company going wrong, the fascinating details of which must be passed over here. Speculation was high on such projects as the discovery of perpetual motion, the import of jackasses from Spain, and, most remarkably, a project "for carrying on an undertaking of great advantage, which shall in due time be revealed." A crash followed this uncontrolled and fantastic speculation. The disillusionment accompanying the crisis caused a run on the Bank of England, which consequently was not in a position to help bail out anyone else. This again was a case of a crisis running its course without any effort to arrest it, but once the speculative commitments had been allowed to reach the heights they did, nothing could have prevented the collapse.

Except for a minor crisis in 1727, there was relative calm until 1745. In that year the Jacobite uprising under the leadership of Prince Charles led to a panic known—like so many since—as "Black Friday." Charles' army was moving from the north and French invasion was feared from the south. When a politically motivated run on the Bank of England was instigated, the Bank resorted to a ruse it had used in 1720 when it paid out cash to certain persons who had agreed to bring it in again by the back door, giving a good impression of the Bank's cash position. This ruse is a distant cousin of the standard method of giving unlimited official cash support to arrest a run on banks, except that now the money comes back in by the front door and without collusion. In the course of the 1745 run, the merchants of London signed a manifesto in which they declared they would not refuse to accept Bank of England notes in payment of any sum of money owing them, a step attesting that there was something special about Bank of England notes.

Although the crises of the first half of the eighteenth century were primarily financial, and induced by political factors or speculation, they reflected characteristics of a growing industrial economy which did not yet have a sound credit basis. There is no evidence of any significant retarding influence of the crises on industrial expansion. The role of the Bank of England was passive; it did not intervene in crises, regarding itself as little more than an ordinary bank, and it did not influence credit conditions or assume any responsibility for monetary stabilization.

The crises of the second half of the century and the methods used to cope with them were different. The difficulties stemmed from or involved home production and foreign trade. The responsibility of the central bank and the government to intervene was gradually recognized.

After the Seven Years War (1756-1763) the first modern-style crisis developed, and it affected all of Europe. England's business had expanded during the war as new markets arose in conquered territories, as supplies were sold to Frederick the Great, England's ally, and as the manufacturing of munitions grew. Exports rose from £10 million to £13 million during the war. When peace came, extensive speculation in stocks and government securities began. An intense demand by the Continent for funds for commercial and colonial development created a stringency of cash and continental countries started selling their British securities. The money market became tight. As orders for British goods declined and exports already shipped could not be paid for, Britain had no choice but to curtail production. There was a general fall in commodity prices, and British merchants found themselves with credits frozen in unmarketable goods. All this has a familiar ring to modern ears.

This crisis, which as it worked out did not cause deep difficulties for Britain, is historic because for the first time the Bank of England took action to arrest it. It made almost £2 million available to commercial firms in London, Amsterdam, and Hamburg. This was only a beginning of the Bank's recognition of its functions as a central bank, a lender of last resort, a banker's bank. There were to be later occasions on which the Bank stood by while credit shortage caused distress throughout the nation.

The crisis of 1772 may rank as the first modern market and industrial crisis. It started melodramatically with speculation and embezzlement involving the failure of the banking firm of Heale and several associated firms dragged down with it. Soon the number of failures reached 525. The failures of some of the important firms in both England and Scotland were the result primarily of overproduction or a decline of consumption. The East India Company was heavily involved, but was able to obtain governmental assistance. The Scottish linen industry drastically curtailed production, and many of the unemployed emigrated to America. Dutch merchants, Imperial Russia, and the Bank of Stockholm provided important tide-over credits. Belatedly, the Bank of England provided credit.

In 1783, after the end of the American Revolution, there was a boom in foreign trade as markets were reopened. As Britain's economy expanded it imported raw materials on a large scale and again ran into balance of payments problems. Government flotations contributed to the swollen income stream. A reserve crisis developed quickly. To arrest it, the Bank of England restricted the note issue and refused to buy government securities from private individuals. The Bank had begun to recognize that a shortage of notes would bring back into circulation coins shipped abroad or hoarded in the provinces. The corollary was that when the external and internal drain of precious metals was reversed credit should be eased, and this was the case later in the year. Crisis was averted and what later came to be known as "the rules of the game" instituted. It was the first occasion on which the Bank successfully exercised control over the money market with the deliberate aim of stabilization.

In 1793, however, the Bank evinced little understanding of a credit stringency resulting from an internal drain of reserves. There had been a crop failure in 1792; technological advances had led to a market glut. When France declared war in 1793, there was an intense demand in the provinces for redemption of provincial notes. In the general alarm London banks refused to assist their correspondent banks in the country, and the Bank of England—itself under pressure—restricted its note issues and raised the discount rate. The government, under William Pitt, stepped into the disorder with commodity-secured credits and the panic was stopped.

The century ended with a hard lesson in the mechanics of monetary policy. The government drew freely on a somewhat reluctant Bank of England to finance the Napoleonic wars. Even larger amounts were sent by England to its continental allies. By 1796, gold reserves were £2 million, or a quarter of what they had been three years before. The Bank limited credit and the government increased the proportion of borrowing from the public. These measures reversed the outflow of gold from England. But within England the gold flowed out of London into the country. The Bank faced the dilemma of restricting credit to keep gold coming in from abroad or relaxing credit to halt the internal drain. A rumor of French invasion touched off a run on country banks in 1797. The run spread rapidly and within a week the credit structure of the nation was paralyzed. The government suspended the gold redemption of bank notes. When the situation improved in the course of the year, the Bank expressed willingness to resume payments, but the government preferred to extend the restrictions rather than risk unknown difficulties in war finance. Britain was off gold for almost 25 years afterwards. Private bank notes were convertible into Bank of England notes, but the latter were officially convertible into nothing, or at least not into the sought-for precious metals. The century ended in soaring prices and a further loss of bullion to foreign countries.

1800-1900: The Golden Age

The nineteenth century was the century of Britain's greatest world influence and sterling's greatest international prestige. In the second half of the century times were so stable and prosperous that poets grew melancholy with longing for the disconcerting days of the past. Childe Roland could seek again his dark tower, but he was more likely to come upon Maud brooding over happiness in her garden. It seemed too good to last, and as it turned out, it was. Nonetheless, it was the only protracted period in which the credit facilities provided by a single country met the credit needs of a lively and expanding world commerce. This had not happened before and it has not happened since.

In the course of the century the predominance of the British merchant in international trade had been growing. Already the bill on London had come into vogue; a foreign exporter would not draw a bill on his foreign importer, but instead on a British merchant, something in the manner of buying a certified check today. London thus financed trade which never touched British shores. As in the course of these commercial practices the British merchant gradually became a banker he gained increasing knowledge of the credit standing of the foreign traders he was willing to accommodate, and eventually stood ready to endorse obligations written against him. A market grew in London where these foreign trade obligations could be bought and sold. The guiding rate for this important market was "Bank rate," or the Bank of England's interest charge in buying bills. A high interest rate at the Bank set the level for the market, and if the rate was higher than in other markets funds would flow to London. Early in the century it was recognized that a lifting of Bank rate would tend to reverse a reserve drain and correct a balance of payments deficit. The converse, that a lowering of Bank rate might eliminate a balance of payments surplus, was not recognized because the problem was not recognized. What could be better than a surplus?

Thus according to the generally accepted version of the "rules of the game" of the gold standard, the raising or lowering of interest rates, keyed to Bank rate, would correct undesired inflows or outflows of gold reserves. Professor R. G. Hawtrey questions this. In *A Century of Bank Rate* he argues that this particular rule of the game was probably not very effective. The alteration of London interest rates could be and was easily offset by the actions of other financial centers, but the internal effects of the interest rate changes were important. The scattered evidence suggests to Hawtrey that Bank rate changes may have been much more important in their repercussions on domestic incomes and expenditures than on movements of funds to and from other financial centers. It is certainly true that in some instances Bank rate changes were completely ineffective in correcting the flow of gold into or out of the country. In recent years the trend of opinion is the opposite: Bank rate changes, in present circumstances, are almost immediately effective in influencing the flow of *short-term* international funds but only indirectly effective in influencing the domestic income stream. But these times are not the golden age, and there are no golden rules of the game.

Reserves, whether they are in individual hoards or in banks, are costly in the sense that they yield nothing. Not being put to work, they earn nothing. Fort Knox with its buried gold is costly to the United States; the Exchange Equalisation Account with its immobilized metal is costly to Britain. This general principle was well realized in the nineteenth century and reserves of "cash" were kept at a low level. But the policy of holding only small reserves tended to intensify domestic instability, since the supply of cash to guarantee domestic convertibility was very short in times of recession. Moreover, interest rate policy came to be geared more to small changes in small reserves than to the state of business activity.

Until the middle of the century Britain's commercial policy followed traditional lines of protection of British industry. It took the form of tariffs against imports of food, but freedom for imports of the raw materials needed by industry. Industry in turn was protected in the domestic market by high duties against foreign manufactured products. This standard policy had been controversial since the middle of the preceding century and British manufacturers made an organized attack on it. Agricultural protection meant higher food costs and therefore higher wages to be paid by British industry, thus putting British manufacturing at a cost disadvantage in foreign markets. Eventually Britain gambled on its industry and the advantages of free trade. Its action, starting with the repeal of the Corn Laws in 1846, touched off a cycle of international liberalization. For instance, Richard Cobden, as Britain's plenipotentiary in France, carried free-trade views to Napoleon III, who, anxious for better relations with England, agreed to a reciprocal ending of duties. The British duties which remained in force after 1859 were only those with mainly a revenue purpose.

As for monetary policy, the debate between those who favored control of money supply in relation to the credit requirements of an expanding economy and those who favored tying it to the inflow and outflow of precious metals was resolved in favor of the former, known as "the Currency School." A flexible credit base for a rapidly growing market was thus encouraged, and in the course of developing this flexibility London became the leading financial center of the world.

At the middle of the nineteenth century, then, Britain's economy was guided by policies providing flexible credit to foreigners as well as to Britons, a minimum of restrictions on foreign trade, and a solid gold basis for sterling in world markets.

How did it work? There were economic and financial crises which rocked Britain at roughly ten-year intervals throughout the century. These are probably to be regarded as the ups and downs to be expected in the dynamic expansion of Britain's markets at home and abroad and the inevitable posing of new monetary problems for which the solutions were not inherited but had to be figured out.

In 1810 there was a crisis arising mainly from the continental blockade during the Napoleonic wars. Britain had turned its attention to Latin American markets as a susbstitute and put new emphasis on trade with the United States. Indiscreet financing of Latin American trade was largely responsible for a rapid rise in monetary circulation. Imports into Britain increased with the reopening of the Baltic ports and British exports declined as the blockade was tightened. Prices began to fall and unemployment rose rapidly. The government intervened by placing £6 million in exchequer bills on the market. Panic was averted but in the last analysis the adjustment was by deflation. Deflation continued to set the tone of policy for more than a decade at the end of which the Bank of England resumed gold redemption of notes. The deflation which made this step possible caused considerable unemployment, distress, and stagnation in production.

In order to relieve distress and unemployment, the government engaged in deficit finance. The revival that followed reached a peak in 1825 and was paced by a wave of foreign lending, speculation on imports, and inflationary banking practices throughout the country. Early in 1825, as gold was being drained from the country, the stock market collapsed and there was a general financial crisis. The Bank of England for the first time fulfilled the central banking function of a lender of last resort and provided credit on easy terms. The Bank got into temporary difficulties but ultimately the crisis served to place British banking on a sounder basis and further edged the Bank of England out of its original character of a commercial bank competing in the market with other banks and into its leading role as a central bank with credit control responsibilities.

Again in 1839 the Bank was confronted with a rapid drain of reserves. They fell to £4 million from £10 million the year before. To meet the situation, the Bank raised its discount rate to 6 per cent, sold securities in the open market, and borrowed funds from abroad. These actions were successful in stopping the reserve crisis but at a great deflationary cost. Commercial and banking failures continued until 1842 and trade, production, and employment remained depressed. Excessive and uncritical foreign lending, general speculation, and tardy central banking measures, cost the economy a prolonged loss of production.

In the 1840's the great railroad expansion took place and there was an extended wave of stock market speculation in which the Bank of England itself was deeply involved. The reckoning came in 1847 when the Bank was again losing reserves at a rapid rate and imports, facilitated by the repeal of the Corn Laws, were running high. Once again there were commercial and banking failures. Raising the discount rate did not arrest the downward trend. Toward the end of the year the government permitted the Bank to increase its fiduciary note issue and confidence returned to the market. But essentially the crisis ran its own course leaving on the plus side of the ledger the fact that the railroads did get built.

The crisis of 1857 was largely foreign-induced as a result of excessive railroad speculation in the United States. The effects of the United States crisis were quickly transmitted to Britain. In the years immediately before there were some signs of financial difficulty in Britain—bad harvests, a decline in foreign investment, and distress signals from European markets. After the outbreak of the Crimean War in 1855, the Bank raised its discount rate to 7 per cent for a short time to forestall excessive monetary expansion. But basically the Bank felt confident enough with its £10 million reserve to negotiate with the East India Company for the export of a million in bullion to the Orient. It took about two weeks for news of the United States crisis, which toppled more than 60 banks in New York, to reach London. British investors were holding large amounts of American railroad securities and exports to America represented about a fifth of total British exports. In the surge of attempted liquidation of American investment the Bank of England raised its rate, but the pressure did not subside. By the end of the year its reserve was down to £1.5 million and within four months it had added £5 million to its discounts, but the market still pressed for accommodation, even on these expensive terms.

The government was forced to step in. Following the precedent of 1847 it notified the Bank that indemnifying legislation would be passed to protect the Bank in case it became necessary—as it did—to exceed the statutory limitation on the issuance of notes. A 10 per cent discount rate was made a condition for granting the indemnity. But as in previous crises, the significant increase in Bank rate occurred *after* the outflow of reserves had taken place and had already been halted by the force of the crisis itself. Also, on this occasion the effect of the Bank's policies was weakened by the competitive raising of discount rates on the continent. After the crisis, the Bank was cautious in reducing its rate; until reserves reached £15 million the rate was not allowed to fall below 5 per cent.

May 11, 1866 is another of the days known financially as "Black Friday" in England. Touched off by the failure the day before of one of the most respected discount houses, Overend, Gurney & Co., it was a day of hysterical demands on banks to redeem their notes in cash. The roots of the difficulties are traceable to the American Civil War which disrupted the cotton trade and caused gold to flow to Europe. The gold became the basis for considerable monetary expansion supporting a new wave of speculation. Meanwhile, the railroad boom continued and speculative investment was encouraged by the Companies Act, which eased the formation of limited liability companies whose investors saw unlimited profits as the counterpart of limited risks. In this period the Bank of England wielded its control over interest rates in an orthodox and responsible central bank way. The raising of Bank rate, however, seemed to be more effective in attracting funds from the country banks than in attracting them from abroad. When the rate was lowered in 1865 the Bank's reserves promptly flowed back to the provinces. On the other hand, when the rate stood at the high level of 9-10 per cent as against 4 per cent in France, gold was not attracted from abroad.

There were, no doubt, special circumstances to explain why the manipulation of Bank rate in this period appeared so ineffective an instrument in protecting reserves. There may not have been a sufficient appreciation abroad that the suspension of the Bank of England's legal limitation on issuing notes is different from a suspension of gold redemption of issued notes. It may be that there simply were not sizeable funds abroad to flow to Britain. But whatever the reason, the events cast doubt on the automatic efficacy of a high Bank rate in starting a flow of gold to London.

The last quarter of the nineteenth century—like the early thirties of the twentieth—is often called the "Great Depression." This is probably a misnomer. Prices were falling and Britain lost its virtual monopoly of industrial leadership as other industrial countries developed, but the gains in British living standards were substantial. In fact, one noted economist told me that in his opinion the tremendous productive gains achieved in the course of the industrial revolution were never passed on to British agricultural and industrial workers until this "depressed" last quarter of the century. There were crises, but the period as a whole was not one of underemployment of resources and commercial stagnation. The falling prices appear now to be the result of technological advances and corresponding increases in productivity. Prices fell in periods of high employment as well as in the cyclical dips. Throughout, real wages rose. A general shortage of monetary gold was blamed for the financial difficulties.

In 1873 a financial crisis in the United States brought pressure on the Bank of England and within four weeks reduced its reserves by £5 million. Of this drain, probably 80 per cent was internal—gold going to the country. Interim increases in Bank rate were ineffective, and only after the rate had been pushed to 9 per cent did the gold start flowing back to the Bank. But the Bank was beginning to learn the complicated task of dealing with internal drains, which high interest rates might well intensify, and external drains, which high interest rates might correct.

There were sporadic difficulties in the remainder of the century, but no dramatic lessons. In the 1880's the Bank found again that low interest rates might stimulate domestic activity but at the cost of a drain of reserves to country banks, and that high interest rates might attract funds from abroad but at the cost of domestic employment. More significantly, Britain learned that conditions on the continent and in America could well be the circumstances that alter cases. The British fear of American economic cycles probably stems from this period.

The Early Twentieth Century

At the opening of the twentieth century it was clear that monetary policy should be geared to the prevention of crises even though the methods available might have to give clear priority to domestic stability rather than the state of the balance of payments. Financial and economic problems had become so enmeshed in political, social, and military considerations that the automatic adjustments of the preceding two generations were no longer fully acceptable.

Although the operation of the "rules of the game" was not perfect in the nineteenth century, there were conditions in the twentieth century that made them practically impossible to follow. In the 1920's a large amount of gold flowed to the United States where deflation and the restoration of the gold standard were attracting it. In contrast to earlier practices, most of the influx was not permitted to exert a direct influence on the volume of credit. United States authorities held that the influx was not the old-fashioned kind, in settlement of trade deficits, but more in the nature of a commodity which foreign countries were in a position to export. The Federal Reserve Board stressed its heavy responsibilities to maintain a sound credit system, and this clearly implied that domestic stability would have first priority in monetary policy.

The Bank of England itself no longer played the gold standard game according to the old rules by which a gold inflow would be translated into a domestic credit expansion and an outflow into a contraction. The Bank's accounts between 1925 and 1931 reveal a systematic policy of neutralization of gold movements. Throughout the interwar period the attitude of bankers in England, France, and the United States was one of apprehension over gold movements. They were regarded as temporary and as threats to financial stability. Although neutralization was to some extent automatic, in the sense that gold accumulation made money markets more liquid and thus led to a repayment of indebtedness, it was far from complete.

Immediately after the first World War it was clear that the inflation created throughout Europe by war finance was a major source of financial instability. The rise in price levels diminished the purchasing power of gold, discouraged new output from mines, and narrowed the gold base of the international credit structure. In addition, the peace settlement had created a multitude of new states, each wishing to maintain its own independent gold reserves. The scramble for gold put extreme pressure on world payments. An international conference was called at Genoa in 1922 to deal with the gold problem. It recommended economy in the use of gold by adoption of the so-called gold exchange standard, a system in which central banks would maintain part of their reserves in gold-convertible foreign exchange rather than in gold. The desirability of restoring the gold standard was not questioned; the gold exchange standard was conceived as an alternative to deflation. As events turned out, deflation was merely postponed until 1922. In 1931, when economy in the use of gold was most needed, it was completely neglected and the gold standard was abandoned altogether.

After the first World War, London's acceptance business declined and the volume of foreign demand deposits in London rose. Britain became more vulnerable to a foreign run. A more important difficulty was the apparent overvaluation of sterling on the restoration of the gold standard in 1925. Convertibility of sterling into gold at the old rate could be maintained only at the cost of deflation and unemployment. There were those in Britain, notably Keynes, who pointed to the dangers of the old parity. In the end it was still considered a matter of prestige in England to maintain the traditional gold rating of the pound. The French franc, on the other hand, was undervalued in relation to gold, and the Bank of France consequently accumulated large holdings of sterling bills which might be liquidated at short notice. The Bank of France began in 1928 to withdraw its London funds systematically—a step which eventually contributed to the demise of the postwar gold standard system.

Under the pressure of world depression Britain suspended gold payments in September 1931. Meanwhile the raising of Bank rate was a signal that the Bank of England was prepared to defend the pound sterling and the inflation which everyone feared would result from the abandonment of gold did not materialize. The fall in price levels increased the purchasing power of gold and induced large-scale dishoarding of Indian gold to the benefit of Britain. The depression also tended to improve the terms of trade and the institution of imperial preferences in 1932 helped maintain the volume of sterling area trade. On the whole, Britain hoped for a regime in which a managed dollar-sterling rate, varying from time to time, would serve the needs of the economy. At the beginning of the period in the depression and at its end at the outbreak of war there were great fluctuations in the sterling-dollar rate, but through the rest of the period it proved impracticable to allow the rate to fluctuate except within narrow margins. The disruptive effects on trade, as argued through diplomatic and governmental channels, made the fluctuating rate an international political anomaly. Beyond that there was the incessant problem of how to manage an unfixed rate of exchange. At what point should the authorities withdraw their support of the pound? At what point should they resume support? As it worked out the "managed" rate was very like a fixed rate.

Then the beginning of World War II put an end to the debate.

Chapter 3

THE IMPACT OF WAR ON STERLING ARRANGEMENTS

> If it should come to the ear of the court, how I have been transformed, and how my transformation hath been washed and cudgelled, they would melt me out of my fat, drop by drop, and liquor fishermen's boots with me . . .
>
> THE MERRY WIVES OF WINDSOR

THE PRESENT sterling system grew out of wartime controls. Its distinctive feature compared to earlier years lies in the difference in substance and formality of rules governing the spending of sterling by owners living in different parts of the world.

In its evolution, sterling has passed through three periods: first, the development of a national currency system from coins to credit; then, its internationalization as an effective British market area carried beyond the geographical confines of England; and finally, in this last generation, a kind of regional retreat as the British economy shrank in relation to the rest of the world. The first phase was highlighted by arbitrary interferences in the monetary setup with considerable distinction between British residents and foreigners; the second by the establishment of more or less common financial facilities in London for Britons and foreigners alike; and the third by a regrouping of sterling facilities along lines that made transactions among sterling-associated countries easier than transactions with countries whose currencies were not coupled with sterling.

During the thirties the regionalization was based on the difference between the fixed exchange rate for sterling bloc countries and a variable sterling rate for transactions outside the bloc. For Empire countries, dependent and independent, this preferment of sterling transactions was reinforced by discriminatory tariff policy. In the postwar period the policy of a uniform rate for sterling against all countries was adopted, but the regionalization was made far more decisive through the operation of direct controls on imports, more or less coordinated throughout the sterling world.

The Present Types of Sterling

The Midland Bank of London has devised a diagram, published from time to time, showing generally the transfers permitted between various types of accounts. The latest version (January 20, 1955) available at the time of writing, is reprinted, with the Bank's permission, on the following page, slightly revised to take into account Turkey's subsequent membership in the transferable account area.

Official sterling regulations now (February 1956) distinguish three broad classes of sterling holders; the differences lie in the purposes for which each class of holders can use its sterling. The first, and inner, group is the sterling area. As a rule, members of the area place almost no restrictions other than tariffs on their trade with one another, and very few on capital movements among themselves. It is not quite clear who in effect owns the gold and dollar reserves of the area. They are centralized in London, and legally form part of the United Kingdom's Exchange Equalisation Account. But sterling area countries consider these reserves as automatically available for their use on the basis of rules mutually agreed upon. As a counterpart to this mutual access to reserves they keep their international spending policies on roughly similar lines in the entire range of transactions which might involve pressure on these reserves. They also base their own currencies primarily or entirely on a variety of sterling obligations issued by the British Treasury.

Next in order of the relative freedom with which their sterling can be used are the transferable account countries. These countries, which include all countries outside the sterling and dollar areas, can use their sterling with a high

UNITED KINGDOM EXCHANGE CONTROL REGULATIONS: OUTLINE OF PERMISSIBLE TRANSFERS

→ The arrow indicates directions of transfers, permitted without individual approval by the Control, between different categories of sterling accounts. All other transfers require separate approval.

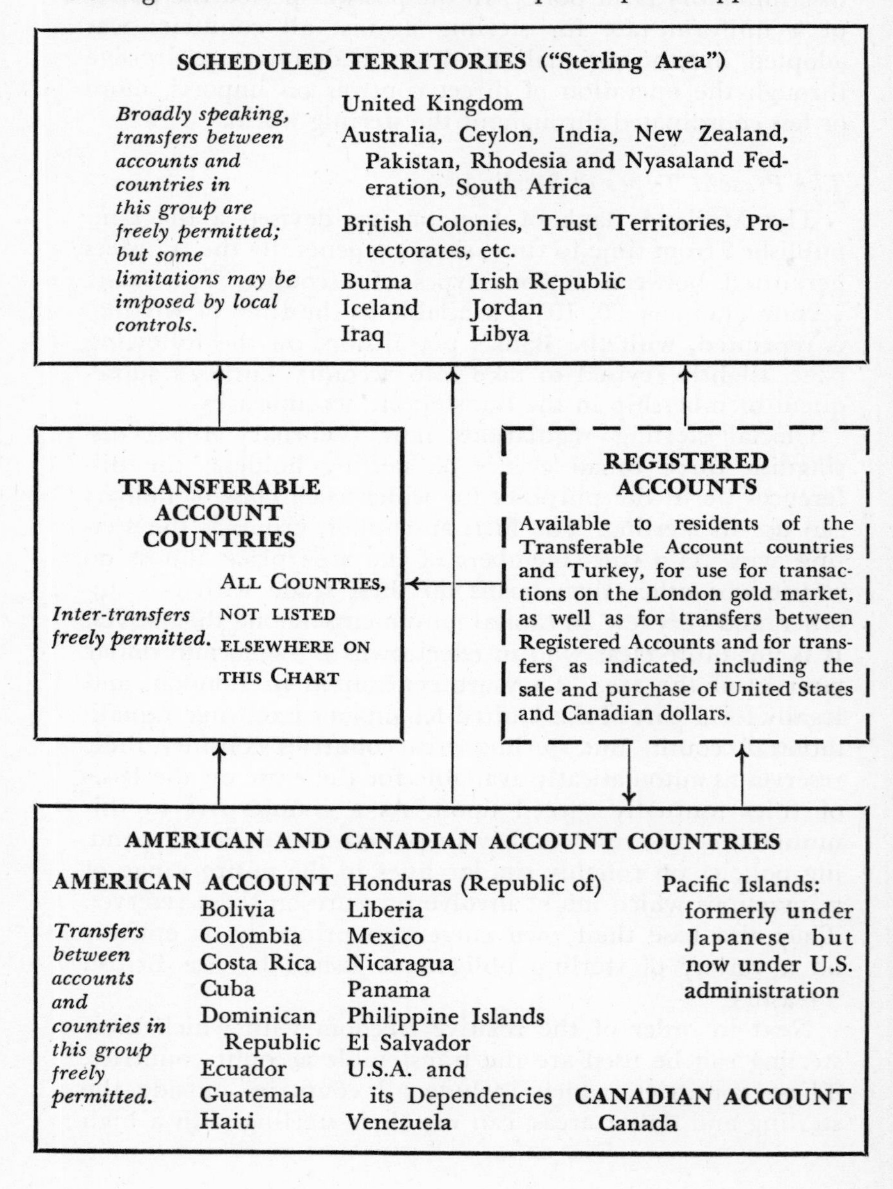

degree of freedom for both current and capital transactions with the sterling area and with one another. They have, however, no direct access to the foreign-exchange reserves in London. This difference from the facilities available to sterling area members has declined continuously as free sterling markets outside the sterling area have been first tolerated, then encouraged, and ultimately even supported by the United Kingdom.

Finally, there are the dollar countries, who enjoy complete access to the foreign-exchange reserves of London for conversion of all of their current earnings of sterling and to a considerable degree for the sterling they hold on capital account.[1] In selling their goods and services, however, the dollar countries enjoy only limited access to sterling markets. Since under these rules all sterling earned by dollar countries constitutes a potential direct call on reserves, sterling rules limit the ability to enlarge these earnings through import quotas and exchange controls imposed more stringently against dollar expenditures than against other expenditures.

The sterling held by each of these classes of owners is usually described as, respectively, "resident sterling," "transferable account sterling," and "dollar account sterling." The first two are now virtually interchangeable—at least as far as the United Kingdom is concerned—for both current and capital transactions. Because of the existence of free sterling markets for both sterling securities and sterling bank credits, there is a considerable degree of convertibility between transferable accounts and dollar accounts at a varying but small discount against sterling. "Registered sterling," a fourth type, is acquired by payment of gold or dollars to a British bank by someone living outside the dollar area. Registered sterling is convertible into dollars, and was created as part of the machinery of the free gold market reopened in London in 1954.

The rationale of these practices, stated so bluntly, may

[1] Repatriation is permitted for all direct investment and appreciation of investment made after 1949. But private firms may agree to accumulate sterling or use it in the sterling area, as the oil and movie companies have done.

seem elusive. In the light of wartime and immediate post-war experience the significance is clearer.

The Wartime System

Apart from the negative aim of preventing any use of sterling in a way harmful to Britain's war effort, the objective of wartime rules covering the use of sterling in foreign markets or by foreigners was to augment Britain's war potential as much as possible. This was not just a monetary problem; it was a problem of arranging for maximum availability of resources for war purposes. In financial practice it meant a policy of buying abroad wherever possible against promises to pay later rather than against cash. In a sense this policy was the counterpart of the domestic financing of the war through governmental borrowing, although domestically the idea was to finance through borrowing as little of the war cost as possible while internationally the idea was to borrow as much as possible.

As it worked out Britain enjoyed two major types of credit abroad, both without definite limitation. The monument of the first type, namely payments to other countries in sterling not then usable, is seen now in the remains of the large wartime accumulations of sterling by other countries. In exchange for goods and services furnished Britain during the war, sterling countries accepted British IOUs ("sterling balances") to the extent of some £2 billion; other non-dollar countries accepted another billion. Because of the nature of the currency structures of the sterling countries, a virtually unlimited line of credit was automatically available to Britain; to limit it would have called for positive action by these sterling countries in reshaping their normally sterling-based monetary structures. All these countries were accustomed to accepting sterling without question and to regarding it as a suitable basis for a corresponding issue of their own currencies. In the case of sterling countries operating their currencies on the basis of a 100 per cent sterling reserve, the credit was completely automatic. Britain could acquire their currencies to meet current expenditures by buying it from the local monetary authorities and paying for it in British Treasury obligations, since these obligations

—"sterling"—were legally acceptable as the basis for a corresponding increase in the local currency issue. The real economic aim and consequence was a net current transfer of resources from these countries to Britain, but the method of doing it differed sharply compared with the less inflationary methods pursued in the United Kingdom itself in the course of achieving a similar transfer of resources from British consumers to the government.

This account of how sterling countries accumulated sterling balances during the war is, of course, oversimplified, but the basic picture is, I believe, correct and it would not be worth our while to catalogue all the exceptions to it. Sterling countries did accept United Kingdom obligations, and they did permit close to an equivalent currency expansion locally without a matching increase in production. At the end of the war the consequently inflated price levels in many sterling countries gave them their most formidable financial problem.

Besides this important line of credit in the sterling world, Britain enjoyed an open line of credit in the dollar world through lend-lease arrangements with the United States. The intention of lend-lease, as in the case of the sterling credits available to Britain through the sterling system, was to facilitate the net transfer of real resources to Britain for war use without holding up the process while working out the ultimate terms of repayment. Lend-lease was not just a credit to Britain but a part of the general machinery of the allied war effort in which Britain sacrificed much of its export trade in order to concentrate on war production with the help of goods lend-leased from abroad.

There were limiting factors on this net transfer of resources, chiefly shipping, production bottlenecks, and United States decisions as to what could be spared from its own requirements. The effect of lend-lease was to rule out *finance* as a limiting factor. By the end of the war this line of credit to Britain amounted to $23 billion. (Total American lend-lease aid to Britain came to $29 billion but reverse lend-lease by Britain reduced the net figure.)

The wartime objective was not to minimize Britain's international deficit but almost the opposite. Under these conditions, the peacetime objective of following policies leading to a balance of accounts with the rest of the world played little part in financial decisions. But the wartime system developed along lines that were to influence strongly the nature of the postwar system of controls, and were, as I see it, to bias that later system somewhat against effectiveness in achieving and maintaining balance in international accounts.

Certain aspects of the wartime sterling system also played a part in the postwar system. The exchange rate between sterling and dollars was fixed, as was the rate between sterling and the currencies of the sterling area countries. Britain's international deficits, which were internationally agreed among the allies to be the necessary consequence of achieving the desired extension of Britain's effort beyond the limits of Britain's own production, were covered by the unique and almost automatic credits available in the sterling world and by other credits from the United States and Canada. Direct controls on imports were relied upon to assure priority for purchases important for warfare and to save shipping. These features of the wartime system were retained, though with many qualifications, in the postwar system.

The end of hostilities did, however, involve a very important change in the circumstances under which the sterling system had been operating. The automatic line of credit for Britain in sterling countries, although perhaps continuing to exist in theory, could not be utilized in practice. On the contrary, the recognized problem was how Britain might reverse the direction of the flow of credit and make it possible for her wartime sterling creditors to spend their accumulations. Similarly, lend-lease was suddenly terminated in August 1945. No longer was Britain to enjoy an almost unlimited charge account in the dollar world. Further help there was to be, but from now on there was to be revived emphasis on current earnings as a general limit of expenditures.

Lend-lease was viewed in the United States as a purely wartime measure; Congress authorized this extraordinary technique of aiding Britain and other allies on the explicit understanding that it was purely a wartime exception to normal methods of international finance. But the end of the war came faster than anyone expected before the power of the atomic bomb was demonstrated. The main means of wartime financial cooperation between Britain and the United States thus disappeared before a satisfactory means of peacetime cooperation, envisaged by both governments, could be brought into existence. The abrupt and unexpected ending of lend-lease was bitterly received in Britain; it precipitated discussion of a large credit.

The effect of this fundamental alteration in Britain's credit availabilities abroad was to restore traditional priority to the problem of achieving international balance as a prime concern of financial policy makers. No more sterling chits were to be signed in the non-sterling world for the time being, and the possibility of signing them even in the sterling world was not promising. In effect, Britain had suddenly to turn to the normal problems of international finance at a time when her economic posture was still far from normal. It is probably not surprising that the methods adopted were a continuation of the "abnormal" methods of war.

Postwar Alternatives

As seen in Britain, the central economic problem was to maximize production and employment. But the termination of major credits abroad meant that Britain would have to find a satisfactory means of limiting its expenditures abroad to an amount that could be covered by earnings plus much reduced borrowings and whatever might be spared temporarily from the small pool of reserves.

Theoretically a number of alternative techniques could have been adopted to bring about this sort of balance. Any limiting of expenditures on imports and any raising of earnings from exports would be in the direction of balance. *Devaluation* was one possibility. At the fixed wartime rate of 4.03 dollars per pound, the amount of sterling which owners would want to convert into dollars clearly exceeded the supply. If dollars were priced too cheaply in terms of sterling, why not raise the price? Would not such an action automatically make it possible to sell British produce abroad at the same price in terms of sterling but at lower prices in terms of other currencies? Would it not automatically raise the sterling price of foreign produce? Would not this broad alteration in price relations between Britain and the rest of the world restore balance in international sterling transactions? To such straightforward and simple questions, only qualified answers were to be found.

Another possible approach was *deflation,* or the reduction of the supply of sterling available for expediture anywhere, including foreign markets. This had been more or less the traditional approach to reestablishing balance in international accounts. If a country is spending too much abroad, then a reduction in the incomes of purchasers is bound to curtail expenditures on imports and at the same time bring domestic costs down so that domestic produce can be sold more cheaply abroad.

The third possibility was to make use of wartime *controls* to limit directly by quotas the amount of foreign exchange, particularly dollars, that would be sold to an owner of sterling. This technique is simply rationing, in much the same way that limited food supplies during the war were rationed according to government-determined priorities rather than by a free price system. Total expenditures abroad could be limited by the imposition of import quotas on goods and the maintenance of exchange controls to limit expenditures on services and capital transfers.

In the event it was the last method that was chosen and consistently pursued in the first four years after the war. Whether devaluation or deflation would have worked cannot be known, but there is a likelihood that they would not have and the virtual certainty that if they worked at all it would have been at a needless and socially intolerable cost in terms of production and employment. There was the risk and perhaps even the clear presumption that if the restoration of international balance in sterling accounts could be achieved at all through devaluation or deflation it would only be at so low a level of production as to impoverish the sterling area.

The Problem of Balance

In economics, financial balance is not an end in itself but a means of arranging for a more productive market. An extreme form of financial balance achieved for its own sake would be no trade at all. The real problem for the sterling area and especially for Britain was to reestablish and extend production. It was obvious that export capacity had been greatly shrunken by war damage and by the monopolization of resources for war production. Export capacity was far short of basic import needs, now swollen by the shortage of consumer goods and the needs of reconstructing damaged or obsolescent plant and adapting it to peacetime demands. If the termination of foreign credit facilities made it necessary to face the financial problem and accept the grim notion that Britain would have to live on what it could produce at the moment, then it was doubly important to assure priority to projects promising enlarged output. The technique of control was not only already in operation and familiar; it seemed the only way by which production could be guided upward.

In the circumstances Britain decided to keep sterling officially related to the dollar at the wartime rate and to ration dollars at this price for the essentials of consumption and for the reconstitution of production. The maintenance of the wartime exchange rate was not a matter of believing that this rate had any immediate market reality, but rather of believing that a higher price on dollars would be equally arbitrary in a deranged economy and might entail a prolonged period of difficulty in rearranging the economy for a satisfactory level of production. The hope was that the $4.03 rate would eventually be validated by the growth of dollar-earning power and by the reduction of dependence on dollar sources of supply, both of which were the anticipated results of the revival of production.

There was no real conflict of opinion among the allies as to the necessity of maintaining import controls immediately after the war, regardless of the rate question. At a time when the dollar world alone was physically able to supply the vital core of goods and services needed from outside the war-damaged countries to provide for a decent level of consumption and a hopeful rate of reconstruction and development, dollars would be scarce and their use would have to accord with carefully established and controlled priorities.

Britain, like other non-dollar countries, saw its dollar problem as the need to make the best possible use of a very short supply of dollars and to protect and strengthen the central reserves of the sterling system so that day-to-day balancing of international accounts would not be necessary. But the dollar problem was only part of the problem which controls on imports were intended to meet. The tremendous accumulation of sterling by other countries during the war posed an obvious threat of drain on low-geared and distorted British production. Somehow, the use of these balances would have to be regulated; sterling as well as dollars would have to be rationed. Beyond this there was the problem of trying to revive traditional prewar trading relations with countries which were in neither the dollar nor sterling worlds, notably continental Europe. What sort of a credit structure could be pieced together so as to permit this traditional trade to start again? The partners in this former trade were not now in a position either to extend continuous credits to one another or to make their settlements in dollars or gold.

Britain's immediate approach to these three aspects of its postwar balance of payments was tailored to the differences in the problems. The dollar problem was handled by an administrative rationing of dollars on the basis of consultation and negotiation with sterling colleagues, taking into account their requirements. The wartime practice of pooling in London the dollars earned by all sterling associates was continued—partly out of habit, partly out of a sense on the part of the outer sterling area that it should do what it could to ease the obviously difficult situation of the United Kingdom, partly out of a common persuasion that the pooling process would be best adapted to covering the essential needs of all the parties, and partly because it seemed to sterling creditors to be in the interest of an eventual conversion of their sterling balances. The sterling-balance problem was handled by negotiated understandings of varying degrees of formality and detail on how far old sterling claims might be used for current purchases. The problem with traditional trading partners in Europe and elsewhere was handled through a series of bilateral agreements envisaging reasonable current account balance and providing modest and temporary credit accommodation for small imbalances.

That the fundamentally regional character of such arrangements would be a persistent feature of postwar British finance was probably not appreciated at the time. The special handling of financial transactions with this and that area was seen mainly as a temporary and necessary aberration from the multilateral system that was seen as the ultimate objective. In fact, the aberrations were regarded as moving along the right track; almost every restriction could be described as less restrictive than what existed before.

For example, the understandings between the United Kingdom and the sterling countries provided for freedom of payments and capital movements within the area, and envisaged growing freedom to buy in the dollar area. British negotiations with third countries (non-sterling, non-dollar) were in behalf of the entire sterling area, not just the United Kingdom. Moreover, the British bilateral agreements, which typically took the form of providing modest mutual credit margins through the central banks as a means of getting around the lack of mutually acceptable foreign-exchange reserves, also provided for a modest degree of gold convertibility for debts in excess of the margins and for the margins too in the event of the termination of agreements. In addition, renegotiation and alteration of the bilateral understandings was usually explicitly provided for in case either party joined a wider (multilateral) clearing arrangement. The constant aim was to increase the freedom of payments over an ever widening area; in other words, to restore the international use of sterling as rapidly as possible.

This was in keeping with the multilateral aims that inspired the Bretton Woods negotiations in 1944. This was the letter and the spirit of the large loans from the United States and Canada to the United Kingdom in 1946. But for all that, the result of the actual practices in the immediate postwar period was a partial consolidation of an international non-dollar area, and a clearer definition of the barrier between that area and the dollar world. The practices adopted in pursuance of the policy of freeing payments virtually guaranteed that the policy could not succeed beyond a certain point.

The Anglo-American Financial Agreement

Under the terms of the Anglo-American Financial Agreement, a very broad freedom of payment between the sterling and dollar worlds was recognized as the aim of financial policy. Wartime lend-lease aid to Britain was written off; repayment of the lend-lease money used to finance the pipeline of civilian goods flowing since V-J day was funded on a long-term basis; United States surplus property in British territory was sold to the British government at bargain rates. Britain undertook formidable obligations to alter the sterling system so as to conform to the agreed multilateral principles of trade and payments within a year after ratification. Ratification came on July 15, 1946; on July 15, 1947 Britain was obliged by the terms of the Agreement to make foreign-earned sterling convertible into dollars for current purposes. This meant simply that the rationing of dollars among current earners of sterling and for current (as contrasted to capital) purposes was to end. After July 15, 1947 anyone living outside the sterling area who had earned a pound of sterling was to be entitled to go to a bank and get approximately 4.03 dollars for it, if he intended to use the dollars and not just hoard them or invest them. This short statement of the British obligation is oversimplified, and the obligation perhaps was not as definite as this, but since our concern for the moment is with the preparatory steps which Britain took during the year of grace before the obligation came into effect, it will serve as a reasonably fair generalization about the sort of freedom of payments envisaged in the Agreement.

It seemed apparent in 1946 that the dollar-convertibility obligation would move toward the elimination of the differences existing between one type of sterling and another. If

Britain was to be obliged to give 4.03 dollars in exchange for a pound offered by anyone anywhere, then the difference between a Finn's pound sterling and an American's would disappear; they would be equal at least in their dollar-buying power. It seemed the most logical sort of preparation for this basic change in the existing sterling system of controlled transfers to eliminate progressively the differences among various types of sterling. A wide "transferable account system" was created in response to this logic. While the final plum of being able to buy dollars with sterling was withheld for the time being, sterling holders in transferable account countries were given more room to practice up for this promised event. They could swap sterling among themselves without getting specific permission from British government authorities.

This was not an insignificant concession, nor one without obligation on the part of those receiving it. A transferable account country's obligation was to accept sterling from other transferable account countries without specified limit. The concession was to permit residents of these countries to transfer sterling among themselves, or to and from the sterling area, or to and from the residents of countries with which the United Kingdom maintained bilateral agreements. In effect this meant that anyone in the transferable account area could use his sterling for current business almost anywhere except in the dollar world.

Under these arrangements, sterling smacked of the old days of general convertibility. The area within which a payment could be made in sterling was considerably widened. This had the important incidental consequence of making more people more willing to hold more sterling and to regard it as a currency of final international settlement even though it could not be turned into gold or dollars. Its regional efficiency was increased with the widening of the region and the freeing of sterling's use therein.

From the United Kingdom's point of view, the ideal condition under which to grant transferable account status would involve a seal of approval on the general efficiency of the other country's exchange control system in preventing untoward drains on the British economy or on the sterling area's reserves. If the other country's controls should be judged reliable enough, then London controls would not be necessary. Actually the granting of transferable account status was more a matter of taking a chance that the known inefficiencies of other exchange control systems would not be harmful, or at least that the harm done would not offset the gains from a wider international use of sterling. As in the case of the wartime freedom granted to sterling countries in handling their London funds, the standard was one of a tolerable level of inefficiency of local controls rather than an ideal level of efficiency. There was no real choice involved for Britain, other than the choice between administrative procedures which would withdraw sterling from international use as a result of policing every transaction and procedures which would yield considerably greater freedom to foreign holders of sterling in determining their use of it. The wartime Anglo-American monopoly of shipping could no longer be counted on in controlling the movement of goods into desired channels, and it became doubtful that the relatively high efficiency of British controls could be maintained in a period of peace.

Inevitably the relaxation of direct British control over the use of funds held in London by other countries led to greater freedom in the use of these funds for purposes not intended by the British. The most important of these unintended purposes was the financing of transactions with the dollar world. British authorities were aware of these dangers. During the war and afterwards there was an obvious black market for sterling currencies which afforded convenient opportunities to exchange sterling at a discount against dollars. Discounted sterling, commonly known as "cheap sterling" in the world of finance, was a familiar commodity in all money markets outside the United Kingdom. The discount tended to rise directly with efforts to eliminate the market, and to fall as the monetary authorities relaxed their efforts to make official sterling the only sterling. The more the authorities tried to make the official rules for rationing dollars stick, the more the premium on the dollar rose in unofficial markets; such efforts dramatized the difference between sterling available for limited purposes from official sources and sterling available for almost unlimited purposes from unofficial sources.

There are other interesting features of the year of preparation for dollar convertibility under the terms of the Agreement. First, a negative one. None of the preparatory arrangements involved any increase in freedom of access to London's gold and dollar reserves by either sterling or non-sterling countries. In the course of negotiating the Agreement it was foreseen that the £3.4 billion in sterling balances held by other countries at the end of the war would have to be controlled in some fashion. If these claims were to be recognized as claims against central gold and dollar reserves, they could quickly overwhelm the several billion dollars which the United States was willing to lend in support of those reserves. But it was only *other countries'* holdings of sterling that constituted a point of concern in the Agreement. There was not a word about *internal* finance, which later appeared to most economists as the heart of the matter. This silence was no doubt due to the traditional diplomatic convention under which no country would be rude enough to suggest changes in the way in which friendly neighbors ran their households. The problems of internal inflation, open or suppressed, were at least partially understood, but they were not a subject for negotiation.

The preparatory arrangements to prevent too fast a use of external holdings of sterling were of two kinds. First, the dollar earnings of sterling countries would continue to be pooled in London and their drawings from the pool controlled by gentlemen's agreements or definite dollar allocations. In either case local controls on dollar imports were the rule. Second, understandings of varying degrees of formality were reached about the use of past accumulations of sterling by the sterling balance holders. In the case of some of the big creditors—undivided India, Egypt, and Iraq—the agreements involved the principle of distinguishing what net amount of sterling would be considered as expendable within the next year, and what would be "frozen." In other cases—Australia and New Zealand for example—this principle was not reduced to definite quantities of expendable sterling but was nonetheless recognized as the main guide for local policy.

All this was roughly, but only roughly, the way the negotiators of the Agreement envisaged a proper handling of sterling balances. The United States was in the course of writing off its claims against the United Kingdom. The negotiators of both countries had in mind a series of settlements in which friendly countries which had provided help on credit to Britain during the war would write off a substantial amount of their claims—perhaps typically a third—and then agree to present their remaining claims only over a long period of time so as not to overtax the tautly strained British economy. But the two largest creditors, India and Egypt, which together had sterling claims of some £1.5 billion, were deaf to suggestions that some of their claims should be written off. They reasoned that they had sorely deprived their peoples during the war in order to provision Allied forces and that in any case they were basically poorer than the temporarily belt-tightened British populace. The more extreme British optimists saw a good part of the leaning tower of sterling balances as being cut off in sportsmanlike recognition of the excessive burden borne by Britain for all associated countries during the war. Other Britons were more concerned about the disruptive effects of an expected United States recession, and some even felt that the sterling balances would, if left intact, be an important offset to a depressed state of United States buying. In the event nothing was written off except the lend-lease debt to the United States and various Canadian claims arising from wartime aid to Britain, plus £46 million of the Australian and New Zealand claims. The rest—well over £3 billion—still loomed over the British economy like a black cloud whose sudden burst was forestalled only by loose arrangements, so long as Britain rejected the disastrous final sanction of repudiation.

Egypt left the sterling area in the course of these preparations. The Egyptian government was unwilling to be in the position of blocking its own residents' holdings of sterling, and Britain was unwilling to be in the position of blocking the holdings of a member of the sterling area. This issue over who would do the blocking was a technical one and probably would not have become important except for the general atmosphere of political contention which prevailed between the two countries. As it worked out, Egypt left the area, Britain did the blocking, and Egypt operated a general control of imports in exchange for concessions on the use of its sterling and for modest allocations of dollars from the United Kingdom. Egypt's relationship to sterling was not significantly affected by this technical departure from the area, although the departure may have reflected Egypt's general drift away from British relationships.

At the time, these arrangements between Britain and the various classes of sterling holders both in the area and outside it looked like the steps one would expect in preparation for Britain's implementation of the dollar-convertibility obligation. The United Kingdom went as far as it could in isolating the current pressure from sterling debts on resources and reserves. Sterling was made easier to use in the whole non-dollar world. In a sense, the non-dollar world was consolidated under the aegis of sterling, and the mold was set against dollar convertibility. The consolidation took the broad form of payments arrangements supported by import controls under which it became increasingly easy to conduct business within the non-dollar world but remained difficult to conduct business with the dollar world.

Convertibility Under the Agreement

The Anglo-American Financial Agreement spells out in considerable detail (but with considerable ambiguity) the obligations identified with the Agreement's concept of current dollar convertibility for sterling. The Agreement was for the most part silent on the conditions which would have to exist if the new convertible regime were to work. It is understandable that international negotiators from two countries would shy away from prescribing the internal financial policies to be pursued by sterling area members and the relations to be established between Britain and countries not party to the Agreement. In the one instance in which the Agreement did make a specific bow to the United Kingdom's negotiations with countries other than the United States—namely in Section 10, dealing with the envisaged neutralization of the sterling holdings of the United Kingdom's wartime creditors—the provision led to bitterness in other countries toward both the United Kingdom and the United States.

In later instances international negotiators and even international administrative authorities did not hesitate to focus their attention very sharply on internal financial policy. Examples are the periodic and special reviews of the policies of members made by the Organization for European Economic Cooperation (OEEC) in connection with the operation of the European Payments Union (EPU) and, in the case of the sterling family itself, the historic communiqué issued at the end of the Commonwealth Economic Conference of finance ministers in December 1952. (Appendix) In looking now at the Anglo-American Financial Agreement as an expression of international financial policy, it is hard to resist the impression that the authorities of the two countries did not foresee the size of the external problems or the extent to which these problems were linked to internal financial policies. Reading the lines and in between the lines of that Agreement now, one gets the impression that it embodies a diagnosis of the obstacles to further dollar convertibility of sterling entirely in terms of, first, the menace of un-neutralized sterling war debts, and second, Britain's limited though recuperating production and export capacity and therefore its probable deficit in current trade with other countries. Accordingly, to deal with the former the Agreement suggested what the negotiators consider an appropriate pattern of agreements which would neutralize Britain's sterling war debt. To deal with the latter, the Agreement provided a substantial dollar credit. With these problems presumably taken care of, it was thought that a satisfactory basis for dollar convertibility would exist.

The United Kingdom's obligations under the Agreement looked toward a basic shaking up of sterling practices. The most important changes are contained in Sections 7, 8 and 9 of the Agreement. Section 7 dealt with the United Kingdom's relations with the sterling area, and called upon the United Kingdom to give to all sterling area *countries* (presumably but not explicitly excluding the colonies) freedom to use their current earnings of sterling for current transactions in any currency area without discrimination, within a year after ratification of the Agreement. The effect of this freedom was specifically equated in the Agreement with the end of "discrimination arising from the so-called sterling area dollar pool." Once this obligation had come into force it was to continue indefinitely.

Section 8 dealt with the United Kingdom's other foreign-exchange arrangements and provided first for a removal of exchange controls limiting payment for "permitted" imports into the United Kingdom from the United States or limiting the use of currently earned sterling in the hands of United States residents. These provisions were perhaps largely unnecessary because United States exporters could have accomplished much the same result by resorting to dollar invoicing in the absence of a right to use current accumulations of sterling freely. This British obligation to United States sterling holders differed from its obligation to other sterling holders in that United States holders would have the right to cash currently earned sterling for dollars whether or not the purpose was to finance a current expenditure. More importantly, Section 8 defined generally the dollar-convertibility obligation of the United Kingdom toward all holders of sterling outside the sterling area countries and the United States. The obligation, subject to minor exceptions, was to make currently earned sterling convertible into dollars for current purposes not later than July 16, 1947. The United States undertook an obligation to make the dollar internationally convertible in the same sense—an obligation to go on doing what was already being done with the dollar.

The British obligation was defined exclusively with reference to controls over payments and transfers and not with reference to import controls. The latter were dealt with in Section 9, in which both governments agreed, subject to certain exceptions, that as soon as possible and not later than the end of 1946, they would not impose discriminatory controls against imports from each other. Both Sections 8 and 9 were to operate until December 31, 1951, which date was also the end date for the United Kingdom's access to the line of credit provided under the Agreement.

This was the core of what the United Kingdom agreed to do in return for the American credit. The United States agreed to operate according to the same principles, so the Agreement was an exchange of mutual obligations, but in the case of the United States these obligations entailed no modification of current policy, while for the United Kingdom they spelled out a decisively changed regime for sterling.

This summary of the crucial obligations undertaken in the Agreement does not do justice to its specific terms. A close look at the exact terms raises some questions which have great interest in the light of how things worked out. What sort of obligation would the United Kingdom have after the expiration of the obligations to be assumed under Sections 8 and 9? To what extent under Section 7 were the colonies to be identified with the United Kingdom rather than treated as "countries" of the sterling area? Under Section 8 and 9 how far could the United Kingdom go in curtailing the dollar expenditures of its own residents or colonial residents? A number of other contingencies, mostly related to the possible failure of convertibility, were not foreseen. What would the United Kingdom be permitted to do in case the dollar credit should be—as it was—prematurely exhausted? Further, the Agreement, being bilateral, could not preclude discrimination against dollar imports into other sterling countries or into other non-dollar countries which would presumably be interested in the new conversion facilities.

Sterling on the Eve of Convertibility

During the golden age of sterling in the late nineteenth century, anyone who had a pound sterling had many options as to its use. He could use it to buy something from the United Kingdom or from anywhere else in the world. He could hang on to it with the feeling that when he did want to spend it, he could spend it pretty much on anything and pretty much anywhere in the world. He could buy gold with it if he chose—gold coins, or gold to wear, or gold bullion to hoard. He could buy dollars with it. All he had to do was to express his preference to his bank.

On the eve of the 1947 convertibility experiment the situation was radically different. Before using his sterling the holder would have to consider where and how and when he got it, and where and how and when he wanted to use it. His choices also depended on where he was making his home. If any of these wheres, whens and hows involved a possible swap of sterling for dollars, the proposed use would be especially closely scrutinized. Before he ever got to the market, he might have to go through an arcade of official bureaus and arm himself with more permits than money—a circumstance to no one's liking. If his sterling was "current," that is, if he had earned it since a given cut-off date, he could use it more easily than if it were part of a past accumulation. If he proposed to use it to make payments for newly produced goods or newly rendered services, he would have easier going than if he wanted to repay an old debt or make an investment abroad. Finally, he would find differing degrees of difficulty depending on his geographic residence and that of the person with whom he proposed to do business. For example, if he himself were a resident of the sterling area and so were his proposed trading partner, he would encounter almost no difficulty; if he were a resident of continental Europe and he proposed using his sterling to make a payment to the United States, he would encounter almost insuperable difficulty.

This system of classified sterling accounts was a compartmentalized system of international payments, like a large house divided into many rooms of varying size and with corridors providing easy access between some, inconvenient access between others, and no access between still others. The steps taken in the year of preparation for dollar convertibility were in the nature of knocking out a few partitions, widening a few corridors, and opening a few doors. But the doors to the outside dollar world remained guarded, though occasionally the guards fell asleep or looked the other way. It may seem that this sort of preparation had little relationship to the security of the house once the outside doors were opened, as they had to be under the Agreement on July 16, 1947. The improvement of internal communications in the sterling house in some ways may have adversely affected the brief experiment with dollar convertibility. But the nature of the preparations was nonetheless logical. Dollar convertibility would automatically provide an interlinking of all sterling accounts; it seemed obviously reasonable to establish and experiment with as much of this interlinking as possible before facing the more dangerous possibilities that dollar convertibility would entail.

The objective of the compartmentalization was to assure that foreign exchange, including reserves and the small amount of mutual credits which had been arranged among central banks, would be effectively used without the need of raising its price (i.e., devaluing sterling). The principle of operation was to favor the purchase of essential goods and to stimulate the rejuvenation of trade throughout the non-dollar world. The technique involved a network of import licenses; once granted, they automatically entitled the recipient to purchase any necessary foreign exchange from the central pool at the official rate. Whether a license should be required for a given class of transactions depended on the authorities' estimate of whether such transactions would overtax British productive facilities or threaten the central gold and dollar reserves or in any other way be inconsistent with the priorities assigned to assuring an adequate influx of essential goods.

The problem of preparation was seen implicitly in the Agreement as one of neutralizing the danger which the large volume of sterling balances would otherwise bring to Britain's reserves under conditions of dollar convertibility. If the balances could be effectively handled, then the only remaining problem would be in financing the sterling area's *current* deficit, and this deficit probably was thought of mainly as a matter of Britain's deficit with the *dollar* world. In any case, the negotiators envisaged a British deficit on current account, even if the problem of the sterling balances could be gotten out of the way. The inevitability of such a deficit was the main reason for negotiating an agreement. The deficit was foreseen as being in the magnitude of some $5 billion over some four years, a serious underestimate. Under the Agreement the United States provided a credit of $3¾ billion, and under a collateral agreement Canada provided a credit of $1¼ billion.

Ironically, Britain's long series of negotiations with both sterling and non-sterling trading partners prepared Britain for everything but dollar convertibility. The danger from possible expenditure of sterling balances at too rapid a rate was not removed by the formal and informal understandings reached with Britain's creditors. Worse, it is possible that these understandings led to Britain's following two principles that may have been more detrimental to her later current position than if there had been no agreement at all.

The first was acceptance of the principle that most creditors should be allowed an annual release of sterling (i.e., a right to spend annually a certain amount of their sterling balances). In some cases the amount was defined, in others just informally understood as falling within reasonable limits. There were two difficulties with this principle. It was a recognition by Britain that all sterling creditors should be given the right to run a current deficit in sterling, i.e., to spend more sterling than they currently earned. This of course is the only way a debt could be liquidated. But the spelling out of the principle imposed on Britain the necessity (perhaps welcome to British traders) of giving high priority to the repayment of war debts rather than to the reconstitution of a trade that would lessen its anticipated dollar deficit. The other difficulty was that the implicit or explicit amounts to be released were large relative to the export capacity of Britain. Later, the situation became familiar in which creditors were unable to get deliveries up to the contemplated ceiling. The existence of these relatively large agreed ceilings on expenditure very likely operated as a means of assigning higher priority to the liquidation of old sterling claims than would otherwise have been the case. The net effect was to edge sterling in the direction of greater usefulness in the non-dollar world at some cost to the strengthening of the position of sterling in the world as a whole.

The second doubtful principle followed by Britain in postwar understandings with sterling area partners before dollar convertibility, was the annual hard currency allocation. With some exceptions, the allocations took the form of limits on the permissible *gross* dollar expenditures by the sterling countries. They got the agreed allocation of dollars regardless of the number of dollars they earned. This left them with no incentive to improve their position in dollar markets; if anything the incentive was the opposite—to minimize their dollar earnings. Some of these countries found themselves highly inflated at the end of the war and hungry for goods, goods both to combat inflation and to make up for the losses in wartime abstention. Their general policy was anti-export; the presumption was that every potential export could be put to better use at home. Under these circumstances, there would be little point in exporting to the dollar world since such exports could not add to the dollars they would have to spend. It seems most likely that this technique of gross allocations of hard currency contributed to the weakness of the sterling area vis-à-vis the dollar world.

The inadequacy of the preparations for dollar convertibility cannot be blamed primarily on a failure of British negotiations before July 16, 1947. The main technical weakness was in the inadequate immobilization of the sterling balances—a point given major emphasis in the loan negotiations and in the Agreement. The loan negotiators, and especially the United States negotiators, seem to have had unrealistic ideas about the readiness of major sterling creditors to accept any impairment of their sterling claims. These creditors were mostly poor countries, and in negotiations they resisted even the smallest concessions and resented any suggestion that they do otherwise. They argued also that any concession to British requests for scaling down the credits would be politically unacceptable to the peoples of creditor countries. The only possible means by which the sterling balances might have been handled along the lines hoped for in the terms of the Agreement would have been through unilateral action by the United Kingdom with the open backing of the United States. Such an action would have amounted to a partial repudiation of the debts and a forced refunding of the remainder over a long period of time. The United Kingdom was unwilling to take this step, which might have been seriously detrimental to the future international status of sterling. It might well have been fatal to a continuance of the sterling area, and perhaps to the political cohesion of the Commonwealth.

I remember the situation in Egypt, where I was living at the time. Egypt was obdurate during the pre-convertibility negotiations with the United Kingdom and the course of negotiations illustrated most of the points about the war-accumulated holdings of sterling. Egypt was the second largest wartime creditor of the United Kingdom. Its sterling balances at the end of the war stood, by Egyptian reckoning, at £440 million, or something more than £20 per capita—a figure not much below the per capita annual earnings of Egyptians and in sum equal to more than 4 per cent of the United Kingdom's annual production at the time. During the war Egypt had accepted sterling in exchange for Egyptian pounds needed by the British and American armies. For the most part these pounds were newly issued and constituted an increase in the supply of Egyptian money. The money supply expanded continuously during the war, while goods for the Egyptian market were at a low level, partly due to shipping difficulties and the resultant interruption of imports, and partly due to the preemption of Egyptian production for allied consumption. Egypt approached the negotiations with the knowledge of its intensified poverty, its inflation, its £440 million nest-egg, and its political antipathy for Britain. Egyptian negotiators had no intention of "scaling down" the country's sterling balances; lend-lease cancellation was a decent gesture for the rich United States, but it ill became a poor country like Egypt. Behind this adamant stand against cancelling any of the debt was the conviction that the proper prescription for Egypt's real needs as well as for its inflation was to increase the volume of goods available locally, and this meant a policy of importing as much as possible and exporting as little as possible. Egyptian export controls were even tighter than the controls on dollar imports; it was practically impossible to buy a bauble in the market and send it out of the country as a Christmas gift, even though one could offer a precious dollar for it. What Egypt wanted was the biggest possible import surplus, to be financed with the wartime accumulations of sterling. In brief, Egypt wanted to spend its sterling balances, and to spend as much as possible of them in the dollar world.

The Egyptian argument against cancellation of part of the balances carries considerable weight. The Egyptian people were, and still are, demonstrably poorer than the British in the depths of the war. The cancellation of sterling claims against Britain would have involved local financial operations of a most difficult sort—the cancellees would have had to be recompensed, and this would have entailed a large, disagreeable and probably unsuccessful operation on a very limited money market. The only part of the Egyptian holdings of sterling that could have been cancelled easily was the sterling held in the note-cover against Egyptian pounds. This could have been handled easily only in the technical sense that the Egyptian government could have substituted its own treasury obligations for those of the British government. This would not have involved any recourse to the market, but it would have been scant comfort to either Egypt or Britain. It would have cancelled claims quite unlikely to be presented against Britain, and so would have afforded no real economic relief to Britain; it would have weakened the Egyptian pound, which in the inflated condition of the country derived considerable strength from its sterling backing, even though it was not clear just what that sterling could be used for; it would have weakened sterling, since one of the major demands for sterling has been as note-cover for other currencies.

The "moral" argument that Britain had saved Egypt from German tyranny worsened the general atmosphere of negotiations. Egypt had never known German tyranny but had known what it regarded as British tyranny. To extreme anti-British elements this moral argument was close to a claim that Egypt had been saved from paradise. Less extreme elements—and these too were anti-British, as most of Egypt was—took the view that it had been Britain's war, that Britain had managed to end up on the winning side, and that now was the time to straighten out the postponed accounting. To me all of this seems so understandable that it leaves only the marvel that the British and American negotiators of the loan could have seriously entertained the likelihood of a voluntary, lend-lease style, scaling down of poor countries' claims against Britain.

Apart from the unrealistic approach to the handling of the sterling balances, the other great defect in the preparations for convertibility as arranged in the loan agreement with the United States was the serious underestimation of the amount of dollar credit that would be required for the effort. This was to be learned from harsh experience. It may be argued that the fault was in the optimism of the negotiators and therefore in the inadequacy of the credit, or it may be argued that the fault was in the failure in the course of preparations for dollar convertibility to concentrate on measures that would have confined the sterling area's dollar deficit to the magnitude of the credit. There is something in both arguments. Certainly the rise in dollar-world prices was not foreseen or provided for. But looking back, one is especially impressed with the inattention to inflationary and potentially inflationary factors in the sterling area and in the United Kingdom itself. The British system of controlled prices, rationing, and subsidies obscured the force that inflation would inevitably exercise, particularly under the freer conditions of dollar convertibility. It is hard to believe that even a very much larger credit—which would have been politically impossible to obtain—would have prevented the failure of the 1947 convertibility experiment. The moral may be that timely and vigorous attention to internal sterling area finance would have saved the experiment, or the moral may be that Britain's and the sterling area's production and trade simply had not progressed far enough to make the obligations of dollar convertibility feasible.

The judgment of financial students differs as to which moral is the correct one. Understandably perhaps, the former moral has the greater appeal in the United States and the latter in the sterling world. One thing is clear. The unreadiness of the sterling area to add dollar convertibility to its system of transfers on the basis of a $5 billion credit from the United States and Canada was scarcely appreciated anywhere on the eve of the attempt. Production in the sterling area, and critically in Britain, was still far short of validating the $4.03 rate at the existing level of income in the sterling world. This difficulty was increased by the similar troubles of most of the area's non-dollar trading partners, especially in Europe, who had as great if not greater a hunger for dollars than Britain and who were impatient to convert sterling assets into dollars. The convertibility trial was premature.

Chapter 4

THE POSTWAR SYSTEM OF CONTROLS AND CRISES

> I would with such perfection govern, sir,
> To excel the golden age.
>
> THE TEMPEST

ON JULY 16, 1947, sterling became convertible into dollars, as required by the terms of the Anglo-American Financial Agreement. The degree of convertibility was still limited; the United Kingdom undertook to exchange dollars for sterling only in the case of certain types of sterling and only for certain purposes. Broadly, the Agreement required the United Kingdom to make this exchange only for sterling earned after July 16, 1947, and for sterling "released" in accordance with British agreements with war creditors. Even in these cases the exchange for dollars was required only if the dollars were to be used to finance current transactions. With the exception of fourteen countries with which the United Kingdom had not been able to complete negotiations, these obligations were given practical effect on the specified day. The emphasis on confining the convertibility obligation to an exchange of dollars for current purposes for sterling currently earned reflected merely the intention of both parties to the Agreement that the United States credit should be used in the interests of trade and not as a means of settling old debts. This idea seems straightforward and reasonable enough but in practice the distinction between old and new claims is very hard to define and harder yet to enforce.

The United Kingdom did not undertake, and the Agreement did not require it to undertake, an unlimited obligation to exchange dollars for sterling held by its own residents, although there was such an obligation to other residents of the sterling area. Also, there was nothing explicitly said in the Agreement to prevent other sterling area members from limiting their dollar expenditures by means of direct—and even concerted—controls on dollar imports. This may have been the strong implication of the terms concerned with the termination of dollar-pooling arrangements and the discrimination against dollar imports woven into pooling practices, and it may also have been more than implicit in the Agreement's various references to the Articles of Agreement of the International Monetary Fund, under which members assumed obligations not to discriminate against other members. But all that was spelled out in the Agreement was that the United Kingdom should not impose a limitation on the access of sterling holders elsewhere in the area—or elsewhere in the world—to dollars held by the United Kingdom authorities, as long as the sterling was currently earned and the dollars were wanted for current transactions.

Even with these qualifications the new regime of greater dollar convertibility was a marked departure from the previous phase of sterling operations. The United Kingdom lost a great deal of its freedom of maneuver in protecting dollar supplies against excessive demands. The supply of "current" sterling held outside the United Kingdom now became the crucial determinant of the potential demand for dollars, and the authorities in London could not, as before, arbitrarily sort out the demand to fit the supply. The United Kingdom could continue to limit its own expenditure of dollars, as before; it could exhort its colleagues in the sterling area to do the same; it could ask other countries holding sterling to be moderate. But it could no longer be the final arbiter in providing dollars to the various claimants; it could no longer ration them unilaterally.

This marked change was not entirely the result of the loan agreement. The United Kingdom's postwar negotiations with other countries as to their use of sterling had already strongly hinted that the days of London's control of recourse to the dollar pool were numbered. Keynes made a strong point of this in pleading for the British Parliament's acceptance of the loan agreement. The "marked change" the Agreement would involve in operating procedures was, he argued, far more apparent than real. He said:

> I wonder how much we are giving away there. . . . What we undertake to do is not to restrict the use of balances we have not yet got and have not yet been entrusted to us. It will be very satisfactory if we can maintain the voluntary war-time system into 1947. But what hope is there of the countries concerned continuing such an arrangement much longer than that? Indeed, the danger is that these countries which have a dollar or gold surplus, such as India, and South Africa, would prefer to make their own arrangements, leaving us with a dollar pool which is a deficit pool, responsible for the dollar expenditure not only of ourselves but of the other members of the area having a dollar deficit. . . . We cannot force these countries to buy only from us, especially when we are physically unable to supply a large quantity of what they require. [1]

The new freedom to convert sterling into dollars in July 1947 was introduced in an unfavorable atmosphere. The sterling area's own dollar position was deteriorating. During the first half of 1947 its dollar deficit was running at the *daily* rate of $10 million, some ten times higher than the year before. Meanwhile, with the date for convertibility well advertised ahead of time in the terms of the Agreement, most holders of sterling were anticipating a feast at London's convertible table and were guarding their appetites; they did what they could to settle their sterling debts in inconvertible sterling and to postpone their sterling earnings until they could be received in convertible sterling. On June 30, 1947, the eve of dollar convertibility, the sterling area had $2.3 billion left, or less than half, of the United States and Canadian credits. It had another $2.4 billion in official gold and dollar reserves—a total of $4.7 billion. But against this reserve, the sterling area in the first half of 1947 was running a dollar deficit at the annual rate of almost $4 billion, and sterling debts stood at over $14 billion, of which almost $5 billion were in the hands of people outside the sterling area.

These figures suggest an unhappy prospect for sterling's

[1] House of Lords *Debates*. v.138 n.41 (Dec. 18, 1945), col. 788-9.

dollar convertibility at the time, although they do not indicate the impossibility of it. The important factor left out of this accounting is British production, far and away the most important asset—if not the only real one—behind the international status of sterling. Total British production on the eve of convertibility was running at the rate of about $40 billion a year (in dollar equivalence at $4.03 per pound.) If a sufficient portion of this production could be made available to those with sterling claims and on terms making them uninterested in alternative dollars, convertibility could work. But this was a faint hope. The British were not near the point of proving that their postwar gains in production had validated the $4.03 rate.

When in August the drain on Britain's dollars had reached the point where only $400 million was left of the United States credit, the new convertibility was called off and Britain returned to the old system of choosing administratively among the various claimants for dollars. It now seems clear that Britain was not ready for the convertibility attempt, that the year of preparations had not increased that readiness but rather may have lessened it, and that the manner in which the negotiators of the United States and Canadian loans pre-arranged convertibility was an unhappy one. The credits were double the sterling area's reserves. They were fundamentally an addition to reserves—a dollar availability other than current earnings. But they were accounted for separately from reserves and invited Britain and Britain's creditors to regard them as charge accounts—something to be used rather than husbanded. The credits were in fact provided to be used, not saved. But had they been merged with British reserves, it might have become apparent much earlier that the rate of expenditure in 1947 was inconsistent with international solvency.

Another sorry feature of the architecture of the credit was that the date for convertibility was specified, and implicitly the rate was, too. This deprived Britain of any room to maneuver in negotiations and gave great maneuverability to speculators. The amount of the dollar credit was universally known; Britain's creditors expected to be cut in for their share. The date for current dollar convertibility was known, and this put Britain's trading partners in a position to take advantage of it.

The 1947 crisis which wiped out the new United States and Canadian credits and threatened remaining British reserves was the result of an excessive demand for dollars. The effectiveness of this demand was partly due to the substitution of foreign (especially European) controls for British controls; other countries were less solicitous of sterling's difficulties than Britain was. What they wanted was dollars, and they took a liberal view of what qualified as a "current transaction" in the context of Britain's obligation to convert sterling. In the half-year before convertibility and during the short life of the experiment, something like $500 million may have been withdrawn from London by other countries simply for the sake of getting out of sterling while the getting was good. This sort of drain was at the time much blamed for the failure of the try. But to assign primary importance to this cause is unwarranted. The normal give and take of the market must be expected to involve leads and lags in payments, and these leads and lags will appear in the form of short-term capital movements. It seems doubtful whether they can or should be prevented by exchange controls; they are normal, they are part of the meaning of convertibility. That they took place inconveniently in the summer of convertibility demonstrates the unreadiness of sterling for dollar convertibility rather than the unreadiness of other countries to cooperate in effective sterling convertibility. Moreover, these movements were small in comparison to the tide of the exchange of sterling for dollars for purposes intended under the Agreement.

It is still not possible to quantify precisely from published data the various sources of drain on Britain's dollar availabilities in mid-1947, but the picture is something like that shown in Table 1.

The core of the problem was simply that at $4.03 per pound sterling dollars were a bargain. Dollar-world production was attractive and the delivery dates decisively better than for sterling production. Quite apart from the greater degree of freedom in converting sterling into dollars during the brief experiment, the trends of the first two quarters of the year pointed to an early exhaustion of the new credits.

Table 1

DRAIN ON BRITAIN'S DOLLARS, 1947

	Total Dollar Drain	*UK's Dollar Deficit* [a]	*Rest of Sterling Area's Dollar Deficit* [a]	*Other Calls on Gold and Dollar Reserves*
	(millions of dollars)			
1st quarter	917	592	170	155
2nd quarter	973	631	179	163
3rd quarter	1,537	996	279	262
4th quarter	704	454	131	119
TOTAL	4,131	2,673	759	699

Source: Cmd. 8976. Full citation of the official British *Command Papers,* frequently referred to in following tables, is found in the bibliography.
[a] Breakdown by quarters estimated by prorating quarterly totals on the basis of known share of annual deficit.

So after five weeks of greater dollar convertibility, the experiment was terminated on August 20, 1947. The British authorities suspended further automatic sales of dollars for current purposes in exchange for current sterling and the rules of the sterling system reverted to the rules prevailing before July 16th. The cardinal features of the system were now: the fixed exchange rate (as before); the use of sterling for settlement within and between certain limited regions; the covering of other deficits (namely, ones that could not be covered by the use of sterling) out of central reserves on the basis of agreed limitations of dollar imports in the case of sterling area countries and on the basis of specific understandings with non-sterling countries. Once again, the only real means of adjustment when the claims presented against London for foreign exchange exceeded the supply was the tightening of direct controls on imports. The direct controls took the form of quantitative restrictions. Once again the problem of maintaining dollar equilibrium was handled through dollar pooling, and the problem of arresting deficits was handled through segregation of dollar transactions from other foreign expenditures and establishing separate, and more severe, quotas for dollar goods than for other goods.

Considering the depth of the 1947 crisis and the length of time in which a disquieting dollar drain had run even before the convertibility experiment, Chancellor of the Exchequer Dalton's cheerful statement in late 1946 seems unaccountably lighthearted. He said that he had been able to meet all the demands on the public purse "literally with a song in his heart." If the British held together as they had since V-J day, shortages and frustrations would disappear "like the snows of winter, and give place to the full promise of springtime." [2]

Technically, the 1947 convertibility crisis did not involve a drain on official reserves but rather a drain on the United States and Canadian lines of credit. Public and even official opinion might have been alerted to the untenability of Britain's dollar posture if the rapid drainage of the credit had been seen as exactly the same thing as a reserve drain. In any case, a very great impairment of irreplaceable dollar supplies—i.e. the credits—occurred, and probably had to occur, before action was taken to rectify the position. This degree of impairment probably had to occur because as long as a substantial amount of the credit remained unused, United States opinion would have been sorely taxed to understand and acquiesce in a reimposition of the restrictions which the credit had been intended to obviate; and very likely British opinion would have shown reluctance to accept a slash in the import of essential goods and raw materials as long as the means of finance still remained.

A somewhat similar situation prevailed in the two following reserve crises in 1949 and 1951. These crises are fascinating and widely studied cases in the postwar development of British financial policy. The discomforts and anxieties attending their occurrence prompted much study and debate, and ultimately produced important changes in British and sterling area thinking about the best lines of international financial policy.

[2] *The Times*, Oct. 21, 1946, p. 3.

1949: The Devaluation Crisis

In early 1948, the United States line of credit was exhausted. For a few months, until Marshall Plan dollars first became available to the United Kingdom, the central reserves of the sterling system were without any basic United States support. Since the beginning of lend-lease in March, 1941, this situation had existed only once before, during the ten months between the termination of lend-lease in August 1945 and the establishment of the line of credit under the Anglo-American Financial Agreement in July 1946. The full burden of financing the whole sterling area deficit with the rest of the world was placed on the central reserves in London. After the convertibility experiment, these reserves were counted officially at $2.4 billion (September 30, 1947), or about half of the sterling area's dollar deficit during that one year.

Despite this somewhat unpromising prospect, export trends in 1948 were favorable and earnings rose by about half. Restrictions on imports were effective in bringing down expenditures by about a third. The reserve position was maintained, as was the exchange rate. Rising production suggested that at long last the policy of trying to validate the $4.03 rate was being vindicated. However, by early 1949 external deficits again made recourse to reserves necessary. In spite of Marshall aid, then running at an annual rate of a billion dollars, there was an uncovered deficit of close to the same amount.

The pressure on sterling area reserves was aggravated by the United States recession of that year. United States sales in the sterling area (supported in part by Marshall aid) were steady during the first half of the year, but the value of United States purchases fell by half. Some students consider this reversal the major cause of the 1949 reserve crisis. The statistics hardly support this view; the decline in United States expenditures was far less than the increase in the drain on reserves. It might be argued, however, that the decline in United States buying may have been the proverbial last straw.

As the basic reserve drain continued, it was worsened by

growing speculation against sterling in anticipation of a forced devaluation. Public concern in Britain was allayed by official references to the improving picture of production and by official assurances that sterling would not and need not be devalued. By this time the opinion of most United States officials was that the sterling-dollar rate did not satisfactorily reflect the two countries' respective cost structures in production for the international market, and that a devaluation of sterling would help check Britain's tendency toward persistent external—and particularly dollar—deficit. Alternative methods of arresting the reserve drain without outside financial assistance would have been the then-forgotten and later-recalled raising of interest rates, or a further tightening of restrictions on dollar imports. In a period of already stringent restrictions in imports the attractiveness of making further cuts was slight. It could even be questioned whether further cuts might not adversely affect British production, which was as always heavily dependent on imports of raw materials for its machines and food for its workers. By the end of June 1949, reserves stood at $1,651 million and the sterling area's dollar drain was running at a monthly rate of over $200 million. Britain had either to raise the price of dollars or suspend their automatic sale for authorized purposes, including a large volume of imports contracted for but not yet paid for. On September 19 the dollar price was raised. A pound sterling would now purchase only $2.80 rather than $4.03 as previously. The rest of the sterling area followed suit, except for Pakistan. A step that had been successfully resisted through seven years of war and four years of recovery was at last forced.

If we may consider the three major means of correcting an external deficit to consist of tightening controls on imports, devaluation, and tightening controls on internal incomes, Britain had now tried the first two in dealing with the reserve drains of 1947 and 1949. The shortcomings of the technique of adjustment through tightened import controls in 1947 were of two sorts. The controls reduced the amount of current sterling incomes which could be translated into foreign exchange, but they did not in themselves reduce the amount of these incomes nor provide adequate alternative uses for the portion which was denied the use the owners would have chosen—the purchase of foreign exchange. Nor were the controls accompanied by sufficient collateral measures to make up for this defect, although as far as incomes were concerned Sir Stafford Cripps made some significant beginnings in this direction through his sterner budgetary measures. This may have intensified the very problem the controls were imposed to solve. The unsatisfied and yet imperfectly immobilized buying power remained a constant pressure against holes in the control structure, and also—probably more importantly—a factor increasing the absorption of current production into domestic uses and away from foreign markets, all to the detriment of foreign-exchange earnings.

Beyond all this, import controls usually require three or four months before their effect shows up in the desired form of lowered payments abroad. We have already noted the difficulty governments have in getting popular acceptance of belt-tightening measures against imports prior to a dramatic demonstration of their necessity through a major reserve drain. This delay in the imposition of controls plus the delay before the controls bring about a fall in expenditures abroad make them very crude weapons against an intolerable external deficit. First the authorities wait until it becomes clear that the deficit is not a temporary difficulty, then they wait until it gets bad enough to enlist popular support for the new controls, and then they can only wait further until the chosen controls, which they cannot be assured are the correct ones to adjust the situation, gradually reveal their consequences. Bulk-purchase commitments to pay for imports contracted for on government account present another barrier to timely reduction of expenditures. In this slow-moving strategy of adjustment, it is perhaps surprising that every external deficit does not grow into a reserve crisis, and every reserve crisis into confidence-impairing deterioration of sterling's international status.

Devaluation was scarcely more convincing as a means of coping with the tendency toward external deficit, although a strong argument can certainly be made as to its technical desirability—even necessity—in 1949, and a fairly strong argument as to its appropriateness to Britain's and the sterling area's general international economic position. It is probably correct to say, however, that the 1949 devaluation was not so much decided upon as a means of reestablishing equilibrium in the future balance of payments as it was forced on Britain by the lack of any attractive alternative in handling the immediate discrepancy between the supply of foreign exchange in the hands of the authorities and the demand which even under their own rules they were obliged to meet if the $4.03 rate were to be maintained.

The effects of devaluation are in practice unpredictable. They may, as in the case of adjustment through controls, even worsen rather than correct the external position. The hope in devaluation is that in making exports from the country generally cheaper abroad and imports generally more expensive at home, the imbalance in external accounts will be corrected. However, the stimulation of production for export may be offset by pricing policies adopted by exporters. To the extent that this does not happen, the stimulation may be undesirably general, giving a new lease on life to industries which are unprofitable. The discouragement of imports may be offset by government subsidies and domestic price control policies. To the extent that imports become more expensive to the domestic producer, the difference may be absorbed fairly readily in a swollen income stream. Meanwhile, the government's expenses are likely to rise—the cost of servicing foreign debt rises immediately and in proportion to the higher price of foreign exchange. The cost of imports on government account rises, and this rise may be, but usually is not, offset by policies to reduce other government expenditures. To the extent that devaluation is followed by a rise in the domestic level of prices, it is a nice question whether the government's increased revenues will be as great as its increased expenditures. It is always possible that devaluation will cause or be followed by an aggravation of the inflationary conditions which presumably led to its adoption.

Whether these untoward effects of devaluation can be

prevented depends on many circumstances. Among the most important are the understanding of the governmental measures needed to check unfavorable developments while retaining the advantages of devaluation and the political will and ability needed to take such measures in the face of strong counter pressures. Though the 1949 devaluation was virtually forced on the British, they set out to get as much advantage as they could from this necessity. The severity of the cut in the dollar price of the pound, which surprised many, was an act of policy. One of its advantages was that it gave some leeway for accommodating pressures in the economy without wholly offsetting effects of the devaluation in cutting costs. In other fields as well, the policies of the British government were adapted to retain as much as possible of the advantages of the devaluation in adjusting the relations of the United Kingdom—and the whole sterling area—with the dollar world.

The prevailing opinion of British officials and of financial observers in Britain and elsewhere at the time was that devaluation was necessary technically and probably desirable economically. A less widespread opinion was that an earlier devaluation, which perhaps might have been a more moderate one, would have been more effective. I think there is much in the opinion some British economists expressed to me in the middle of 1954 that the favorable position of Britain and the sterling area in 1953 (the first postwar year in which the biennial reserve crisis was avoided) might be to an important degree a reflection, though belated, of the favorable effects of devaluation on the competitive international position of British and sterling area production.

Import controls and radical exchange rate adjustment were at best clumsy means of straightening out the balance of payments. In the absence of measures bringing about a relationship between sterling incomes and sterling production comparable to the relationship prevailing in other countries, these methods were bound to fall short of bringing external accounts into order and keeping them so. Lionel Robbins wrote colorfully:

> Before we resign ourselves to the view that we have done all that could have been done and that everything that has happened

has been unavoidable calamity, it is desirable to inquire a little further concerning the mechanisms which have been operative and the policies that have been in vogue. Our inquiry is not limited to the problem why there have been disturbing influences. Even more important is the problem why these influences have not been met by a sufficient response. . . . We have been attempting to drive our car through this difficult postwar country with the steering gear out of action, the wheels lashed rigidly in one direction, our only means of equilibration an occasional stop, every few months, for the wheels to be unlashed and turned at another angle—while ministers stand on the roof and deliver salutary exhortations.

And a bit later he added:

But, beyond this, there is the difficulty of administration. It is a fact of experience that direct control of this sort always tends to be behind the gun. The process of decision-making cannot be continuous. The plan cannot be altered from day to day. It is only when a crisis is on the way that action is taken—and that in circumstances when small adjustments are ruled out by the nature of the problem. Hence the vulgar spectacular nature of this side of economic life nowadays, with its big men flying about wildly in aeroplanes, its grandiose conferences, its last-minute compromises, and its penumbra of high politics even over consignments of canned meat and sardines. [3]

It seems possible, though not inevitable, that the devaluation of 1949, which seems to have surprised the most enthusiastic proponents of devaluation by its severity, would have been followed by a much more balanced period in sterling's international status had it not been for new external problems created by the Korean War. Whether the British position and that of the sterling area would have been one of balance in the absence of problems associated with the trouble in Korea depends largely, I think, on whether Britain would have achieved an internal income structure and level more in keeping with a balance between its external needs and earnings, and a better coordination of sterling area expenditures. It may be that one more crisis, which in fact

[3] Lionel Robbins, *The Balance of Payments*. The Stamp Memorial Lecture delivered before the University of London on November 20, 1951 (London: Athlone Press, 1951), pp. 17, 21, 25-26.

occurred in 1951, was essential to focus attention on the neglected field of internal finance. What seems clear now is that the Korean War produced new problems which made it much more difficult to avoid inflation and large external deficits.

United States economic aid to the United Kingdom (and through it to the sterling area) was terminated in June 1951. Following the outbreak of the Korean War in June 1950, the United Kingdom announced that no more aid would be needed after 1950. Military aid of significant proportions was started in July 1950, but this was in the nature of a partial offset to the new defense obligations undertaken by the United Kingdom. The basic dollar support to the economy of Britain and the sterling world was removed, as it had been briefly twice before. The termination of economic aid was the result of the favorable balance of payments achieved by Britain—in fact by the entire sterling area—in 1950. An incidental irony of this timing is that the United States made a substantial amount of "economic" aid ($706 million) available in 1950 when it was not needed, and relatively little ($174 million) in 1951 as Britain was heading into its most severe postwar balance of payments crisis. However, a new and important element of external support for sterling had come into existence in this same period. This was the volume of credit available to the United Kingdom under the arrangements of the European Payments Union.

1951: Reaction to Prosperity

The 1951 reserve crisis was particularly shocking because it developed so rapidly and deeply after a year of great prosperity for the sterling area. The raw material producing countries of the sterling area profited from boom prices as the Western industrial nations, paced by an almost insatiable United States demand, bought heavily. The United Kingdom, too, did well in the international market, partly due to a delay in the buying soon to be necessary for purposes of gearing up production for a higher level of armaments. The United Kingdom not only postponed buying but actually ran down existing stocks, apparently seriously. In the course of the short-lived prosperity, the sterling area countries imported more liberally. Then, as the market neared its peak, the United Kingdom had to import to replenish stocks as well as to feed its geared-up industry. By late summer 1951 it was clear that a first-class reserve crisis was in the making. Raw material prices dropped drastically, while the sterling area countries continued to buy heavily under the liberalized import policy. Now, in a falling market, the United Kingdom had to sell the goods it had produced from raw materials bought at peak prices.

The rise in international commodity prices following the outbreak of the Korean War favored the raw material sales of the outer sterling area which earned half a billion dollars net from the dollar area in the next twelve months. For six months the United Kingdom itself earned a surplus in transactions with dollar countries, the first time since World War II that the United Kingdom's transactions with the dollar area had produced anything but substantial deficits. But the prosperity was temporary. In the first half of 1951 the United Kingdom again was in deficit with the dollar area and by the second half of the year the outer sterling area, normally a dollar earner, was also in deficit. The sterling area's favorable position in trade with Western Europe was also reversed. Between July 1950, when the operations of the European Payments Union commenced, and May 1951, the sterling area had earned a cumulative surplus of $450 million; after that the current monthly deficits ran as high as $250 million, and by the beginning of September 1952 totalled $1,700 million. When offset by the previous surplus, this left Britain with a cumulative deficit of over $1,200 million. In the early summer of 1951 these trends began to show up in the form of a major reserve drain; during the summer reserves fell about $200 million a month. The Labour government lost the October 1951 elections and for the first time since the end of the war the United Kingdom had a Conservative prime minister.

The first steps to meet the crisis were familiar ones. Import controls were tightened against imports from both the dollar world and the EPU area. The finance ministers of the

Commonwealth were assembled in emergency session in London. The gloomy, even alarming, facts were put on the table, and the sterling countries agreed that immediate and substantial cuts in imports once more had to be made. In the case of dollar imports, a 25 per cent slash was generally accepted as the standard.

The conference recognized the emergency situation as the first and main item on the agenda and accepted the technique of tightened import controls as the only measure which at that stage gave promise of arresting the crisis before reserves dropped so low as to impair, perhaps permanently, international confidence in sterling. What was new about the crisis was the unanimous feeling that the recurrent riches-to-rags life of the sterling area was intolerable and could not be cured by emergency measures. It was the general understanding that once the crisis had been arrested, the Commonwealth would have to consider longer lasting therapy for the international stabilization of sterling. Some of the more cynical observers felt that this vision of a freer and more stable sterling was merely an indefinite British promise made in order to obtain the help of restive sterling partners in another season of import slashing. Actually, the understanding set the tone for international sterling policy ever since.

The reserve drain was not arrested for four months after that, another demonstration of how long import restrictions take to become effective. British officials discussed the situation with United States officials when Churchill and Eden visited Washington in January 1952. Minor United States assistance was arranged; major assistance could not have been given without the lengthy legislative procedures required to get funds for the purpose.

The Conservative government took certain other steps which hinted that its conception of rectifying sterling's position went beyond restrictions on imports. Interest rate changes had not been an instrument of monetary policy since before the war. But one of the first acts of the new government was to raise Bank rate from 2 to 2½ per cent in November 1951, and in March 1952 to 4 per cent. These steps suggested that the government not only recognized excessive internal incomes as an important factor in external deficits but, more important, intended to wield the traditional monetary weapons to bring about a correction. On December 17, 1951, the government established a foreign-exchange market in London; for the first time in twelve years authorized dealers were permitted to buy and sell foreign exchange on their own account. Both spot and forward dealing were permitted and in order to give the market needed flexibility the official spread between buying and selling rate was widened to the equivalent of $2.78 (selling) and $2.82 (buying) per pound, compared to the previous narrow spread of $2.79⅞ to $2.80⅛. The reopening of a foreign-exchange market suggested that the new government regarded a private foreign-exchange market with slightly more flexible exchange rates as a useful instrument in international dealings and as a useful indicator of trends. On March 11, with reserves still falling but at a slower rate, the first Conservative budget was announced. It featured lower food subsidies, lower taxes, and various measures intended to increase incentives to production. The budget suggested that the government would strive for an economy in which the market's voice would be listened to more attentively.

The main significance of the 1951 crisis is that it dramatized for the sterling association the neglected relationship between internal and external financial expenditures and underlined the unfavorable effects of inflation, economic rigidities, and the lack of coordination in the financial policies of sterling area members. Flexibility was now to become a synonym rather than an antonym for economic stability—the most important shift in emphasis that had yet occurred in postwar financial policy.

The Meaning of the Crises

In the first six postwar years a great deal happened to sterling, but not very much happened to the rules governing its use. The drama of a reserve crisis every two years, of a convertibility experiment, of a puritanic Cripps and an indiscreet Dalton, all create an aura of great changes that are not borne out by the facts. The rules were much the same at the end of 1951 as they were in the beginning of 1945.

The period is memorable to us mainly for the recurrence of crisis, but even this feature is an ephemeral one. It seems likely that some years from now these crises will strike students of sterling as a fairly minor embarrassment in a period of postwar adjustment. The chances are the crises will be described in terms of how the sterling system functioned in this period, rather than how it staggered. But for now fresh memory makes crisis the distinctive trait of these years. Not very much else happened.

The statement that not very much else happened during this period may be misleading. It is correct in that the rules governing sterling transfers were little altered, but the reason was because so much else happened to make changes unnecessary. Marshall aid was instituted and the European Payments Union invented. Both institutions bore directly on Britain's twin preoccupations in restoring production and the international status of sterling. Marshall aid was in effect a resumption of lend-lease in a toned-down form. Unlike lend-lease, it was not a blank check for financing dollar deficits, but it was a big one, based on calculations (or guesses) as to what might be a reasonable dollar deficit for the sterling area to run. It underpinned the status of sterling in the non-sterling world. Intra-European payments arrangements, sponsored by the United States in connection with Marshall aid and effective from the middle of 1949, performed a similar service to the status of sterling in most of the non-dollar world.[4]

[4] In the European Payments Union, which in 1950 succeeded the earlier payments arrangements for Western Europe, the sterling area was recognized as a unit, and the United States even undertook a limited obligation to indemnify the United Kingdom for any loss of gold and dollars arising from the use of sterling in settlements among members of the Union. Under EPU rules, such settlements could—and did—involve partial payment in gold and dollars. Similarly, the 1945 negotiations with the United States for the dollar credit were conducted on the basis of estimates of the drain of gold and dollars from the area's central reserve pool. The treatment of sterling as an *area* currency rather than a *national* one was in sharp contrast to the United States stand in the Bretton Woods organizations where the argument has been made consistently that the independent sterling countries, including the United Kingdom, be judged by their own performance and not by that of the area as a whole. The issue has considerable significance in such problems as whether a member of the International Bank would be in a position to service sought-for loans in dollars.

Given sterling area arrangements plus the European Payments Union plus Marshall aid, sterling countries had a broad basis for settling international deficits. Deficits with one another would be settled in sterling, deficits with Western Europe in the EPU combination of credit and gold, and deficits with the dollar world through Marshall aid. In this happy situation, why the three reserve crises?

The answer to this is surely a complicated one, but important components of the answer can be distinguished. First, the means of financing deficits were limited while the factors making for rising deficits were almost unlimited. Second, under modern parliamentary conditions and with a highly controlled economic system, effective action against mounting deficits is not popularly acceptable until a severe run on reserves, with the consequent threat of international insolvency, makes the necessity obvious. In such a situation a serious drain on reserves becomes the instrument of adjustment. Third, the rigidities inherent in a system in which important changes in the economy can be made only by administrative decisions, which are likely to be unpopular and cannot in any case be immediately effective, led to a kind of off-beat timing in decisions about expenditures abroad. Under typical licensing procedures it was the volume, not the value, of imports that could be planned and controlled. Even more important, it turned out that the decision to reduce imports by issuing fewer licenses and by other means (for instance, importing less under government contracts) required something like three or four months to become effective. This lag between official decision and actual expenditure created the continuous possibility that more liberal policies toward expenditures would become effective at times when foreign-exchange availabilities were particularly worrisome and that import austerity would become effective when the need for it might not be at all clear. This possibility came close to being the continuous fact during the period of biennial crises. Finally, the looseness of coordination of policy among sterling countries intensified all of these factors, creating the possibility of increased sterling expenditures in the rest of the world while at the same time the uncertainties of earnings from the rest of the world grew.

The sterling system of controls was an effort to build a foreign-exchange budget on the basis of an unknown timing and volume of either receipts or expenditures. As Professor Hawtrey has written:

Theoretically, import restrictions should be a safeguard against an adverse balance, but in practice they are not easily adjusted with precision to changing requirements. While it is the total that has to be adjusted, each imported commodity has to be considered separately. Each has to be considered with reference not only to the needs of the home market but also to the rival claims of foreign suppliers, both the individual producers and the exporting countries. Any desired increase or decrease in the total quantity of imports has to be distributed among the various imported products, and in the case of each the interests affected have to be taken into account. And, when quantities have been decided on, the money value of the whole is liable to be altered by price movements.

Import restrictions work by trial and error. Error can only be estimated from the experience of a considerable period, probably several months, and the correction needed, when an error is revealed, can only be approximately estimated. Successive revisions, extending possibly over several years, may be necessary to arrive at a balance, and, before the adjustment is completed, new and unforeseen disturbing factors are likely enough to supervene. [5]

1952-1955: Sterling without Tears

The reserve drain which grew to such alarming proportions in 1951 was finally arrested in April 1952. From then until the end of 1954 the reserve position was generally good. The growth of reserves has become as popular a barometer of returning strength and confidence as the downward drift was of weakness and worry. Many, if not most, students have interpreted the reserve drains as a sign of deep distortion in the allocation of British and sterling area resources, even as a harbinger of Britain's decline and sterling's collapse. In my view, the periodic reserve crises were essentially the only remaining means of adjustment to international conditions in a system which ruled out other means of adjustment. The relative economic strength of Britain and

[5] R. G. Hawtrey, *Towards the Rescue of Sterling* (London: Longmans Green & Co. Ltd., 1954), pp. 25-6.

the rest of the sterling area may better be measured by such standards as progress in production, international solvency, export earnings, and so on. By these standards, the story of Britain's postwar economic development and that of most of its sterling associates can be made out pretty convincingly as a success story. Even in the international orientation of sterling, the weaknesses can be seen as temporary lapses in a general trend toward greater freedom short of dollar convertibility and toward stability of sterling. It is interesting that if one looks at two-year periods the crises disappear and the general picture is one of import deficits more or less of the magnitude generally recognized as appropriate to the task of recovery from war.

It is possible that the future will reveal the postwar sterling crises as the first signs of a secular decline. I know of no way of disproving this gloomy forecast. Those who make it strike me as reading a history of disaster into a few minus signs in the bank account. But this is a point better considered in the final chapter.

On the other hand, while trends since the arresting of the 1951 crisis have been encouraging—production rising, employment steady, prices steady, sterling stable on international markets, exports well maintained, imports in a more balanced relation to exports—it is too early to put the seal of permanent success on the policies which accompanied these developments. What seems clear is that the cycle of reserve crises was an extremely uncomfortable way of conducting international business. Sterling area policy since 1951 has been directed at the problem of eliminating crises without getting into worse problems, such as depression or widespread unemployment. So far policy has been accompanied by success. To what extent that success may be attributed to policy is not clear. It may be a case of good luck attending good sense, or it may be a case of sheer—and temporary—good luck. But it would be ungenerous to deny pride of achievement to the conscientious and concerted efforts made throughout the sterling world to get rid of the curse of crises and restore sterling to a comfortable international balance.

In tracing the thread of policy from the reserve crisis of 1951 to the end of 1954 there are few dramatic incidents, but the thread runs in a generally consistent direction and it extends an impressive length. For the sake of brevity we will limit the consideration here to the types of measures taken rather than their detailed order. More will be said about the events of 1954 and 1955 at the end of Chapter 5.

The first type of step has already been mentioned—*the changing of Bank rate*. In the period we are considering—1951 through 1954—it was raised twice and subsequently lowered twice (from 4 percent to 3½ percent in September 1953, and from 3½ percent to 3 percent in May 1954).[6]

A change of Bank rate does not by itself automatically result in a tightening or easing of domestic credit availabilities, and the extent to which accompanying measures and the response of the financial community are effective in translating Bank rate changes into money-market changes has been questioned. Whatever effectiveness may be attributed to a flexible Bank rate policy as a direct instrument of domestic credit control, it seems clear that this flexibility has been demonstrated to be effective in controlling the flow of short-term foreign funds into and out of London. It therefore has provided at least a partial alternative to a reserve drain as the signal that international accounts require adjustment.

As I read the circumstances, these increases of Bank rate were undertaken as part of a policy of tightening credit and thereby easing the pressure of excessive demand for foreign exchange; they at least gave notice to the banks and to the public that lending policy should be stricter. The increases also had the objective of making London a more attractive place for foreigners to keep their funds. The decreases similarly seemed to have both domestic and international objectives—to stimulate business activity in a period of tapering off, and to arrest the flow of speculative foreign funds

[6] In January 1955 it was raised to 3½ per cent and in February, to 4½ per cent. This move, which caused surprise in financial circles, was apparently motivated partly by concern over a possible resurgence of inflation and partly as a direct means of coping with a loss of reserves. It signified to the market that Bank rate had been made the effective center of the credit atmosphere.

attracted to London in anticipation of greater dollar convertibility.

The second and perhaps most significant type of step had to do with *the mechanics of foreign-exchange dealings.* These measures all contributed something to the further dethroning of reserve drain as the ruler of balance of payments policy. The first such step, already mentioned, was the reopening of a private foreign-exchange market in London in December 1951. The importance of this market was considerably extended in May 1953 when Britain reached agreement with seven continental countries (Belgium, Denmark, France, Netherlands, Sweden, Switzerland, and West Germany) on the basis for a common arbitrage market. Each of the countries involved in the scheme agreed to permit authorized banks in any of the other countries to buy and sell its currency for permitted current transactions. The step was not a radical alteration of prior conditions, nor was it intended to be. In effect the arrangements meant simply that a bank in Paris, for example, could sell sterling to a bank in Brussels on mutually agreeable terms without getting official permission in London. The arrangements did not involve any significant loosening of sterling rules in other respects. The spread between buying and selling rates of the participating countries was widened and made uniform, just as the sterling spread had been widened when the private exchange market was reestablished almost two years earlier. The effect—and the intended effect—of the new arrangements was to refurbish private means of handling international payments traffic, not to widen the paths such payments could travel. A considerable volume of day-to-day dealing was taken out of bilateral channels between the central banks and out of the channels of the European Payments Union. The new market brought the incidental advantage of harmonious cross rates among the eight currencies. The transactions of the new market were limited for the time being to spot transactions [7] arranged through authorized banks within the general restrictions of prevailing import policy in all of the countries. But if anything these limita-

[7] Dealing in futures was permitted after mid-October, 1953.

tions were overstressed in financial comments at the time, and even in the official playing down of the significance of the new market. In transferring a large volume of transactions from bilateral central bank channels to multilateral authorized bank channels, central control must inevitably have been weakened and the importance of short-term flows of private funds from one center to another strengthened. Most significant of all, there would have been little point in reestablishing this limited private market except as a step toward a further relaxation of exchange controls.

In March 1954 a major change in sterling rules occurred. Virtually all sterling held by non-residents of the sterling area was made "transferable," and capital transfers as well as transfers for current payments outside the dollar world were officially sanctioned. According to *The Economist* (November 20, 1954) in looking back on this step:

> The extension of the transferable account area was the greatest single simplification in the exchange control regulations that has taken place since their introduction in 1939. With a few temporary exceptions, two of which have since been discontinued, the whole fabric of bilateral accounts was swept away and all non-resident sterling other than that held on American, Canadian and blocked accounts was unified. That is, sterling could be transferred without restriction throughout virtually the whole non-dollar area; the one remaining restriction on transfers was that on payments from non-dollar to dollar accounts. No longer could the irreverent speak lightly of sterling's "fifty-seven varieties."

The extension of the transferable account area, which elsewhere in the press was described as making 79 varieties of sterling into one, may not have been the greatest simplification in exchange controls since 1939. The convertibility experiment in 1947 and even the creation of the transferable account area prior to that experiment come to mind. But the consolidation of transferable accounts was a most interesting step. It made sterling convertible into almost every currency other than dollars (at the official rate). Basically the new rules simply recognized a *de facto* transferability that already existed through the tolerated free markets in sterling and through the various exchange control dodges that the international commercial community had found to be effective. The trend in these markets, with the feasible dodges, gave strong support to the notion that "bilateral" sterling was essentially the same thing as "transferable" sterling, and that such moderate capital transactions as might be anticipated were not necessarily inimical to the strength of official sterling. This unification of the international market for sterling was considerably advanced again in February 1955 when British authorities decided to support the foreign value of sterling securities, so that trade in "security sterling" was placed on the same terms as trade in transferable sterling.

Immediately after the consolidation of this larger transferable account area, a free market in gold was reopened in London. The market was opened at a time when the familiar postwar premium on gold in free markets had fallen to a nominal figure. Therefore, in practice the new gold market scarcely changed the terms on which gold could be bought and sold. But in principle it legally reestablished a large traditional market where gold might be bought and sold at prices other than the prices set by various countries in defining the gold (or dollar) value of their currency units. The new market was not intended to increase the possibilities of converting sterling into dollars and the facilities of the market were carefully circumscribed to prevent any such tendency. Foreigners holding sterling could purchase gold with it only if that sterling had been obtained as a result of the sale of gold or dollars; such sterling was earmarked either as "American account" sterling or as special "registered" sterling. But, as *The Economist* commented (November 20, 1954), ". . . the very fact that even these restricted varieties of sterling could be converted into gold on the open market appeared to make the ultimate goal of full convertibility of sterling far more realistic than it was when dealings in gold were still the strict preserve of the authorities." An incidental curiosity of the new gold market was that with the disappearance of the effective free market premium on gold, the whole South African output, so vital in prior days to London's gold availabilities, started to flow to London, and South Africa participated *de facto* in the sterling area's dollar pool almost on a 100 per cent basis.

Neither of these first two types of changes—the adoption of a more flexible interest rate policy and the relaxation of rules inhibiting the circulation of sterling in the non-dollar world—directly increased the possibility of converting sterling into dollars, although these changes were generally interpreted as part of the move toward dollar convertibility and must have expanded conversion channels. In fact, United States banks were given to understand that the Bank of England would no longer frown on trading in transferable sterling. The third type of change—*reestablishment of international commodity markets in London*—did provide limited possibilities of converting sterling into dollars. Such possibilities were very limited. The general rule applied to the purchase or sale of international commodities in London was that commodities purchased for dollars should be sold for dollars. Even on this strict basis, British traders would expect to profit as middlemen, particularly as the improvement in the dollar position of other countries continued. There were three important exceptions to this dollar-for-dollar rule: copper, lead and raw sugar. These commodities, all of which originated in substantial measure in the dollar world, could be freely exported to any currency area; in effect they could be bought for dollars and resold elsewhere for sterling. The final purchaser could use his sterling freely to purchase a dollar-origin commodity. Stated more simply, the London market in these commodities became freely international once more; buyers could buy wherever prices were lowest, regardless of currency-area barriers, and sell where prices were highest, regardless of currency-area barriers.

In addition to these "convertible" markets in copper, lead and sugar, private markets in a number of other commodities were reopened. The significance of these markets in the evolving sterling system is hard to pin down. Their reopening seems to express mainly the determination of the Conservative government in Britain to put business in private hands rather than governmental ones wherever possible, and also the expectation that such steps would swell the volume of Britain's earnings as a middleman in the commodity commerce. But the reopening of the "inconvertible" commodity markets also seems to express a policy of making sterling as usable as possible internationally without exposing the sterling system to greater reserve drains. The theory of this policy seems to have involved the notion that the commodity markets, though operated with the dollar wall still standing, would somehow serve as preparation for the eventual convertibility of sterling into dollars and, in any case, would expand Britain's traditionally important earnings as broker, middleman, insurer, shipper, and banker.

A fourth type of change during this period was *the consolidation of procedures and policies toward greater sterling area self-sufficiency*. There are few specific measures to be cited, yet the conception became more prevalent throughout the sterling world that its further integration should be pressed. The golden cup of plentiful dollars was always seen at the end of the rainbow, but the rainbow itself shone over a sterling world. The most important development of this sort occurred in the Commonwealth conference of finance ministers toward the end of 1952. The conference produced an agreement that the strength of sterling is broadly dependent on satisfactory internal financial practices of sterling countries and that the more convertible sterling could be made internationally, the better for all concerned. Meanwhile, the more specific agreement was that the thing for all sterling countries to do was to put the balance of payments of the entire area in order and to give priority to this objective in plans for economic development. Projects which promised to earn or save foreign exchange, especially dollars, were to be preferred to projects having less immediate impact on the balance of payments.

Finally, there was *a series of measures designed to reduce the rigidity of the British economy*. The machinery of price-subsidy and rationing was almost entirely dismantled in the period of two years after the 1951 crisis struck. The government withdrew increasingly from state trading practices.

Where did all this leave the sterling system? The significant neighborhoods making up the sterling system were really reduced to three—the sterling area, the dollar area, and the rest of the world. Residents of the sterling area could use their sterling with a high degree of freedom for any purpose within the area, and with almost as much freedom anywhere except in the dollar area.[8] The residual countries described as "the rest of the world" could use their sterling freely in transactions with one another, almost as freely in transactions with the sterling area, and with considerable freedom in dealing with the dollar world through world financial markets. The dollar area holders of sterling could use their sterling freely in any currency area and for virtually any purpose.

In this parade of freedoms, what was left controlled? A lot was. The general scheme was that sterling payments within the non-dollar world should flow freely, but between that world and the dollar world they should flow only when the authorities deemed it necessary. In the controlled flow of payments with the dollar world, the central reserves of the sterling area would be available, on a pooled basis, to provide a limited measure of dollar convertibility for residents of the area but not for "the rest of the world." The policies of the governments of sterling countries, however, would be expected to prevent any net drain of reserves by sterling holders having recourse to reserves. How such a drain might be prevented in the case of "rest of the world" holders of sterling was not spelled out, and was in fact a considerable source of worry as sterling officials tried to establish a plan for greater payments freedom between the sterling world and the dollar world.

The period was one of loosening the rules of sterling, up to a point. The hope, the thought, the intention, was that any freeing of sterling must be an appropriate part of the final design to restore sterling to its former role of general international usefulness. But what was accomplished was actually the consolidation of sterling as a currency of almost unlimited usefulness in the non-dollar world. To revert to the analogy of the sterling house, partitions were knocked out and doors created for almost perfect sterling communications

[8] Subject to such restrictions as the ceiling on travel expenditures, the control of investment, and the policing of East-West trade.

among the non-dollar roomers,[9] but a guard was left at the slightly widened dollar door.

Summary: The Character of the Sterling System

Here are the basic features of the sterling system as we know it now. In the first place, it is an informal association whose rules develop out of day-to-day decisions, not fully coordinated, of the members. The informality is in fact one of the recognized problems of the system. As Hugh Gaitskell put it:

> Another striking fact about the sterling area is the absence of any definite central control. I often find in talking to Americans that they cannot really believe that; they think of the sterling bloc (which is the phrase they usually use—perhaps there is something in the difference of phraseology) as something which moves as a unit, directed from the centre, by instructions from someone, whether from the Governor of the Bank of England or some mysterious body, or even from the Chancellor of the Exchequer, which all members of the sterling area obey. It does not work like that at all. No formal authority or body controls the sterling area. There is not even a regular committee of the governments concerned. It works on the basis of contacts between the central banks which are pretty continuous, and occasional meetings, which are quite a new feature, of the Finance Ministers of the member countries—even here the meetings are usually of the Commonwealth Finance Ministers, and the non-Commonwealth sterling area Finance Ministers are not present. Therefore it is a very loosely knit affair without any constitution, without anything being laid down in black and white at all.[10]

Gaitskell's point is well taken. The system is informal, and the many gaps in coordination of financial practices among members have often increased sterling difficulties. Nonetheless, there has been and is an impressive degree of coordination of practices. Contacts between central banks and the existence of a common banking tradition are not necessarily much less than a constitution; in operation they can amount to an unwritten constitution, in something of the same sense

[9] Non-residents of the sterling area may be prevented from spending in the sterling area by the controls of their own country.

[10] Hugh Gaitskell, "The Sterling Area," *International Affairs,* v. 27, no. 2 (April 1952), p. 171.

that the statutes and law cases and traditions of the United Kingdom itself provide an unwritten constitution of recognized coherence and effectiveness. Also, while it is true that the United Kingdom certainly cannot dictate monetary policy in the independent countries of the area, it wields great influence as custodian of the area's foreign-exchange reserves and even more as the controller of the London capital market—a market that is an *area* credit market almost as clearly as the reserves are *area* reserves. In general, the informality of operations does not spell the absence of system, but rather the presence of certain non-contractual flexible techniques of monetary concert that have proved effective.

A second important feature of the system is that it operates on the basis of a sharp distinction between the freedom of transactions which do not press directly on gold and dollar reserves and the limitation of transactions which might. Given reasonable cooperation in carrying out import policies which obviate persistent and excessive calls on the central gold and dollar reserves, the members have automatic access to the reserves and hence a limited degree of dollar convertibility for their sterling holdings. In contrast, they have considerably greater freedom in their use of sterling in making payments in the non-dollar world and almost complete freedom in their use of sterling to make payments within the sterling area. This last has always been the cardinal point of postwar sterling area policy, and the increase of freedom of use of sterling in the rest of the non-dollar world has been, as we have seen, a consistent objective of sterling policy since the war. The difference in the degree of freedom with which sterling can be used in the three monetary groups it distinguishes—the sterling area, the dollar area, and the rest of the world—is the most important factor influencing the specific decisions of all sterling countries with respect to their payments abroad. It pervades thinking about the pattern of current transactions, about the international equilibrium of sterling countries with other countries, about reasonable balance with the dollar world—i.e., any commerce requiring dollar settlements or yielding dollar earnings is to be considered apart from the over-all balance of payments problems of members. It also pervades the thinking of sterling countries about the general pattern of their economic development.

The recognition of different monetary areas is not just a matter of *separating out* the dollar world. An equally important facet of this regional approach—perhaps the other side of the coin—is the *"including in"* of sterling countries. The important balance to be achieved in dollar transactions is not the balance of individual members but the balance of the group as a whole. It is this group balance to which the technique of dollar pooling applies, a technique which has become the symbol of sterling regionality and which the Anglo-American Financial Agreement was so explicitly concerned to dismantle.

A third important feature of the sterling system is the primacy given by sterling countries (like most of the rest of the world) to quantitative restrictions on imports as the means of overcoming regional and global deficits in the balance of payments of the group as a whole and of each individual member. The importance of quantitative restrictions has diminished somewhat in practice since 1952, as the problem of external deficits diminished for one reason or another (including renewed attention to the importance of internal monetary balance as a factor in external balance). But QR—as quantitative restriction is called in the trade—still remains the adjustment factor of last resort whenever an important deficit appears, and the importance of QR in policy at any given time will reflect the state of the sterling area's balance with the rest of the world. The importance of QR that discriminates against dollar transactions will similarly reflect the extent to which dollar deficits turn out to be greater than general deficits. QR and discriminatory QR will not, in short, be dethroned unless a happier means of adjustment appears on the scene. Credit from or investment by the rest of the world in the sterling area are probably the only substitutes that the sterling world would regard as happier.

A fourth important feature of the system, and perhaps its most unique feature as an international monetary system, is the intimacy of the relationship of the various monetary and credit systems of the outer sterling area to that of the United

Kingdom. British Treasury IOUs are of first importance in national currency and credit structures of sterling countries, including the independent countries. This importance is expressed in a number of practices. The rest of the sterling area looks to the London market for both short- and long-term accommodation and, as we have seen earlier in considering the wartime accumulation of sterling balances, London too can get important accommodation in other sterling countries—almost mechanically in some (notably the colonies) and on the basis of a long tradition of banking cooperation in others. The intimacy of monetary relations is also illustrated by the importance of sterling in the currency reserves of sterling countries, although the degree of importance varies from country to country depending on the extent to which independent central banks, treasuries, and local money markets have developed. On the whole the degree of importance of sterling as a currency reserve in sterling countries is high. The intimacy is expressed in the inbred channels of private investment of one sterling country in the area of its sterling associates. The volume of such investment is extremely hard to guess, for reasons we will consider later, but it is certain to be large in relation to the flow of sterling area funds to the rest of the world.

A fifth distinctive feature of the present sterling system is the importance of sterling as an international reserve and a means of final settlement of deficits of sterling countries with one another and with many non-sterling countries as well. Habit, agreement, statutes, and the lack of a better alternative contribute to sterling's role as a money of at least *de facto* legal tender in a wide area of international transactions.

Finally, the present sterling system is distinctive as a trading area in which a member has a preferred status in the markets of the other members. This preference is formalized only to a minor extent in actual tariffs (the pattern of imperial preference). It exists more simply as the consequence of the features already noted and is underlined by a long history of commercial and political cooperation.

Chapter 5

THE METROPOLE, CENTER OF THE SYSTEM

> I think, by some odd gimmors or device
> Their arms are set like clocks, still to strike on;
> Else ne'er could they hold out so as they do.
>
> KING HENRY VI

THE UNITED KINGDOM is the center of the sterling system. Historically, Britain created sterling as its national currency and has supervised its international uses. The centrality of the United Kingdom in the sterling system turns on the fact that the pound sterling is first and foremost the national currency of Britain. Other sterling countries base their national currencies on sterling in a number of ways, but sterling itself is based only on the solvency and reliability of the British Treasury. The fact that sterling has wide international uses reflects the belief of foreigners that it serves and will serve conveniently in making international payments. In the case of countries which are members of the sterling area, it reflects the further belief that their currencies will gain strength and stability from being based completely or partially on sterling. These beliefs are held in differing degrees by both sterling and non-sterling countries. Obviously, once a country is deeply committed to sterling as a result of accumulating substantial amounts of it, the strength of its sterling habit may be a more powerful determinant of its monetary policy than the strength of its belief in sterling's convenience and solidity. The conceivable losses, uncertainties, and inconveniences of breaking an established sterling tie prevent sterling countries from doing so lightly.

As the center of the sterling system, Britain and its economy necessarily have special importance. It is not just another part, albeit a large part, of the sterling system. It is the part with the most critical bearing on the strength of sterling. The monetary authorities of Britain alone can determine how much sterling shall come into existence and how such sterling may be used. As the sterling area has broadened—some have said weakened—with age, British authorities have had to make their policy decisions with the interest of other countries very much in mind, and the trend has been toward increased consultation with sterling associates before making important decisions. For example, when the last war was imminent officials of the central banks of the Commonwealth met to plan jointly the financial controls which the outbreak of the war would require. Nonetheless, the fact remains that sterling is the national currency of the United Kingdom and the administration of this currency is a function of Britain's national sovereignty. Later we will want to consider some of the ways in which Britain, in the exercise of this sovereign function, finds itself confronted with what is—or appears to it to be—a conflict of interests between its national monetary interest and the interest, particularly in sterling area countries, of other countries holding sterling.

Sterling grew gradually from a national currency to become the currency of an international and basically maritime market which Britain organized, supervised, and dominated. Britain's dominance, based on the extraordinary productive advantages arising from its early lead in agricultural and industrial techniques, was promoted by naval power. Britain's increasing difficulties in this century in maintaining the international stability of sterling have not been primarily the result of any absolute decline of Britain's economic power —although war losses twice in this century have certainly entailed temporary setbacks of large order—but rather the result of the *relative* decline of British economic power in comparison with gigantic consolidated domestic markets, especially in the United States. The effect of this change has been to establish the sterling system, still growing though it is, as merely *one* of several monetary areas. Its main traits—coordinated exchange controls and quantitative restrictions on imports from various parts of the world—bloomed as a matter of war necessity. After the war, and even after war losses had been made good and production had reached unprecedented heights, the controls were continued because of the apparent convenience of handling the region's problems by such means and to an important degree in fear of new international instabilities. The region has behaved like a region for the good reason that it considers itself to be a region.

These views differ from other familiar and perhaps more widespread ones that the restrictive practices of the sterling area (especially those of Britain) are unnecessary, unfair, and perhaps harmful interferences with international commerce. The sterling area is seen in these other views as a group of countries which are not an economic region but which have followed an inappropriately regional monetary policy to the detriment of advantages which they and others could gain from freer policies in international trade.

It is not possible to make a decisive demonstration of the correctness of either of these very broad views. They concern the central problem of sterling's international role for better or worse in the world, which will be the concern of the last chapters of this book. The present chapter is concerned with the role of the United Kingdom as the central economy of the sterling area and the economy which underpins the whole sterling system.[1]

The Nature of the British Economy

The population of the United Kingdom is about 50 million; these people produce about £18 billion of goods and services a year. Similar figures for other sterling countries are full of gaps, and insofar as they exist their comparability to British figures is not clear. But roughly, the United Kingdom seems to have about a twelfth of the area's population and it accounts for something like half of the area's production. Per capita production in Britain is about £350 ($1,000), compared to about $2,400 in the United States.

The first notable feature of the British economy is the low

[1] An adequate description of any national economy is a subject for a specialist, which I am not. In my efforts in this chapter, I have relied greatly on a number of sources mentioned here or in the bibliography.

proportion of people working on the land. In 1952, even after war and postwar emphasis on farm production, agriculture accounted for less than 6 per cent of total production and about the same percentage of employment. Over a third of British production was accounted for by manufacturing, and nearly a quarter by the distributive trades and other services. The most distinctive trend since the war has been a shift away from the production of textiles and other consumer goods and into the engineering industries. But the basic pattern of high industrial specialization has continued, with Britain remaining dependent on foreign sources for about half of its food requirements. This is one measure of the second broad feature of the economy—its orientation to foreign trade. In 1952 British exports accounted for 30 per cent of total production, and even in 1946 when the export industry had not yet been rebulit for peacetime needs the percentage was 17.

This description of the structure of production, though oversimplified and excessively abbreviated, suggests the essence of Britain's role as the economic center of the sterling system. The pattern appears to have been developing in a consistent direction for 300 years—a story that E. A. G. Robinson, working with very limited data and frequently with only intuition as a guide to the comparability of data, tells with striking ingenuity.[2] In 1688, about as far back as he feels sensible information permits us to go, the population was about a fifth of today's and production per capita may have been in the order of £10 a year. Some two-thirds of the population were agricultural. Imports were a little more than 5 per cent of production and were largely raw materials, scarcely at all food. England was. in fact, a net exporter of food. Foreign trade was marginal in the economy, rather the way it still is in the case of the United States. The largest export was wool (two-thirds); the rest were mostly coal, lead and tin—indigenous resources. People spent half their money on food and another quarter on clothes.

By a century later (around 1800) production had risen eightfold, and retained imports were a good bit more im-

2 E. A. G. Robinson, "The Changing Structure of the British Economy," *The Economic Journal,* v. 64, no. 255 (September 1955), pp. 443-461.

portant—some 15 per cent of the nation's income. Textiles were still the heart of exports (about two-thirds) although cotton had replaced wool in importance. England imported about a seventh of its food and had ceased to be an exporter of grain. Manufactures of all kinds, including textiles, were 90 per cent of total exports, and the trend was away from the export of raw materials. Imports of raw materials, largely for the textile industry, were 60 per cent of the total. The proportion of the population engaged in agriculture had fallen to about a third, or by half. Professor Robinson comments:

> Thus the economy had already moved a long way from the pattern of 1688. It had no longer in anything like the same degree as then the features that we now associate with an "underdeveloped country": the relatively large proportion of population engaged in agriculture or engaged in the trading and handicrafts associated with it; the chief imports composed of manufactures and chief exports of primary products (that feature had largely disappeared before 1750). But the structure was still a long way from that which developed later in the century.

This was the beginning of the century in which Britain's international economic power and influence came to their peak and Britain became the major supplier of manufactures to an agricultural world in exchange for raw materials and food. The population of the world was less than half what it is now, and it was most heavily concentrated in the Far East (40 per cent) and Western Europe (29 per cent). Of total world manufactures, Britain produced 40 per cent and enjoyed a correspondingly large share of world trade in this category. The United States accounted for only 10 per cent of world production; the day of the large inland non-agricultural markets was still a couple of generations away, as was the fierceness of competition which manufacturing in those markets would entail for Britain. Compared to the twentieth century, Britain's industrial leadership, together with still moderate dependence on international trade, made for a greater degree of stability in its international transactions.

British agricultural population continued to diminish; in 1870 it was down to 14 per cent, in 1913, 8 per cent, and nowadays typically 5 or 6 per cent. The other side of this trend is the increase in Britain's dependence on food imports which amounted to a third of retained imports by 1880. By 1900 only half the food requirements were coming from domestic sources; in 1913 this had dropped to a third, and for the first time food imports became more important than raw material imports. Since the last war the proportion of domestic food supplies to total needs has been brought up to 50 per cent again. Since 1850 imports in general continued to increase in relation to national income to a peak of 33 per cent in the 1880s, after which the ratio declined somewhat and stands now at around a fourth.

Professor Robinson has called the British economic structure as it developed in the second half of the nineteenth century "inherently fragile" because the nature of the trade (export of manufactures, import of food and raw materials) involved a specialization of British resources in response to a fortuitous lead in manufacturing which could not indefinitely be retained as other countries developed, and because it made Britain increasingly dependent on foreign sources of supply as a result of increased needs and diminishing indigenous supplies. As an illustration of the latter he gives these figures for the proportion of requirements supplied from indigenous British sources.

	1857-1863	*1907-1913*
Lead	100%	11%
Tin	88%	21%
Copper	71%	1%
Wool and flax	58%	22%

Moreover, Robinson finds that the available evidence negates the widely accepted and rarely challenged notion that Britain's concentration on manufacturing reflected a comparative advantage over agricultural production. From all this he concludes that the structure of the British economy is still far too closely disposed to an international situation which has passed. This he illustrates with a half-dozen simple and arresting tables. His figures indicate a trend since 1820 in which imports in general played an increasing role in the British market, reaching a peak in 1880, and since then declining slightly; of food imports playing a pretty consistently growing role in the British diet; of British exports dominated by manufactures at a fairly consistent level, although the portion accounted for by metal and engineering products has grown rapidly while that accounted for by textiles has undergone a corresponding decline.

Remedies for structural imbalance are difficult to be sure about economically and even more difficult to carry out politically. Britain's loss of leadership in manufactures implies the need to foster an economy less dependent on imports; that that must be done he has little doubt. His fear is that failure to do it by a satisfactory reallocation of British resources will mean that it will be forced as a part of a general contraction in economic activty.

But what is the relevance of this inquiry into Britain's secular problems to the sterling area and sterling as a system? It has to do with the manner in which Britain goes about coping with the trends to which Professor Robinson drew attention and which are already widely (if vaguely) acknowledged in Britain.

The decisions for economic policy makers are harrowing, however clear may be the inevitable general direction which the British economy must follow. In attempting to create an attainable and maintainable economic structure, public policy makers have at least three broad lines of possible movement to consider. The most attractive, if the least convincing, is to try to create a structure that would permit Britain once more to play the sort of dominant role in international economics that it did in the nineteenth century. Sterling once again would become fully international, convertible, and desirable to all fund-holders. This line of movement is appealing because it involves the least change in the habits of financial thinking in Britain and because it suggests a picture of reconstituted British leadership in the world.

Almost the converse of this approach would be a policy concentrated on the national rather than the international function of sterling, that would in effect recognize a conflict between the two. The British government would concern itself with its national economic position. It would drop the notion that the country would profit from efforts to improve the usefulness of sterling in settlements among non-Britons (even among sterling colleagues), and devote itself to establishing a solid national currency rather than an international one. In short, it would forget the grandeur of its international financial past and the risks attending that degree of international influence and responsibility. Conceivably this line of approach might, as in the case of Switzerland, actually lead to a much broader and more easily supportable convertibility of sterling, as the currency of a compact and presumably soundly-run nation rather than the currency of a melange of countries with different objectives, practices, and notions of financial right and wrong.

The third possible line of movement in steadying the British economy lies somewhere between the first two. The major goal would be the establishment of a region, larger than the United Kingdom but smaller than the world, in which financial policy could be coordinated and economic development influenced so as to bring new strength to one part of the region to offset a current weakness in another part. In short, to consolidate a sterling region on the assumption that such a policy might involve less painful adjustments for Britain and give greater promise of attainment and maintenance.

A logical case can be made out for any of these possibilities and it would be almost impossible to calculate which would bring the greatest, earliest, or most lasting success. An important fact influencing the choice under modern democratic procedures is that deliberations must take account of the government's overriding responsibility to maintain a stable economy and to achieve a rising standard of living. No step may be taken in carrying out the general line of policy if that step suggests to the voting public the risk of substantial unemployment or impairment of the current standard of living. And yet which line of policy carries the least risk is never free from questions to which the answers are uncertain.

Britain's Postwar Balance of Payments

Before considering these alternatives any further, as we shall do in Chapter 9, we need before us the basic facts of the United Kingdom's balance of payments since the war. The state of the United Kingdom's balance of payments critically reflects the manner in which it, as the center of the sterling system, has discharged its central obligations, and also provides a basis for estimating its ability to continue the discharge of these, or even enlarged, functions.

The central functions are the achieving of a maximum degree of ease and convenience for sterling countries in their use of sterling for current payments to other countries, and the providing of credit facilities for the development of the metropolitan economy and the diverse economies of the sterling association. Obviously any number of factors will affect how well the center may discharge these functions but the broad general considerations can be stated briefly. The usefulness of sterling in financing the foreign payments of sterling countries depends heavily on the center's ability to provide long-term credit. Both short- and long-term credit could be provided by expanding the supply of sterling; this process has been significant in the postwar years, but continued inflation works against the monetary integrity of the system and ultimately worsens problems of credit supply it initially solves. The level of reserves and the flow of new savings into the metropolitan market establish the limits of the center's ability to provide short-term credit to cover the temporary deficits of the members in their accounts with *non-sterling* countries, and long-term credit for the betterment of their production. Such savings may originate in the central economy, or in the economies of the associated countries, or elsewhere. The larger the savings available from the metropole, the more outside savers will be willing to place their funds in the center. The extent of any bank's assets, and especially its liquid assets, affects its popularity with depositors. So in a very real sense, it is the capital position of the metropole and its own savings which determine its ability to perform effectively as the center of a monetary system.

The center's foreign-exchange reserves—that is, its uncommitted holdings of non-sterling currencies—obviously can result only from an excess of receipts from the non-sterling world over payments to it. The supply of longer-term sterling credits for economic development is determined by more complex factors, but nonetheless is critically affected by the center's ability to produce more than it consumes. The success with which the United Kingdom can operate a monetary system that goes beyond its own borders depends fundamentally on its own capacity to save—domestically in the sense that production must exceed consumption, internationally in the sense that it is able to sell more abroad than it purchases. Hence our concern with British production and with the British balance of payments.

The United Kingdom's current account with other countries since the war is shown in Table 2. The surplus with

Table 2

UNITED KINGDOM BALANCE OF PAYMENTS ON CURRENT ACCOUNT

(£ millions)

	With the Sterling Area	*With OEEC Countries*	*With the Dollar Area*	*With Other Areas*	*Total Current Account*
1946	− 28	+ 80	−301	−49	−298
1947	+127	+ 6	−510	−66	−443
1948	+254	+ 88	−252	−89	+ 1
1949	+293	− 16	−296	+50	+ 31
1950	+287	+115	− 88	−14	+300
1951	+343	−201	−431	−96	−385
1952	+367	− 26	−172	+86	+255
1953	+179	+104	− 4	−54	+225
	+1822	+150	−2054	−232	−314
Annual Average	+228	+ 19	−257	−29	− 39

Source: Cmd. 8976, 9119.

Note: In the three years 1951-1953 the United Kingdom received "defense aid" amounting to £227 million from the United States. I have followed the official British practice of treating this amount as a current earning.

sterling countries was about the same as the deficit with the dollar area, suggesting—somewhat misleadingly in this particular period—a basic triangular pattern. This is the traditional pattern of British payments abroad—a dollar deficit covered by surpluses earned in the sterling area and elsewhere. In the postwar period, however, the triangulation has not been nearly as direct as the current account figures above suggest.

The United Kingdom has not earned enough dollars from Europe and the sterling area to cover its dollar deficit. Its total deficit payable in dollars has been considerably larger than the figures for the current deficit with the dollar area indicate. In addition to the current deficit with the *geographical* dollar area, Britain has had to make very substantial dollar payments for other purposes. There have been capital transactions, long-term and short-term; there have been net dollar payments to the non-dollar world (for example, under the European Payments Union and the terms of the British bilateral agreements with the non-dollar, non-sterling countries); there have been transactions with the International Monetary Fund; and there have from time to time been substantial dollar payments in behalf of other sterling countries, as we shall note later in examining the operations of the sterling area's "dollar pool." Existing statistics do not permit a precise attribution of all these other dollar pay-

Table 3

UNITED KINGDOM ADDITIONAL DOLLAR PAYMENTS

(£ millions; "+" indicates net receipts)

	Capital Account with Dollar Area	*Dollar Payments to Non-Dollar World* [a]	*Total*
1946	+ 21	+ 46	+ 67
1947	− 43	−249	−292
1948	− 66	− 78	−144
1949	+ 11	− 77	− 66
1950	+130	− 5	+125
1951	− 98	− 59	−157
1952	+ 32	−145	−113
1953	+ 24	+ 64	+ 88
Total	+ 11	−503	−492
Annual Average	+ 1	− 63	− 62

Source: Cmd. 8976, 9119.

[a] On sterling area account as well as United Kingdom account, but apparently mostly for the United Kingdom.

ments to the various members of the sterling area, but the general account in Table 3 is in itself of interest.

Dollar payments to countries other than those usually classed as members of the dollar area have evidently been very large—£503 million in eight years compared with the total British deficit of £2,054 million with the dollar *area.* The figure suggests a substantial degree of *de facto* dollar convertibility for non-residents of the sterling area. This sizable figure is also a reminder that the dollar is not just a currency of settlement between a dollar region and a sterling region, but is—like sterling itself in the nineteenth century and to a lesser degree now—an important instrument of final resort in net payments between currency areas.

Apart from the pressing problems arising because of regional clearing difficulties, the United Kingdom's current account with other countries reveals the general difficulty the center of the system has had in generating any surpluses in foreign trade as a whole. Such surpluses, constituting national savings from international trade, are vital to accelerating the development of the sterling area. Instead of the hoped-for international surpluses, there have been net deficits at the rate of £39 million a year. The working assumption of the British government has been that a minimum of £300 million a year as a balance of payments surplus is needed if the United Kingdom is to function properly as the hub of a large monetary area. This amount is probably minimal, especially if the United Kingdom's current account is read in relation to the capital ("financing") account. The actual current deficit would have been significantly worse but for the volume of United States "defense aid," starting with a trickle of £4 million in 1951 and amounting to over £100 million in each of the next two years. These defense receipts are, no doubt properly, regarded as "earnings," and perhaps under such assumptions as present circumstances entitle us to make about Western defense costs they should be regarded as a stable form of earnings. Nevertheless, in the course of long-range economic arrangements, such earnings have a peculiarly arbitrary character of a sort that a metropolitan monetary center should be reluctant to count on in building the financial security of its system.

Another striking feature of the annual current accounts of the United Kingdom is the magnitude of the swings from plus to minus, particularly in their relation to central reserves. The main facts about these changes are shown in Tables 4 and 5.

Table 4

CHANGES IN THE UNITED KINGDOM'S BALANCE ON CURRENT ACCOUNT

End of Year Compared to End of Preceding Year	*Change in Current Account (£ mils.)*	*Change in Dollar Account Alone (£ mils.)*	*Index of Official Reserves (1946=100)*
1947	−145	−209	78
1948	+444	+258	69
1949	+ 30	− 44	63
1950	+269	+208	138
1951	−685	−343	88
1952	+640	+259	68
1953	− 30	+168	93
Annual Average	±320	±213	
Annual average level of reserves at year's end	£726 million		

Source: Cmd. 8976, 9119. Dollar payments to the non-dollar world are not included in column two.

The size of the annual swings on current account has been large in relation to official reserves, although the use of official figures for gold and dollar reserves significantly understates Britain's foreign-exchange availabilities because it neglects substantial amounts in private hands (perhaps typically a fifth). Moreover, not all the changes in current account balance involve gains or losses of reserves. The swings are underestimated a bit because the figures are year-end figures, rather than the highs and lows of the given year. Nonetheless, the figures fairly illustrate the extent to which changes in Britain's current account position have been accompanied by similar changes in reserves.

In the years 1946-53, year-end figures in dollar terms show annual accretions of reserves ranging from $672 million (1953) to $1,612 million (1950), and drains ranging from $168 million (1949) to $965 million (1951). The magnitude of swings in reserves also appears to be closely related to the magnitude of the shifts in Britain's current account over the period as a whole, although the correspondence is not high in each year. The suggestion is that the state of the metropolitan current account has been closely related to the state of central reserves, but it would require much closer examination to decide whether the correspondence is casual or causal.

Table 5

ANNUAL CHANGES IN THE UNITED KINGDOM'S DOLLAR POSITION

	Changes in Current Account with Dollar Area	*Changes in Level of Central Reserves*	*Level of Reserves*
	($ millions)		
End of:			
1947	−1109	− 617	2079
1948	+ 954	− 223	1856
1949	+ 186	− 168	1688
1950	+1217	+1612	3300
1951	−1599	− 965	2335
1952	+1090	− 489	1846
1953	+ 447	+ 672	2518
Annual average:	± 943	± 678	2232

Source: Cmd. 8976, 9119.

In the years in which there were balance of payments losses, the United Kingdom's current account deteriorated by a total of $2,708 million; in the seven year period the total reserve losses amounted to $2,462 million.

A traditional feature of Britain's balance of payments structure has been the earning of large enough surpluses from foreign investments and services to offset deficits on merchandise account. This structural feature appears to have been weakening for some time, as Table 6 indicates.

Table 6

ANNUAL DEFICITS OF THE UNITED KINGDOM ON CURRENT ACCOUNT, 1924-53

(£ millions)

Annual Average	*On Trade Account*	*Invisible Account*	*Total Current Account*
1924-1928	−381	+448	+67
1934-1938	−346	+325	−21
1946-1953	−261	+221	−39[a]

Sources: Cmd. 9119 for 1953; otherwise, Bank for International Settlements, *The Sterling Area,* Basle, January 1953, p. 21.
[a] Would be —67 if defense aid were excluded.

The figures for the postwar period can be set forth in much greater detail, as is done in Table 7.

Table 7

POSTWAR DEFICITS OF THE UNITED KINGDOM ON CURRENT ACCOUNT

(£ millions)

	Trade Account				*Invisible Account*			
	Dollar Area	*Sterling Area*	*Rest of the World*	*Total*	*Dollar Area* [a]	*Sterling Area*	*Rest of the World*	*Total*
1946	—290	0	+125	—165	—11	— 28	— 94	—133
1947	—437	+ 45	— 23	—415	—73	+ 82	— 37	— 28
1948	—210	+ 90	— 72	—192	—42	+164	+ 71	+193
1949	—247	+157	— 47	—137	—49	+136	+ 81	+168
1950	—115	+ 62	— 80	—133	+27	+225	+181	+433
1951	—348	+ 26	—407	—729	—83	+317	+110	+344
1952	—194	+ 81	— 4	—117	+22	+286	+ 64	+372
1953	— 70	—104	— 23	—197	+66	+283	+ 73	+422
Total	—1911	+357	—531	—2085	—143	+1465	+449	+1771
Annual Average	—239	+ 45	— 67	—261	—18	+183	+ 56	+221

Source: Cmd. 8976, 9119.
[a] Defense aid (£227 million in the period 1951-53) from the United States has been included arbitrarily in invisible accounts. Had it been excluded, the average annual surplus would appear as 193 instead of 221.

The figures for the mid-twenties show a surplus on invisible account comfortably larger than the deficit on trade account, even though the resulting surplus on current account of £67 million a year does not represent a very large fund of metropolitan savings available for international use. In the thirties, the situation had deteriorated considerably, and current account deficits were the rule. In 1934-38, the deficit on trade account was running at about the level of the twenties, but surpluses on invisible account had dropped by almost a third or by £123 million a year. In the postwar period, the merchandise deficits were considerably reduced, although extremely large in the two worst years. The trend toward smaller invisible surpluses also continued; they were only half as much as in the twenties, and were considerably under even the shrunken level of the thirties. Despite the reduction of the merchandise deficit and despite defense aid, the over-all deficit on current account rose to an average of £39 million a year. The surpluses of the twenties were replaced by deficits almost as large.

Trade Account versus "Invisibles"

Can the key to Britain's and sterling's difficulties since the war be found in the deterioration in net invisible earnings? This, it has been argued, is the main difference between the days when sterling's international status was unrivalled and the unsteady days of the present generation. If this diagnosis were correct, the therapy would be directed at a strengthening of invisible earnings and a lowering of invisible expenditures, and in particular at a restoration of London to its former world leadership as a center of international services —shipping, insurance, banking, and middlemanning.

No one questions the great importance, traditionally and currently, of invisible payments and receipts in Britain's current international position. About a fifth of the total payments to other countries is on invisible account; about a third of the total receipts is from invisibles, excluding defense aid from the United States. Disregarding defense aid, net receipts from invisibles have run at an annual average of £193 million since the war, compared with an average annual deficit on merchandise account of £261 million. In transactions with the dollar area, invisible payments and receipts are even more important, accounting for a third of the United Kingdom's total dollar payments and about half of total receipts. These fractions understate the importance of invisibles in total transactions because figures for many important invisible accounts are published on a net rather than gross basis.

The details of postwar invisible transactions set out in Table 8 are worth looking at.

"Invisible" accounts are named literally. Unlike transactions in commodities, the object of the transaction cannot be seen. A tourist's hair is cut in England; a profit to a British shareholder declared as the result of sales of Lux soap abroad; a father sends a check to a son seeking his fortunes abroad; an Australian student pays fees at a foreign university; or an American violinist performs in Johannesburg. From the standpoint of pure economics, the distinction between visible and invisible trade is somewhere between elusive and non-existent; one might as well talk about the difference between trade that is felt and unfelt, heard and silent, smellable and unsmellable. The services of a gang supervisor in a Rhodesian copper mine enters into the London price of a copper ingot no less directly than does the more visible phenomenon of a Nigerian farmer trucking his home-grown product to Lagos for shipment.

A country's resources lie fundamentally in the ingenuity of its people. If rich physical resources lie ready to hand, so much the better; if not, they can be imported. We have already noted the economic evolution of Britain from a subsistence economy to a market economy processing indigenous resources for its own use, and later to an economy processing imported resources for ultimate use in foreign markets. With each stage in this development the national production of Britain grew, and as the final stage was reached there was little left of the distinction between visible and invisible production. Britain's contribution to foreign markets became primarily a matter of what Britons did in the way of services for foreigners, either directly, as in the case of entertaining foreign tourists, or indirectly, as in the case of fashioning goods out of imported raw materials and then selling them to foreigners. The distinction now between the accounts

Table 8

THE UNITED KINGDOM'S INVISIBLE CURRENT ACCOUNTS (£ millions)

Payments (–) Receipts (+)	*1946*	*1947*	*1948*	*1949*	*1950*	*1951*	*1952*	*1953*	*Annual Average*
Shipping–Payments	141	170	178	191	180	283	299	248	211
Receipts	169	205	255	282	321	422	405	370	304
Net	+ 28	+ 35	+ 77	+ 91	+141	+139	+106	+122	+ 93
Interest, dividends and profits) Payments	100	93	103	106	117	179	212	223	142
) Receipts	162	186	192	200	271	304	289	272	235
Net	+ 62	+ 93	+ 89	+ 94	+154	+125	+ 77	+ 49	+ 93
Travel–Payments	42	76	66	75	85	104	82	86	77
Receipts	13	21	33	42	61	75	80	88	52
Net	– 29	– 55	– 33	– 33	– 24	– 29	– 2	+ 2	– 25
Private transfers (legacies, gifts, etc.) Net	+ 16	– 35	– 34	– 21	+ 5	– 6	– 6	+ 3	– 10
Government–Payments)	487	278	172	174	165	191	217	214	237
Receipts	164	129	96	35	29	38	44	60	74
Net	–323	–149	– 76	–139	–136	–153	–173	–154	–163
Other [a]–Net	+113	+ 83	+170	+176	+293	+264	+249	+298	+206
Total–Payments	754	652	553	567	542	763	816	768	677
Receipts	621	624	746	735	975	1103	1067	1088	870
Net	–133	– 28	+193	+168	+433	+340	+251	+320	+193

Source: Cmd. 8976, 9119.

[a] An official note defines "other" as including "all other current transactions except defence aid, e.g. the overseas transactions of oil companies (other than capital expenditure), insurance, civil aviation, royalties, commissions, banking and other services. It also includes sales of gold at home for industrial use, miscellaneous disbursements in the United Kingdom by international organisations, net current transactions of the United Kingdom Wool Disposals Ltd. (Joint Organisation), and an allowance for profits accruing from abroad to United Kingdom merchants." Remittances in respect of films are also included. Defense aid from the United States is excluded from this table, hence the slight differences in totals for the last three years compared with the

showing commodity trade and other accounts is mainly a matter of the degree of statistical ease in following transactions. The chief economic interest in the various separate accounts is in what the trends suggest about changes in Britain's structure of foreign trade.

The general trend for the surplus on invisible account to diminish over the last thirty years has been noted. The lack of comparable data for prewar and postwar years makes it difficult to follow the trend in the various types of invisible earnings except in the postwar years, but even in that limited time the developments are arresting. The heavy impact of the war on Britain's international earnings immediately after the war is sharply reflected in the smallness of earnings from shipping and investment interest, profits, and dividends, and the bigness of payments on government account. In the first two years after the war, the latter accounted for about half of all invisible payments abroad and military payments accounted for the bulk of all governmental expenditures abroad. In the next six years military expenditures accounted for almost two-thirds of a considerably diminished total of government payments abroad.

Apart from the undistinguishable components of the miscellaneous account called "other," these are the big invisible items: *payments* on government account, and *receipts* from shipping and investment. The postwar trend in these accounts has been favorable, but not favorable enough to suggest a restoration of the traditional position in which net invisible earnings cover net expenditures on commodity imports.

Still, the trend has been encouraging. Invisible payments have not risen, despite the rise in world prices and the costs of rearmament. Invisible earnings have grown steadily, despite the wartime impairment of British overseas investment and the three financial crises. The long-run trend may be toward reduced importance of the invisible transactions in the total international financial position of Britain, but the very great deterioration caused by the war has been corrected.

For several years after the war, there was a general tendency to blame all of the economic difficulties of Britain on the war, at the cost of obscuring shortcomings of financial policy. Professor Lionel Robbins commented in his Stamp Memorial Lecture of 1951:

I must confess to a certain sense of desolation nowadays when I encounter yet again the hackneyed tale of misfortunes which we have heard so often from a thousand public platforms . . . I am tempted to say with Macaulay that 'every schoolboy knows' that during the war we cut down our export industries to a bare minimum and that we sold substantial slices of our foreign property; that, when the war was over there were further drains on our purse in the shape of heavy relief and military expenditure; and that, since then, there have been still further acute embarrassments in the shape of steeply rising prices of essential imports and the losses we have suffered from the depredations of Dr. Moussadeq.

The "hackneyed tale" has grown less familiar as years have passed and a reminder here is in order. In the course of financing the war, Britain liquidated £1 billion of its overseas investments, about half in the sterling area and most of the rest in the dollar area. At the same time Britain increased its foreign debt by more than £3 billion. No figure is available showing the exact effect of this change on income receivable or payable on investment account, but even assuming a moderate earning rate of 5 per cent on foreign holdings and the probable modest rate of 1½ per cent interest on the new liabilities, the net loss of income must have been at least £100 million a year. This one figure alone is large in relation to the size of the annual current deficits which actually developed in the first postwar years. In the case of shipping, Britain came out of the war with less than half of the tonnage it had at the beginning. Earnings from Britain's extensive oil investments around the world account for a substantial part of the transactions included in "other." Oil was the only major source of earnings not impaired by the war.

In 1946 and 1947, Britain's earnings from all transactions other than commodity exports were only about half the prewar strength. But the effect of the war was not confined to earnings. Britain's foreign expenditures for military purposes and for relief were unusually high in these two years. Military expenditures were £374 million in 1946 and £209 million in 1947. These amounts are well above the annual rate of about £140 million in the next six years. Relief expenditures, though not accounted for separately in British figures, can be inferred from other figures; apparently international relief programs cost Britain some £100 million a year in 1946 and 1947. So the unfavorable effects of the war on Britain's foreign transactions other than exports and imports must have amounted to upwards of £400 million a year in 1946 and 1947.

Early calculations based on estimates of how badly Britain's international earning capacity might have been impaired by the war suggested an annual balance of payments deficit in the immediate postwar years of £500 million or more a year. Actually, the deficit in 1946 was £298 million and £443 million in 1947. The explanation for the overestimate is not clear from the information available. What is clear is that the impairment of Britain's international status in current dealings was mercifully below what the wreckage caused by the war suggested at the time.

In Table 7 on page 117, the average annual surplus on invisible account in postwar years was given at £221 million, or about half of the comparable figure in the mid-twenties. Actually, the invisible surplus has been growing, and in 1950-53 averaged about £350 million annually, or £400 million if defense aid is included. Does this favorable development suggest a favorable answer to the question posed initially—are invisible surpluses in the future likely to eliminate a large deficit on current account? Beyond that, is it to be expected that an invisible surplus will exceed the commodity deficit substantially, so that Britain will be in a position again to invest abroad?

These basic questions cannot of course be answered with any certainty. Perhaps from a policy standpoint they do not need to be. No harm would result from efforts to enlarge the invisible surplus, although considerable harm might be done if a continuing substantial deficit on commodity account were tolerated in the unproved expectation of growing invisible surpluses. On the whole there are many reasons to doubt that Britain's balance of payments will revert to the earlier pattern in which invisible transactions played the critical role. We have seen that the significant invisible accounts are shipping, investment income, and "other" (mostly oil). Net earnings from shipping have levelled off in recent years, after a striking comeback from the immediate postwar position. The moderately favorable net earnings in the last several years may represent just about the position Britain can hold in this highly competitive and widely subsidized field. Investment earnings are depressed by the annual interest payments on Britain's large postwar borrowings; these charges, largely on the United States and Canadian credits, have been running over £40 million a year. Whether Britain can expect increased income on foreign investment depends mainly on whether substantial new foreign investments can be made, and this in turn depends directly on whether Britain can develop a substantial current account surplus in its balance of payments. So far, such surpluses have not been forthcoming and probably have not been since before the first World War.

Of the major invisible accounts, then, that leaves "other." Most of the net earnings here are probably attributable to operations in oil, although separate figures are not available. Despite the difficulties in Iran the general trend of oil earnings has been rapidly upward and is still upward, but the future course of earnings is subject to uncertainties of price, competition from other fuels, renegotiation of royalty payments, possible foreign expropriations, and ultimately—a long way off—depletion.

When attention is focused on the changes from year to year in the state of Britain's current accounts, the impression that commodities account for the critical element in international transactions is reinforced. Figures in Table 9 are arranged to show how changes in the various major types of earnings and expenditures account for the improvement (+) or deterioration (—) in the over-all accounts.

The big accounts are commodity imports and exports, and

Table 9

Year to Year Changes in Britain's Current Accounts

(£ millions)

	1946	*1947*	*1948*	*1949*	*1950*	*1951*	*1952*	*1953*
Balance on Current Account								
Trade Account	−165	−415	−192	−137	−133	−729	−117	−197
Invisibile Account	−133	− 28	+193	+168	+433	+340	+251	+320
Defense Aid	—	—	—	—	—	+ 4	+121	+102
Total	−298	−443	+ 1	+ 31	+300	−385	+255	+225
Change Compared with Preceding Year (Deterioration −; Improvement +)		−145	+444	+ 30	+269	−685	+640	− 30
Of which:								
Imports		−478	−234	−184	−405	−1092	+532	+ 71
Exports		+228	+457	+239	+409	+496	+ 80	−151
Shipping		+ 7	+ 42	+ 14	+ 50	− 2	− 33	+ 16
Interest, profits, etc.		+ 31	− 4	+ 5	+ 60	− 29	− 48	− 28
Travel		− 26	+ 22	0	+ 9	− 5	+ 27	+ 4
Gifts, legacies, etc.		− 51	+ 1	+ 13	+ 26	− 11	0	+ 9
Government		+174	+ 73	− 63	+ 3	− 17	− 20	+ 19
Defense Aid		—	—	—	—	+ 4	+117	− 19
Other (oil, etc.)		− 30	+ 87	+ 6	+117	− 29	− 15	+ 49

Source: Cmd. 8976, 9119.

the big changes are in those accounts. Postwar expenditures on imports increased steadily and by large amounts until 1952; except for 1953 earnings from exports increased steadily but by somewhat smaller amounts. In an economy as dependent as Britain's on foreign raw materials, it is to be expected that an increase in exports will entail a substantial increase in imports. However the actual increase in payments for imports over the eight-year period slightly *exceeded* the increase in the value of exports. Part of this unfavorable expansion of payments compared to receipts is attributable to unfavorable trends in import and export prices over most of the period; the prices Britain had to pay for imports rose more or fell less than the prices gotten for exports.

The importance of this deterioration in Britain's terms of trade is considerable. For example the volume of imports which a fixed volume of exports would pay for in 1938 was only three-fourths as large by 1952. Put another way, the volume of Britain's imports in the peak postwar year (1951) was 5 per cent less than the volume imported annually in the period 1934-1938, while the volume of Britain's exports in 1951 was 62 per cent above the prewar period. Yet in that year, Britain's payments for imports exceeded its earnings from exports by £729 million.

Bearing in mind that in the 1946-53 period Britain's average annual bill for imports exceeded export receipts by £261 million, the index for the volume of trade (Table 10) shows dramatically the persistent pinch from international price movements. Against a consistently rising volume of exports and a fairly consistent abstention from imports, a substantial deficit in payments continued. Britain's traffic in commodities on the international market suggests a parallel to a firm whose output is rising beyond expectations, but whose losses grow as costs rise faster than selling prices.

These figures also show a considerable fluctuation in the volume of imports, and suggest that the disadvantageous price-cost relationships in Britain's merchandise trade do not account for all of the difficulty. In each of the crisis years—1947, 1949, 1951—there was a significant expansion in the volume of imports and a relatively smaller expansion in the volume of exports. It is interesting that despite the tendency of authorities to rely on import slashes as the immediate means of coping with the crises, the volume of imports in the years following the first two crises increased or was maintained. After the third crisis, the volume of retained imports was reduced about 10 per cent, but this was a reduction back to the level of recent years from the peak postwar import volume of 1951.

Table 10

CHANGES IN THE PHYSICAL VOLUME OF BRITAIN'S IMPORTS AND EXPORTS

(1938=100)

Volume Expressed as Per Cent of the Volume in 1938	*Retained Imports*	*Exports*
1934-1938 average	97	102
1946	63	90
1947	72	99
1948	75	126
1949	82	138
1950	82	160
1951	92	162
1952	83	152
1953	91	157

Source: Derived from United Kingdom Board of Trade data given in *Monthly Digest of Statistics* (Central Statistical Office).

Regional Accounts

Variations in the United Kingdom's accounts with the various major trading regions were marked, as Table 2 (p. 112) shows. Dividing the United Kingdom's current trade into three parts—dollar area, sterling area, and all the rest—one finds that from 1946 to 1953 the dollar deficit on trade account was nearly as large as the entire trade deficit; in non-dollar trade, the United Kingdom earned from its sterling associates a considerable surplus which was somewhat more than offset by its deficit with non-sterling, non-dollar countries ("the rest of the world"). The deficit with the "rest of the world" is very largely the result of transactions in the year and a half after the outbreak of the Korean War, a period in which the cost of Britain's imports from the rest of the world just about doubled. The great rise in imports was due to the physical requirements of defense expansion, to the booming prices of the period (i.e., the unfavorable terms of trade, from Britain's standpoint), and to the fact that credit facilities available through the European Payments Union made it possible for a growing deficit to go on unchecked. Apart from this one relatively brief episode, Britain's trade accounts—and indeed its whole current account—with the "rest of the world" were in virtual balance in the eight-year period.

So the areas in which British deficits or surpluses have been substantial and persistent are the dollar area and the sterling area. From the sterling area the British earned on trade account £357 million over the first eight postwar years, and another £1,465 million from services—a total of £1,822 million. Roughly these net British earnings from the rest of the sterling area are very close to the same size as its dollar deficit—£1,911 million on trade account and £143 million on invisible account, for a total of £2,054 million. If these figures accounted for all of the transactions between Britain and these two areas, there would be the suggestion of almost perfect triangulation—Britain meeting its dollar deficits by using surpluses earned in the sterling area. But this has been far from the case (although recent trends suggest it is coming to be more the case). For instance, over the period as a whole, the £1,822 million deficit of the rest of the sterling area (conventionally abbreviated RSA) on current account with the United Kingdom was settled in dollars and gold only to the extent of some £500 million (plus current payments and receipts of dollars attributable to the rest of the area's transactions with non-sterling, non-dollar countries which are very hard to determine).[3] The figure of £500 million is the same as the amount of dollar payments which British

[3] An effort to look more closely at these accounts will be made in Chapters 6 and 7, dealing with the other members of the sterling area.

Table 11

The United Kingdom's Accounts with the Rest of the Sterling Area (£ millions)

+ UK receipts — UK payments

	1946	*1947*	*1948*	*1949*	*1950*	*1951*	*1952*	*1953*	*Total*
1. Current Account									
Trade	0	+ 45	+ 90	+157	+ 62	+ 26	+ 81	—104	+ 357
Invisibles	—28	+ 82	+164	+136	+225	+317	+286	+283	+1465
Total	—28	+127	+254	+293	+287	+343	+367	+179	+1822
2. Use of these surpluses									
Investment (—) in RSA	+63	—277	—180	—263[a]	—184	—177	— 94	—158	—1270
Gold purchases (—) from RSA	—82	— 84	—135[b]	— 68	—100	— 78	— 72	— 79	— 698
Dollar purchases (—) from RSA[c]	+73	+306	+ 65	+ 54	—170	—103	— 38	— 77	+ 110
(net gold & dollars purchased (—))	(— 9)	(+222)	(— 70)	(— 14)	(—270)	(—181)	(—110)	(—156)	(— 588)
Other transfers for RSA[d]	+8	+ 59	— 72	— 4	—214	— 44	— 52	—118	— 437
Total	+62	+4	—322	—281	—668	—402	—256	—432	—2295
3. The difference between totals of paragraphs 1 and 2 = increase (+) or decrease (—) in UK's debt to RSA (i.e. changes in the RSA's sterling balances)	—34	—131	+ 68	— 12	+381	+ 59	—111	+253	+ 473

Source: Cmd. 8976, 9119.

[a] The New Zealand and Australian gifts of £30 million in 1947 and £16 million in 1949 are arbitrarily counted here as a reduction of reported United Kingdom investment.

[b] Including £80 million in gold loaned by Australia. The repayment the following year is taken into account in the figure for United Kingdom investment.

[c] This line includes only transactions with the dollar area, and not dollar payments or receipts resulting from RSA transactions with non-dollar, non-sterling countries (e.g., with members of the European Payments Union). These appear in this table as a part of "other transfers."

[d] I.e., transactions with non-dollar, non-sterling countries, handled through RSA accounts in London and resulting in a change in RSA sterling balances.

figures show for settlements with non-dollar countries. Thus, the dollars Britain got out of its large earnings from the sterling area were just enough to finance the dollar payments needed in the non-dollar world, but nothing was left over for financing the large deficit with the dollar world.

Moreover, despite the deficit with the United Kingdom, the rest of the sterling area built up its sterling balances in London by £473 million in this period. To the £1,822 million of the RSA's current deficits with the United Kingdom must be added £473 million increase in the capital assets of the RSA, giving a total of £2,295 million requiring explanation. The explanation available from published figures is set forth in the second part of Table 11.

In Britain's official accounts of its balance of payments, little attention is paid to the details of its transactions with the monetary area for which it serves as the center. The details of its dollar accounts are set forth generously, and its accounts with Western Europe with fair liberality. But even the simplified version of these critical sterling area accounts as set forth above had to be gleaned from figures buried in a number of tables, in contrast to the consolidated official totals for dollar and EPU transactions.

A rough summary of the foregoing information on Britain's position in the first eight postwar years looks like this:

	(£ millions)
British investment in the sterling area	1270
Minus increase in UK liabilities to RSA	– 473
Leaving net investment by UK in RSA	797
UK's current surplus with RSA	1822
UK's deficit on current account with all other areas	–2136
UK's position on total current account	– 314
All this leaving to be financed from outside Britain and the rest of the sterling area:	
Britain's over-all deficit	314
Britain's net investment in sterling area	797
Total	1111

It appears that a little more than half of the £2,295 million which accrued to the United Kingdom from the rest of the sterling area between 1946 and 1953 represents British investment in the sterling area. A little over a third of this investment has been offset by the rise in the United Kingdom's liabilities to the area, leaving net investment of £797 million. This figure taken by itself implies corresponding British savings. However, Britain's total current account in this period was in deficit by £314 million. Obviously its investment in the sterling area could have been possible only because of resources available to Britain from outside the sterling area. The extent of these outside resources will be set forth a little later when we examine Britain's dollar accounts and the operations of the dollar pool.

About a quarter of Britain's receipts from the rest of the sterling area were used in net purchases of gold and dollars from the area, although as we have seen these gains sufficed to finance less than a quarter of the United Kingdom's dollar deficit. The trend has been toward smaller dollar deficits on United Kingdom account, and toward steadier dollar receipts from the RSA. In 1952 and 1953, if defense aid from the United States is treated as a current dollar earning, the net gold and dollar receipts from the rest of the area slightly exceeded Britain's current deficit with the dollar area, and did not fall far short of covering Britain's current dollar requirements in all areas. The *trend* toward current dollar balance for the area as a whole would exist even in the absence of defense aid.

The Dollar Accounts

The postwar dollar accounts of the United Kingdom have usually been regarded as especially critical, although there may be no good reason to consider them as more critical than the sterling accounts. The United Kingdom's position has been polarized between large dollar deficits on current account and equally large non-dollar-yielding surpluses with the rest of the sterling area. But the dollar accounts have *seemed* the crux of Britain's financial problem. For much of the period the United Kingdom was heavily and abnormally dependent on dollar sources of supply, and in exports the United Kingdom found it hard to earn dollars directly or to compete with dollar area producers in other areas. This was to an important extent a matter of delivery dates and the existence of the wartime accumulations of sterling which, as it worked out, kept the order books of British producers greatly overloaded. Moreover, dollars have been needed to finance a portion of the transactions in the limbo between the sterling and dollar areas. Perhaps all of these reasons for the focus of interest on dollar accounts can be described in a general way by saying that the United Kingdom had little control over its supply of dollars other than through the hard process of earning them by exports and saving them by import limitations. In contrast, in the sterling world deficits could be covered (at least for the time being) by sterling, of which the United Kingdom controlled the supply.

To judge how important this distinction may or may not be, we need to look at the United Kingdom's dollar accounts in greater detail. Table 12 should be read with the features of British dollar accounting in mind. The accounts distinguish in considerable detail the *gross* payments and receipts of the United Kingdom in visible and invisible commerce with dollar countries. They distinguish in broad lines the United Kingdom's capital transactions with dollar countries. They distinguish in less detail the gross position of the rest of the sterling area, insofar as it is reflected in transactions through Britain. All these accounts deal with dollar payments and receipts in relation to the *geographic* area where the dollar is the basic instrument of international settlement. The accounts then distinguish the *net* dollar payments or receipts in trade with non-dollar countries (such as the members of the European Payments Union, in which some of the deficits of members with one another must be settled at least partially in gold or dollars) or in transactions with non-territorial organizations (such as the International Monetary Fund). This is the broad form of the accounts—the payments and receipts of the United Kingdom with the dollar area on both current and capital account, the net payments or receipts of the dependencies and independencies, and the net dollar transactions of the whole sterling area with the non-

Table 12

TRANSACTIONS THROUGH THE STERLING AREA'S GOLD AND DOLLAR POOL

(£ millions)

	1946	*1947*	*1948*	*1949*	*1950*	*1951*	*1952*	*1953*	*Total*
United Kingdom's balance with dollar area									
On current account	—301	—510	—252	—296	— 88	—431	—172	— 4	—2054
On capital account	+ 21	— 43	— 66	+ 11	+130	— 98	+ 32	+ 24	+ 11
Total	—280	—553	—318	—285	+ 42	—529	—140	+ 20	—2043
Pool gains or losses as result of RSA transactions with dollar area:									
Independent countries	— 30	—237	— 68	— 52	+114	+ 7	— 28	+ 46	— 248
Dependent territories	+ 39	+ 15	+ 58	+ 66	+156	+174	+138	+110	+ 756
Total	+ 9	—222	— 10	+ 14	+270	+181	+110	+156	+ 508
Total transactions with dollar area	—271	—775	—328	—271	+312	—348	— 30	+176	—1535
Gains and losses as result of transactions other than with the dollar area	+ 46	—249	— 78	— 77	— 5	— 59	—145	+ 64	— 503
TOTAL NET GAIN OR LOSS OF DOLLARS AS RESULT OF ALL OPERATIONS OF POOL	—225	—1024	—406	—348	+307	—407	—175	+240	—2038

Source: Cmd. 8976, 9119. Defense aid from the United States is treated as British earnings.

sterling, non-dollar world. These last cannot be attributed exactly to the various members of the area, but from the supporting partial details in the official statistics they seem largely attributable to Britain's own transactions—mainly with Western European (OEEC) countries and substantially because of the use made of sterling in transactions between other non-sterling, non-dollar countries and the OEEC group.

The British dollar statistics are not and do not purport to be a complete statement of the sterling area's dollar transactions, and it is very hard to guess how much the impression given by the British statistics would be modified by comparison with a complete accounting. Probably not much. The main gaps have to do with the dollar transactions that do not pass through London. For instance, most independent sterling countries handle some of their dollar transactions without resorting to facilities of the central dollar pool; South Africa and Burma handle all their dollar transactions independently. Besides this, many traders outside the sterling area have found it fairly easy to change their sterling into dollars indirectly, but at discount, and these transactions do not pass through official channels, although a substantial part of them must affect the central reserves and therefore get included in official accounts in one way or another. But the United Kingdom's accounting of dollars is necessarily a report only on the known transactions affecting the central pool; considering how both sterling and non-sterling countries handle their dollar accounts, the pool accounts must closely reflect the total dollar position of the sterling area.

In Table 12 the figures are grouped to show the United Kingdom's own dollar deficit (on both current and capital accounts), the extent of dollar assistance which the United Kingdom has received from other sterling countries, and the total net gain or loss of dollars in the central pool. Table 13 shows how these dollar deficits have been financed, according to official British figures.

The summary of the dollar pool transactions in Table 12 suggests a number of interesting things. Most obviously, the deficit of the United Kingdom on *current* account with the dollar area (£2,054 million), was almost exactly the same as the entire net dollar payments from the pool (£2,038 million).

The region's continuing dollar difficulties were, then, measured almost exactly by the difference between what the United Kingdom was able to earn currently from dollar countries and what it spent there. In the 1947 convertibility crisis the United Kingdom's current deficit with the dollar countries accounted for only half the drain (although the proportion is more like three-fourths if you take into account capital transactions and dollar payments to non-dollar countries). In the other two crisis years, 1949 and 1951, the United Kingdom's current deficit with the dollar countries accounted for almost all of the drain (92 per cent and 98 per cent respectively). If the dollar payments to non-dollar countries (£503 million) are added to the United Kingdom's current deficits, it appears that the metropole's net use of dollars exceeded by 25 per cent the net dollar expenditures of the sterling area as a whole. This is another way of saying that the RSA as a whole made a considerable contribution to the central pool in the first eight years after the war—a total of £508 million.

Table 13

FINANCING OF THE STERLING AREA'S DOLLAR DEFICITS

(£ millions)

	Loans and Grants from Outside the Sterling Area	*Use of Reserves*[a]
1946	279	– 54
1947	872	152
1948	351	55
1949	345	3[b]
1950	268	–575
1951	63	344
1952	0	175
1953	0	–240
TOTAL	2178	–140

Source: Cmd. 8976, Table 21; 9119, Table 10.

Notes: [a] Minus sign indicates increase of reserves.

[b] This figure is an oddity of accounting for the devaluation of sterling vis-a-vis the dollar in 1949. The reduction of the sterling-dollar rate from $4.03 per pound to $2.80 per pound on September 18, 1949 resulted in an increase in the *sterling* value of dollar reserves by £149 million. The actual net use of dollars during the year was $168 million.

This dollar contribution is attributable to the dependencies. The independent countries as a group were on balance drawers of dollars from the pool, even after taking into account their gold sales to the pool (mostly South Africa's). Moreover, the dollar accounts of the independent countries were invariably at their worst during the years when dollar help would have been most welcome to the United Kingdom and to the area as a whole.

Dollar difficulties of the various members have for the most part been cumulative. Table 14 shows how the dollar accounts of the various groups of sterling area members changed from year to year. In the table, minus signs indicate deterioration (increase in dollar deficits or a reduction in dollar surpluses), and plus signs show improvement in the dollar position.

Table 14

ANNUAL CHANGES IN STERLING AREA DOLLAR ACCOUNTS FROM YEAR TO YEAR

(£ millions)

		Rest of Sterling Area			*Total Sterling Area*
	UK	*DOTs*	*ISA*	*Total*	
1947	−568	−24	−207	−231	−799
1948	+406	+33	+169	+212	+618
1949	+ 34	+ 8	+ 16	+ 24	+ 58
1950	+399	+90	+166	+256	+655
1951	−625	+18	−107	− 89	−714
1952	+303	−36	− 35	− 71	+232
1953	+369	−28	+ 74	+ 46	+415
Annual Average	±378	±34	±111	±133	±488

Source: Cmd. 8976, 9119.

Note: All of the net payments made from the pool to non-dollar countries, a total of £503 million, have been included in the United Kingdom account.

The dollar accounts are apparently very volatile, changing annually by almost £500 million, for about three-quarters of which the United Kingdom seems to be responsible. With an annual level of reserves running at £726 million, this is surely a large swing. And the average swing understates the swings in particular periods. For instance, in the difficult years 1949-51, dollar accounts for the area as a whole fluctuated by £1,369 million much as they had in 1946-48. The big dollar earners, the dependencies (who made an annual average contribution of £94 million), have also been the steadiest in their performance, although in recent years their net earnings have tapered off.

The first eight years after the war are probably too few and too odd to support any firm speculation of trends, but there are some interesting possibilities. The United Kingdom, to which I have attributed major responsibility (not blame) for the area's deranged dollar accounts, has fairly consistently bettered its dollar position in the course of the period. The independent members have blown hot and cold dollar-wise, but their performance has never suggested that they would solve the area's problem without a considerable shaking-up of trading patterns. The dependencies have performed consistently as net dollar earners, but the amount earned has varied from year to year, and generally in an inconvenient way for the area as a whole—biggest when least needed (1950), declining when most needed (1951-52). But this may be carping. As a group the dependencies have been consistently large dollar earners, and have contributed £756 million in dollars to the sterling area since the war. Apart from the outside support the United Kingdom had from the United States and Canada, the dependencies have been the dollar bulwark of the system.

The Situation in 1954 and 1955

Early in the chapter it was suggested that the United Kingdom, as the center of the sterling system, had three broad lines of choice in financial policy. It could strive to reestablish sterling as a currency automatically convertible into other currencies in the money markets of the world. In this case, the main problem for the sterling monetary authorities would lie in necessary and frequent decisions as to how far they should dip into official reserves in efforts to guarantee the value of sterling in terms of the currencies of other countries. Should the price of sterling be fixed within narrow price margins for purchases and sales, or should the authorities let the money markets set their own price limits, without official intervention? Or should the authorities adopt a compromise policy of intervening in the markets only when the price of sterling rose or fell by a considerable amount?

A second line of policy, and almost opposite to the first, would be to forget about the international role of sterling and instead concentrate on sterling's function as the money of the United Kingdom. The focus of policy in this case would be on internal credit requirements, with priority given to the estimated supply of money needed to keep national production expanding and the standard of living rising.

A third line of policy would be somewhere between the first two, with emphasis placed on a wide but not unlimited use of sterling as an international currency. This is the line of policy described as *regional* in this book and is probably the closest of the three to the orientation of sterling policy since the war.

In the actual determination of policy, the alternatives are far less clear-cut than this description suggests. Any British government must recognize the various alternatives as expressing interrelated aspects of financial policy. The point of emphasis in policy may be shifted from time to time, either because a given government has a political point of view differing from that of its predecessor, or merely because circumstances change and call for a change in emphasis. But it remains true that sterling, like any widely used currency, must be sound at home if it is to be sound in world markets. To be sound at home, it must be prized in the proliferated credit structure which, peculiarly in the case of the sterling system, has made the stability of British banks almost synonymous with the soundness of the closely related banking structures of other sterling countries.

Any financially minded visitor to London in the spring and summer of 1954 would have seen visible evidence of a new sense of well-being. In the financial district, "The City," the banks and the great trading houses, the brokers, the shippers and the insurance companies, all had their traditional window-boxes again blooming with flowers. On sunny days the tortuous streets of the city reflected happiness as well as prosperity, as did the informal talking of the financial community. There were some doubters, mostly on the grounds that the whole pleasant situation was too good to last, but the consensus was one of confidence that the postwar crises could be put out of mind for the time being and full attention given instead to the pleasanter problem of extending Britain's prosperity at home and abroad. The behavior of sterling rates in free world markets was reassuring. For some nine months the discount had been so slight in comparison to the official rate that sterling was regarded in many quarters as dollar-convertible in fact though not in law.

The general view was that the monetary authorities and the financial community were adroitly managing financial affairs in such a way that the national, regional and international positions of sterling were being harmoniously furthered. In the City, the tendency of many financiers as they looked into the future was to favor more aggressive official steps to bring official and unofficial markets for sterling into line—in effect to bring about dollar convertibility soon, while the favorable economic situation would serve to reduce the risks to be expected from placing all sterling at the mercy of free markets. On the other hand, the tendency of many economists and government officials was rather to wait and see and meanwhile concentrate attention on longer-range problems. For who could be certain just how long the situation would remain unharried by a crisis? And if the problem of achieving a regular expansion in production could be solved, would not that be the best bulwark against another crisis?

Fear of the effect of a United States recession on Britain's production and balance of payments continued. But the apparent containment of the recession that occurred in the United States in late 1953 and early 1954 and the notable lack of unfavorable repercussions in the United Kingdom or in the sterling area in general allayed a large part of this fear. The problem shifted a bit in the view of many who were making the effects of external economic conditions their main concern. The possible effects of changes in United States economic activity became a special case, though an important one, in a general problem. Could Britain follow policies directed at raising its own level of production at the hoped-for rate (say, 3 per cent or so a year) if the level of production in countries which were Britain's major trading partners should rise less rapidly?

The question seems important because of a view of international economic relations which, though far from universal, is widely held. This view is that if a country which is engaged in foreign trade expands its production more rapidly than do its trading partners, it is very likely—perhaps certain—to run into difficulties in its balance of payments. The relatively higher production is likely to lead to relatively higher expenditures on imports. Raw materials not produced at home are needed for the increased volume of production. With their higher incomes people feel they can afford more consumer goods from abroad. Meanwhile, there is a lag before increased raw material imports are translated into increased exports. People in foreign countries are not likely to increase their expenditures by as much as Britain does since their incomes have not risen by as much. As a result, Britain's earnings from abroad will fail to cover expenditures.

The issue is very controversial. Against the argument just outlined, it is held that only inflation, not prosperity, could bring about a deterioration in the balance of payments. Less graciously, it is sometimes argued that all this is merely a rationale for a high degree of governmental control over foreign trade. In the absence of government control, would not any tendency of a country to buy too much from abroad be corrected through the mechanism of shifting market prices? The usual rebuttal to this is, Yes, but at what cost to the level of national production?

The events of 1954-55 probably deepened this controversy in the course of illustrating its importance. The evident prosperity of the second half of 1953 was carried further in the first half of 1954. There was a satisfying surplus of £141 million on current account in the six months, and an increase in gold and dollar reserves of $500 million. Production was expanding at an encouraging rate, probably about 4 per cent per annum. Wage rises were moderate, and prices almost stable. There was no disturbing rise in consumer expenditures. Private savings rose substantially. *The Economist* wrote on July 3, 1954:

For more than a year the British economy has successfully defied the most sacrosanct rule of postwar economic policy. Inflation has, to all intents and purposes, been eradicated—the bulging shop windows; shorter delivery dates and shrinking waiting lists; and this week the disappearance of the ration book are adequate signs of monetary improvement. Yet unemployment has shrunk to 1½ per cent of the working population, only ¼ per cent above its nadir in the roaring inflation of mid-1951. The miracle has happened—full employment without inflation, and this despite the heavy burden of defence, the rising burden of the social services, and some reduction in taxation.

Conditions remained prosperous in the second half of the year. Employment and production continued at high levels, and the rise in wage and price indexes was modest. The United States economy was expanding again. But there were some unfavorable signs in the British economy. Expenditures on imports rose, while earnings from exports fell, leaving a trade deficit of almost £150 million, compared to £60 million in the same period a year before and compared to about £50 million in the preceding six months. The traditional surplus on invisible account fell by £28 million compared with the second half of 1953. The balance on current account as a whole showed a deficit of about £5 million, compared with a surplus of over £100 million in the corresponding period a year before. Trade figures, and even to a greater extent payments figures, are available only after the delays of collecting and assembling, and according to early reports the deterioration was greater than it later turned out to be.[4] But there was no doubt of the direction in which the balance of payments was moving. Officially priced sterling, which under present policies is permitted by the authorities to move only within a narrow price range, weakened; transferable sterling, for which there was then no floor price or official support, dropped more significantly, if not alarmingly. In May, at its peak, it sold for $2.79; in December it stood at $2.72.

[4] For instance, the provisional figures for the second half of 1954 published in April 1955 (Cmd. 9430) showed a current account deficit of £38 million. The revised figures published in October 1955 (Cmd. 9585) reported the same item as only £5 million. The difference was due entirely to a change from £106 million to £139 million in reporting the surplus on invisibles. These figures and those in the text exclude defense aid.

When on January 1, 1955 *The Financial Times* of London reviewed the 1954 performance under the title, "And So to 1955," its tone was much the satisfied one of the earlier quotation from *The Economist*:

> In retrospect 1954 looks like the last of the postwar years. It was the year which saw not only the end of rationing and most of the remaining physical controls, but also—what is more important—the end of the frame of mind which sees in physical controls the best method of economic government. In prosperity it has been better than any prewar year on record. At the same time, as the savings figures show, inflation has been kept at bay: the threat of its reappearance has been met with delicate, and as it seems at the moment an adequate, adjustment of the short-term rate of interest.

By this time, *The Economist* was reflecting the mild concern of many observers over lengthening delivery dates, higher consumer expenditures, the slight upward drift of wages and prices, and the threat of inflation in general. By February it seemed to the government that the boom might get out of hand and mild restrictive measures were adopted. Bank rate—which had been lowered from 3½ per cent to 3 per cent in May 1954 in a move generally interpreted as undertaken for technical reasons rather than to ease credit conditions—was raised back to 3½ per cent at the end of January 1955. This was a very mild step at a time when consumption was rising sharply, and sterling deteriorating abroad.

Toward the end of February more decisive steps were taken. Bank rate was raised to 4½ per cent, its highest level in 23 years. In addition, the Exchange Equalisation Account was authorized to intervene in markets dealing in transferable account sterling. The policy of lending official support to transferable account sterling resulted in an immediate rise in rates to a level very close to that prevailing for official sterling. In addition to these measures, a mild tightening of the conditions allowable in installment buying was ordered.

Late in July the Chancellor of the Exchequer announced that the government would be more stingy in giving approval to capital expenditures requiring approval. He wrote the banks requesting them to bring about a "positive and significant" reduction in loans. The required down payment for installment buying was raised to 33⅓ per cent. In October a revised and tighter official budget was introduced. It increased purchase tax rates, abolished certain tax reliefs which had been granted in the regular budget the preceding April, reduced public works expenditures, reduced subsidies for house constructions, and reduced the amount of national lending to local authorities.

There are a number of interesting features in the difficulties that developed in late 1954 and 1955. First, they came at a time when the United States economy was stable. It was also a time when the terms of trade, though moving slightly against Britain, can be blamed for the trouble only to a minor extent. The core of the difficulties seems clearly to have been the inflationary condition developing along with Britain's expansion. Second, although the difficulties were aggravated by similar ones in other sterling countries, there was no Commonwealth conference to arrange for cooperative corrective steps. Third, to meet the difficulties Britain relied exclusively on monetary measures, in contrast to the import and exchange controls which we associate with the handling of balance of payments difficulties in the postwar years.

Britain's gold and dollar reserves fell by $642 million in the course of 1955, from $2,762 million to $2,120 million. They had already declined by about $250 million in the latter half of 1954. Thirty per cent of the reserves were lost in 18 months, compared with over 50 per cent ($1,600 million) from December 1950 to March 1952. Although the largest part of the drop in reserves came in the third quarter of 1955, the situation since the middle of the year seems to have been improving, if but slightly. The trade deficit was reduced, the dollar position improved, and the general position of the current accounts was in "bare balance," as the Chancellor of the Exchequer said, which he termed not enough. Even the most optimistic do not assume that similar difficulties may not recur, perhaps more seriously, in 1956.

In fact, the persistence of difficulties led to a further round of stern measures in February 1956. Bank rate was raised to 5½ per cent, compared to 2½ per cent in the United States. Down payments on some installment purchases were raised to 50 per cent. Bread and milk subsidies were cut. The government reduced its planned expenditure, in particular cutting back investment in the nationalized industries. The *New York Times* reported (February 19, 1956) that, "Laborites feel they have the Government on the defensive. The economic situation, they believe, is a major factor in a Conservative loss of popularity . . ." And so, as this book goes to press, the controversy over deflationary monetary policy is again at the center of British politics. Graham Hutton's conviction that *We Too Can Prosper* has given way to the question, *Are We Prospering Too Much?*

The temporary reestablishment of balance had led some observers to conclude that "orthodox" monetary policy—"flexible" is the more usual word now—had been clearly established as the most efficient way of meeting balance of payments difficulties. Certainly the monetary measures seem to have had some success, although it is too early to say how much or how long-lasting. A more moderate and probably more accurate conclusion is that monetary measures have been shown to be helpful in reestablishing balance in current external accounts if, as in this case, the cause of the imbalance can be related primarily to overspending at home, and if the difficulties are not aggravated by significantly reduced buying by major trading partners abroad.

The events of 1954-55 do not conclusively solve the problems posed earlier. Does British economic expansion lead to balance of payments difficulties if major trading partners are expanding less rapidly? And even if so, can a sufficient therapy be found in monetary measures not so severe as to impair production? There was British expansion, and there were balance of payments difficulties, but did the cause lie in the expansion or in inflationary conditions attending it? There were monetary steps taken, rather mild ones, and at least a precarious balance was restored. But was this the result of the monetary measures, or a series of other factors, including the significant expansion of United States imports in the course of a highly prosperous year? One certain thing is that the controversy will continue. Another certain thing is that the British government will rely on monetary measures rather than control until a situation develops in which such measures are seen to be ineffective or too costly in terms of production.

Chapter 6

THE INDEPENDENT MEMBERS OF THE STERLING AREA

That sir which serves and seeks for gain,
  And follows but for form,
Will pack when it begins to rain,
  And leave thee in the storm.

KING LEAR

THE INDEPENDENT members of the sterling area (abbreviated ISA) are a motley group by almost any standard. They are scattered over four continents, ranging in climate from tropical to subarctic. Culturally some are oriental, some occidental, some in between. Their economic and political institutions vary widely; so do their races and religions. Some are members of the Commonwealth of Nations, some are not. It should not be surprising, then, to find that generalizations about their behavior are subject to continuous qualification. The main thing they have in common is their independence and their membership in the sterling area.

These are the countries:

Commonwealth countries	*Other countries*
Australia	Burma
Ceylon	Iceland
Federation of Rhodesia and Nyasaland [1]	Iraq
India	Irish Republic
New Zealand	Jordan
Pakistan	Libya
South-West Africa	Persian Gulf States (Bahrein, Kuwait, Qatar, and the Trucial States)
Union of South Africa	

[1] The Federation became effective in September 1953. Previously only Southern Rhodesia was included among the independent states in official British statistics. As of 1954, Northern Rhodesia and Nyasaland enter into the statistics. Quantitatively the difference is not currently significant.

From the standpoint of economics it is largely arbitrary to group the independent members of the sterling area together. Most of them draw resources from the system, some contribute resources to it. The apparent behavior of the group as a whole is not descriptive of the behavior of an individual member. Nevertheless, the common fact of independence has economic significance since it bears on the degree of policy coordination in the system. It also bears on the promptness, nature, and severity of measures taken to correct difficulties in the area's balance of payments. It bears on the degree of willingness to pool reserves. It affects local credit structures, which, although based heavily on sterling reserves, have their own flexibility and can produce important variations from time to time in the rate of use of sterling.

In a more general sense, the fact of independence is bound to have an important bearing on the nature of the trade pattern within the sterling world. The traditional pattern, originating in colonial days and involving exports of food and raw materials to the metropole from other sterling members, and exports of manufactures to other members from the metropole, tends to break down; as countries develop they do more and more of the things for themselves that formerly were done by the metropole. Independence sharpens and may hasten the process. These activities are mostly associated with the primary consumption requirements of life—food, clothes, and shelter. The course of light industrial development has become almost standard: textile manufactures, construction materials (particularly cement), food processing, tobacco processing, glass making, matches, furniture, and so on. As the process goes on, countries retain a larger proportion of their own raw materials and the nature of their requirements from the metropole shifts toward machinery and heavier items related to local production rather than to light items related to local consumption. The trend of development which goes with independence and which underpins independence is away from the high degree of manufacturing concentration in the metropole that existed when England's currency was the important money of a very large extranational association, and as such, the important money for all international transactions.

The method of treating the independent sterling countries in this chapter is a mixed one, because the nature of the available information is mixed. The statistics at hand are of three kinds. First, the information published in the United Kingdom's official balance of payments white papers. On the whole, these are the most useful statistics on the external accounts of the independent sterling area. They have a number of shortcomings. They are presented from the point of view of the United Kingdom and are confined to the transactions that pass through London. They do not distinguish the transactions of the various countries. This means that in following the activities of the independent sterling countries through British statistics, the picture is limited to only part of these countries' transactions, set out on a group basis. The United Kingdom could not, of course, presume to publish a detailed account of the external transactions of each of these independent countries, and is not in fact in a position to do so.

The second major type of information available on the external accounts of the independent sterling countries is found in the publications of the International Monetary Fund. The Fund's statistics have the advantage of distinguishing transactions by country, and they are prepared on a uniform basis. In the Fund, however, the independent members of the sterling area stand as nations, not as sterling countries, and the information published by the Fund does not lend itself to an analysis of the financial operations of these countries as a sterling group.

The third type of information is what is available from the countries themselves. More and better information is becoming available all the time, and in the case of almost any given country the information is adequate to reflect the position of that country in its transactions with the rest of the world. The information is not, however, prepared on a uniform basis. For example, it is not possible to add the statistics on the expenditures of one country to those of others and get an accurate figure for the ISA as a whole. There is a lack of detailed information which would permit an adequate analysis of transactions with the various monetary areas, especially the sterling and dollar areas.

In short, from British figures it is possible to distinguish the transactions of the independent sterling area, but not completely and not with any hint as to how each member is performing. From Fund figures it is possible to get an impression of the behavior of most members, but not in their peculiar role as sterling countries. From the figures of the various countries it is, in most cases, possible to get a good impression of their activities as nations, taken one at a time, but the information cannot be added to yield an accurate impression of their activities as a part of the sterling community. In the course of trying to portray here the activities of the group as a whole, the partial statistics of the United Kingdom and the non-comparable statistics of the various countries have been used for illustrative purposes. This procedure is subject to many objections. Nonetheless, it appears that the general picture is not basically distorted.

There is another source of information that may in time remove many of the objections to the present sources. It has come to be almost an annual affair for the Commonwealth countries of the sterling area to get together and look at their mutual problems. When things are not going well with the area's dealings with the rest of the world, and particularly when a dollar reserve crisis is brewing, the financial authorities of the Commonwealth get together on the basis of urgency. It has gradually been recognized by the members that meetings provoked merely by the desire to swap views periodically may produce a better coordination of policies than meetings prompted by emergencies. So far, the get-togethers have involved only Commonwealth countries, although it is hard to see why all countries of the sterling area should not come to the table to discuss economic problems. In any case, a great deal of coordinated statistical work has become a regular feature of the preparations for the Commonwealth meetings. Most of the information is not made public, probably because the prospect of publication would seriously inhibit the already difficult task of compilation. This mine of information on the transactions of by far the largest part of the sterling area would furnish the best factual guidance as to the position of this critical region in the world of finance. If the compilation could be extended to cover non-Commonwealth sterling countries, the major objections to present sources of information on the sterling area would disappear altogether.

The Nature of the Tie to Sterling

Why are these countries in the sterling area? In the case of the British dependencies, which will be the concern of the next chapter, the monetary affiliation seems easily understood as a facet of political dependence. But why should countries which have achieved their political independence prefer to continue a degree—and in most cases a fairly high degree—of financial dependence on Britain's monetary structure?

The offhand answer is that most of them were formerly British dependencies, and even those that were not (for example, Libya) have been strongly influenced by British administration. They grew up in a sterling world and now that they have grown up dependent financial relations with Britain have not ordinarily appeared as serious limitations to political independence. When the question is put to British officials as to why the independent countries continue to attach themselves financially to Britain, the answer is likely to be, "Well, it is not because of our pretty blue eyes." Britain assumes that no matter how sterling countries may have come into the area, their remaining in it has to be based on real financial advantages.

In general the financial ties of the independent countries to Britain are more flexible, but not necessarily less deep, than those of the British dependencies. Unlike the dependencies, they have their own central banks, their own local money markets, their own tariffs and import controls free of the control of London. Sometimes controls are directed against imports from other members of the sterling area, as in recent years in Australia, and sometimes against imports from anywhere, without distinction between the sterling and dollar worlds, as in the case with the controls of the Union of South Africa. There is a growing tendency in the ISA to maintain *national* gold and dollar reserves (for example, in Australia, Burma, Ceylon, and South Africa), and thus to rely less on the central pool administered by Britain. Although their common practice is to maintain a fixed relationship between the official value of their currencies and sterling, they do not regard this relationship as unalterable. For example, in 1951 when Britain widened the spread between official buying and selling prices for sterling in an effort to get greater market flexibility and to encourage a new growth of the atrophied private market in foreign exchange, South Africa came close to fixing its own rate vis-à-vis the dollar, rather than following sterling. In 1949 when Britain drastically lowered the dollar price of sterling, Pakistan decided not to follow suit—perhaps mainly out of an urge to demonstrate publicly the greater integrity of the Pakistani rupee in comparison to the Indian rupee, although there was nothing to suggest that the Pakistani rupee was stronger than sterling in gold and dollar terms. Pakistan belatedly aligned its currency with the pound in the summer of 1955. In 1948 New Zealand raised the official price of its currency in terms of sterling; in 1950, Iceland lowered it. In a strictly legal sense, the currencies of India and Ceylon are not tied to sterling at all, although in practice they are.

Another major manifestation of the traditional tie between Britain and other sterling countries has been the habit of basing currencies on sterling reserves. This means that the treasuries of sterling countries have given first preference to the promises (i.e., the securities) of the British Treasury in trying to arrange a confidence-inspiring backing for their own currency issues. In the case of the British dependencies, local currency is backed note for note by sterling and sometimes by more than note for note. But the trend in the ISA countries is clearly toward more moderate holdings of sterling as a backing for their own currencies and toward a greater reliance on the securities of their own treasuries. This trend corresponds with the financial development of more mature economies, including all of Western Europe and the countries of the American continents. From the standpoint of Britain, the trend suggests impending disappointment for that important segment of official thought which assumes that large sterling reserves in the note-covers of other sterling countries represent a permanent withholding of sterling from the market and hence an easing of the demands which otherwise would be presented against British resources.

The ISA countries still rely heavily on London facilities in financing their trade, even trade in the non-sterling world, but this tie with Britain also seems to be loosening, as later tables suggest. A growing volume of ISA trade with the non-sterling world is being financed independently of London. Outstanding examples are South Africa, admittedly a peripheral sterling country and, as a major gold producer, understandably so, and Burma, now handling its dollar transactions on its own account. But a distinction must be made between the availability of foreign exchange in London for ISA countries' expenditures in places where sterling is not accepted and the availability of facilities for financing readily and competitively the trade for which exchange is available. An ISA country may turn to other centers to obtain dollars for purposes which London is unwilling to cover, but it may—and traders confirm this as a commonplace practice—turn to London in seeking channels of finance for which the necessary foreign exchange is available. Many traders in ISA countries state flatly that London terms for handling trade, for short-term credit, and for insurance are more attractive than those of New York, and so they take their business to London. Whether traders will avail themselves less of London facilities in carrying out current transactions depends on how far London proves able to provide services priced competitively with those of other financial centers. Currently London rates appear competitive, but it is still uncertain how much of the business flowing into London is attracted by favorable terms and how much goes there out of habit.

As a group, and unlike the dependencies, the independent sterling countries are net spenders internationally. Since the war they have drawn on their sterling reserves by about £30 million a year, mostly to buy dollars from the central pool to pay for imports from the dollar world. Another group feature is that the ISA countries have been receiving the great bulk of Britain's postwar foreign investment funds. They are the most wayward members of the sterling system in the year-to-year course of their balances of payments. Compared to the dependencies, they are far more important in the disturbing movements of hot money flowing from or through London. They still look to London for official loans and have received the major share of British postwar private investment, but at least the former seems to be declining.

The independent sterling countries are too different to be treated easily in groupings. Australia and New Zealand may have many things in common, maybe mostly a feeling of being at the other end of the present world of affairs. India and Pakistan, sharing a sub-continent and the recent experience of independence, may have many things in common, but these are overshadowed by the bitter experience of partition, which, in the course of giving birth to two independent nations, induced eight million people to go many miles north or south rather than endure the hardships of being minority groups in an atmosphere of new national solidarity. And what is Iceland to Burma, or the Irish Republic to the countries of the Arabian peninsula? In even this variety we are omitting the present dependencies of Africa and the Mediterranean and the Caribbean and South Asia which must become the independencies of tomorrow. What do the independent countries of the sterling area have in common?

In spite of their individuality and the difficulty of subgroupings, it is helpful to consider some of the differences in the historic experiences of independent sterling area countries, and from these differences to try to guess at their future status in the sterling system. The more "British" group—notably Australia and New Zealand and, with some differences, South Africa—are thinly populated, and relatively rich in terms of present output and potential resources. They are in the process of relatively fast economic expansion. British settlers found a standing invitation in their temperate climate, rich land, and sparse native populations. In the course of the nineteenth century these countries became *British* countries, with British political, social, and commercial institutions, and with deep and direct ties to the United Kingdom. These countries although touched by British influence relatively recently, achieved the independent political status of "dominions" relatively soon.

The more important "non-British" countries of the ISA have almost opposite characteristics. These are the poor Asian countries—India, Pakistan and Ceylon. Britain's interest in these countries developed earlier and their independence later than in the British-colonized group. Britain's early interest was essentially, if not exclusively, a trading interest. The link between them and Britain was formed through the establishment of British trading posts in the sixteenth and seventeenth centuries. The countries were well populated and had achieved a relatively advanced stage of civilization and social (though not always national) cohesion when British traders arrived. The commercial aspect of this initial interest inevitably affected the nature of the political control which Britain developed. India, for instance, was ruled by the East India Company until the middle of the nineteenth century, and—to take an African example—Southern Rhodesia was governed by the British South Africa Company until 1923. Although many decades of British rule brought important aspects of British culture, the Asian members of the ISA remain non-British, and since their recent achievement of independence they have made it a point to reinforce the non-British aspects of their national life.

Their status as members of the Commonwealth must still be regarded as experimental. The outcome of the experiment will be strongly suggestive of the future of Britain's third (and doubtless last) colonial empire, the African dependencies. These, too, are non-British countries and the experience of the present Asian members of the Commonwealth may have a strong bearing on the ultimate status of the African dependencies as they achieve their planned independence.

Arresting examples of the British and non-British types of independent sterling countries are India and Australia. India is rated as the eighth industrial country of the world in terms of total output. It has one of the largest steel mills in the Commonwealth. It irrigates, it is claimed, three times as much land as does the United States. However, with a population density considerably *less* than that of the United Kingdom, production and earnings per capita are among the lowest in the world. Seventy per cent of its work force remains in agriculture, despite the extent of industrial development in aggregate terms. Its menacing food deficit continues as the most urgent economic problem in the sterling area. Australia, in contrast, is thinly populated and relatively rich in terms of earnings per capita. Investment per worker and income per capita are much higher than in the United Kingdom. Although only 16 per cent of its workers are agricultural, Australia produces large surpluses of food for export.

It is not argued that the circumstance of British colonization determines whether a country is likely to remain in the sterling area, or, for that matter, the Commonwealth. Of all the countries in the world, the United States and Canada are the most definitely *not* in the sterling area, although Canada continues as a strong adherent to the Commonwealth. The Union of South Africa, also colonized by the British, is a fringe member of both the sterling area and the Commonwealth. What is suggested, rather, is that in a country whose development has been strongly influenced by British colonization, the economic and financial ties to Britain are likely to be deeper and the other ties—institutional, political, family, sentimental, habitual—more important than elsewhere. It is also suggested that the existence of large and poor populations which made the non-British countries unattractive for colonization has created a far more formidable problem for the sterling world than the problem posed by the possibilities of economic development of the British countries. The non-British countries are currently not only less attractive areas for British investment, but also, in the event of food scarcity, the most menacing to the sterling area's balance of payments. Before considering this problem any further, a look at the ISA balance of payments is in order.

The ISA Balance of Payments

Table 15, setting forth the ISA balance of payments on current account, is based on readily available sources; the construction of a more comprehensive and doubtless a more accurate table would have required a major statistical effort not possible in the course of this study. Nonetheless, on the basis of a check of figures for several of the countries against more comprehensive studies, these figures seem to reflect both the trends and the correct orders of magnitude. Since most of the figures have been taken from International Monetary Fund sources they should have the advantage of being as comparable as is now possible among the countries.

Table 15

ISA BALANCE OF PAYMENTS ON CURRENT ACCOUNT

(£ millions)

	1949	*1950*	*1951*	*1952*	*1953*	*Total*
Australia	— 18	—45	—177	—156	+132	—264
Burma	n.a.	+ 7	+ 22	+ 21	+ 6	+ 56
Ceylon	+ 2	+15	+ 12	— 26	— 22 (est.)	— 19 (est.)
Iceland	— 4	— 2	— 4	— 3	— 3	— 16
India	—122	+42	— 54	— 20	+ 19	—135
Iraq	— 6	+ 9	+ 11	+ 13	+ 22	+ 49
Irish Republic	— 26	—45	— 77	— 26	n.a.	—174 (4 yrs.)
New Zealand	— 2	+18	+ 18	— 29	+ 26	+ 31
Pakistan	— 34	— 8	+ 60	— 84	+ 15	— 51
South Africa	—114	— 2	—105	— 59	— 59	—339
So. Rhodesia	— 30	—20	— 51	— 41	n.a.	—142 (4 yrs.)
TOTAL	—354	—31	—345	—410	+136	—1004

Source: International Monetary Fund, *Balance of Payments Yearbook* and *International Financial Statistics;* A. J. Conan, "The Sterling Area after the Boom," *The Banker,* v. 101 (October 1953); Bank for International Settlements, *The Sterling Area* (Basle, January 1953).

Notes: Gold transactions have been included. Conversion rates: Australia, 1 £ = 1.25 £A.; Burma, 1 £ = 13.34 kuyats; Ceylon and India, 1 £ = 13.60 rupees (13.34 after Sept. 1949); Iraq, 1 £ = 1 dinar; Pakistan, 1 £ = 12.25 rupees (after Sept. 1949, 9.27 rupees).

The ISA, and all countries of the group except New Zealand, Burma and Iraq, have been almost continually in deficit over the five-year period starting with 1949. Unlike the United Kingdom, whose over-all deficit has been considerably less than its dollar deficit, the ISA's over-all deficit would have been considerably more but for its surplus with both the dollar area and the OEEC countries.

Table 16

ISA REGIONAL CURRENT ACCOUNT

(£ millions)

	1949	*1950*	*1951*	*1952*	*1953*	*Total*
With dollar area (including gold sales)	— 52	+114	+ 7	— 28	+ 46	+ 87
With OEEC countries	+ 30[a]	+111	+ 25	+ 4	+ 27	+197
Total dollar area & OEEC	— 22	+225	+ 32	— 24	+ 73	+284
Total current account	—354	— 31	—345	—410	+136	—1004
Therefore, deficit with areas other than dollar area and OEEC	—332	—256	—377	—386	+ 63	—1288

Source: Same as preceding table; Cmd. 8976 and 9119.

[a] Estimated by carrying backward the figure for the second half of 1949 onto an annual basis.

Note: This table is fairly rough. The figures for the over-all deficit on current account come from non-British sources and include undistinguished amounts representing deficits settled out of the independently held reserves of the ISA. The effect of this gap is that the dollar deficits in the table, taken from British sources and reflecting settlements through the central dollar pool, must understate the total dollar deficit of the ISA, though probably not seriously. This in turn means that the residual calculation of deficits with all other areas is too high. A minor arithmetical defect of the table derives from the discrepancy between British figures as given in sterling and in dollars for the dollar deficit of the ISA in 1949 (devaluation year). Here the sterling figures have been used; had the dollar figures been used, the deficit would have appeared a bit larger than can be accounted for in terms of the exchange rates prevailing during the year between sterling and dollars. In fact, the conversion rate derived from the two sets of figures works out at $4.11 per pound, which is higher than even the pre-devaluation rate. A more serious defect is that the table begins in 1949; the dollar deficits of the ISA in the three preceding years (British figures for central pool operations) amounted to £30 million, £237 million, and £68 million—a large total deficit of £335 million for 1946-1948. The British figures include some (but not all) dollar capital transactions and the amount of these cannot be distinguished. Chances are that these capital receipts are offset by the omitted current account payments made from the ISA's independently held dollar funds.

Despite the limitations mentioned in the note, the figures in Table 16 suggest that since 1949 the ISA countries have been in surplus with the dollar area and with the OEEC countries, and have been in heavy deficit with the rest of the world, which must mean mostly other parts of the sterling area. It seems likely that much of the deficit was with the United Kingdom itself.

It is not possible to make a satisfactory breakdown of the

dollar accounts by individual countries. Table 17, based on country sources, should be read as a general outline rather than as an accurate accounting of dollar transactions. The figures are limited to known transactions in the dollar pool. As an indication of how much these figures do *not* account for, the official British figures for the ISA as a group are given. The residual item is the difference between the British figure and the figures available from country sources. Among other things it includes the transactions of the other independent countries on which we have no separate information: Burma, Iceland, Iraq, and Libya. For postwar years before 1949, the residual is even larger.

Table 17

ISA OPERATIONS IN THE DOLLAR POOL

(£ millions)
+ = Contribution
− = Draught on pool

	1949	*1950*	*1951*	*1952*	*Total*
Australia [a]	−73	+31	+29	− 50	− 63
New Zealand	−53	+21	+23	+ 1	− 8
South Africa [b]	+55	+190	+151 [c]	+140	+536
India	−69	+77	−12	−118	−122
Pakistan	−46	−20	−72	− 41	−179
Ceylon	+18	+62	+30	+ 1	+111
S. Rhodesia	n.a.	+14	+ 9	+ 32	+ 55
Irish Republic	+11	+11	−39	− 48	− 65
TOTAL	−157	+386	+119	− 83	+265
Total ISA as given by UK [d]	−254	+320	+20	− 81	+ 27
Residual	−97	−66	−99	+ 2	−238

Sources: A. R. Conan, *The Sterling Area* (New York: St. Martin's Press, 1952), p. 190 for individual countries in 1949. Same, "Clouded Outlook for Reserves," *The Banker,* V. 102 (January, 1954), p. 31, for individual countries for the years 1950-1952. Cmd. 8976 and 9119.

Notes: [a] Fiscal years ending June 30.

[b] Net gold sales to Britain; the amounts exclude that portion of gold sales covering hard-currency payments by the United Kingdom on behalf of South Africa.

[c] Estimate based on figures given in *The Economist,* October 24, 1953.

[d] See note to Table 16 on the difference between official United Kingdom's dollar figures, used here, and the sterling figures used in Table 16.

To complete the profile of the ISA balance of payments, it is useful to compare the current account figures with those for the United Kingdom. A fairly good basis of comparison is available for the years 1949 to 1953. As would be expected from previous tables, the United Kingdom managed pretty consistent over-all surpluses, while the ISA ran even larger and more consistent deficits. But in trade with both the dollar area and the OEEC countries, the ISA had surpluses compared with the United Kingdom's deficits.

Table 18

COMPARISON OF ISA AND UNITED KINGDOM TRANSACTIONS ON CURRENT ACCOUNT BY REGIONS

(£ millions)

	1949	*1950*	*1951*	*1952*	*1953*	*Total*
With all areas						
ISA	−354	− 31	−345	−410	+147	−993
UK	+ 31	+300	−385	+255	+225	+426
With dollar area						
ISA	− 52	+114	+ 7	− 28	+ 46	+ 87
UK	−296	− 88	−431	−172	− 4	−991
With OEEC						
ISA	+ 30[a]	+111	+ 25	+ 4	+ 27	+197
UK	− 16	+114	−201	− 26	+104	− 25

Source: Preceding tables.
[a] Annual rate based on July-December figure (Cmd. 8976).

In view of the already noted limitations of all of these figures, refined conclusions would be inappropriate. Still, some broad conclusions seem warranted when the preceding tables are taken in conjunction with other evidence. (1) The ISA's deficit with the United Kingdom has certainly been the main part of its large current deficit and may have been considerably larger than the ISA's global deficit. (2) The ISA's deficit with the United Kingdom probably reflects the order of magnitude of British investment in the independent countries. (3) This investment, in view of the very modest British surpluses on current account, must have been made possible to a significant extent by the existence of Britain's dollar receipts from the dependent territories. The preceding chapter showed the United Kingdom's own dollar deficit to be almost identical with the loss of dollars from the sterling area's pool. (4) The apparent transfer of earnings from the dependencies to the ISA is also strongly suggested by the fact that in this postwar period the dependencies earned a dollar surplus of £756 million, turned it over to the dollar pool, and got in exchange sterling balances (British IOUs) of about the same amount. (See Chapter 7). (5) The ISA has drawn dollars from the pool over the eight-year period but contributed to it in 1949-53. Its accounts have fluctuated considerably, and for the most part in a way inconvenient for the area as a whole. (6) The widespread impression that the ISA's deficits with Western Europe, financed through the arrangements of the European Payments Union, have accounted for a large part of the United Kingdom's debt to the Union, is not borne out by the figures. However, the calendar-year figures do obscure a sharp reversal in ISA accounts with Western Europe during the sterling crisis of 1951-1952:

	£ millions
July 1950–June 1951	+135
July 1951–June 1952	− 85
July 1952–June 1953	+ 54

One of the characteristics of the sterling area has been the high proportion of each member's foreign trade that has been carried on within the area. The United Kingdom as historical mother country, industrial leader, financial and commercial market place,—in short, as the center of the system—has normally been the main trading partner of every other sterling country. With independence and economic development, some of the independent countries of the sterling area have moved somewhat out of the traditional orbit in response to their national economic needs and the currents of the international economy. Several postwar circumstances had a special bearing on the evolution of the United Kingdom-ISA trade pattern. In the first postwar years the United Kingdom was unable to supply many of the things needed by the ISA countries and they, like the United Kingdom itself, had to turn to the United States for a larger share of their imports than in the past. In the interest of the whole sterling area's dollar position there were advantages in each sterling country's trying to sell more to the United States; for the raw materials producers, at least, this conformed to the developments of United States imports during these years. Working in a contrary direction, against an increase in the importance of the United States in the trade of the ISA countries, was the intensification of some of the regional features of the sterling area, notably the emphasis on trade controls that favored sterling imports and discriminated against dollar imports. Desire to use the sterling balances

Table 19

UNITED KINGDOM'S SHARE OF ISA TRADE

(Percentages)

	1913	*1929*	*1937*	*1949*	*1950*	*1951*	*1952*	*1953*	*1954*
Australia									
Exports:	44	38[a]	49	42	37	30	38	38	37
Imports:	52	40[a]	42	50	51	45	42	47	47
Ceylon									
Exports:	45	40	43	33	24	31	29	25	29
Imports:	29	21	22	18	20	22	22	22	21
India									
Exports:	23[b]	21	34	23	22	25	20	28	32
Imports:	64[b]	42	31	25	22	17	19	25	25
Pakistan									
Exports:	with	with	with	13	17	13	13	19	19
Imports:	India	India	India	23	26	21	20	16	29
New Zealand									
Exports:	79	74	76	73	66	57	65	67	67
Imports:	60	49	50	55	60	54	55	57	57
South Africa									
Exports:	81	49	36	25	28	26	30	29	32
Imports:	57	43	43	42	41	35	34	38	34

Source: League of Nations. *Memorandum on International Trade and Balances of Payments, 1912-26,* v. 2; Same, *1930,* v. 3; *Statistical Abstract for the British Empire,* 1931 (Cmd. 3919); *International Financial Statistics,* December 1950, July 1954, February 1956; *Statistical Abstract for the Commonwealth,* n. 72, 1948-1951.

Notes: [a] Fiscal year 1928-29. [b] Fiscal year 1913-14.

that they had acquired during the war also encouraged the ISA countries in the pursuit of intra-sterling area trade.

Without much more intensive investigation than the shape of this book allows, it is impossible to assess the significance of each of these pressures, or of other strands of the world trade web that have not even been mentioned. We shall have to rest content with a summary statement of trends as reflected in some selected figures. While trade outside the ster-

Table 20

CHANGES IN ISA IMPORTS FROM THE UNITED STATES AND THE UNITED KINGDOM, 1934-38 TO 1949-50

	Imports from US	*Imports from UK*
	(in percentages)	
Australia		
Machinery	+50	+300
Vehicles	−80	+1100
All commodities	+10	+100
New Zealand		
Machinery	+40	+150
Vehicles	−75	+150
All commodities	+ 5	+ 60
South Africa		
Machinery	+60	+ 10
Vehicles	−50	+ 50
All commodities	+45	− 8
India & Pakistan		
Machinery	+500	+200
Vehicles	+ 50	+300
Iron & Steel	+400	no change
All commodities	+400	+ 25
Ceylon		
Iron & Steel	+1000	+ 50
Machinery	+500	+300
Vehicles	+ 50	+130
All commodities	+400	+ 66

Source: U.S. Economic Cooperation Administration, *The Sterling Area: An American Analysis* (London, 1951), various tables. The prewar figures are annual averages; the postwar ones refer to the 12 months ending June 30, 1950.

ling area has grown in importance for the ISA, the United Kingdom still is its most important market and supplier. For most of the countries the importance of the United Kingdom on both counts has declined significantly since 1913, as Table 19 shows. The decline of the United Kingdom as a market has been more pronounced. This trend is even more marked since 1937, which suggests—or at least is consistent with the familiar argument—that the sterling balances have played an important, or even crucial part, in sustaining British exports to the sterling markets. Table 20 shows that when Britain and the United States are compared as suppliers the change from prewar to postwar varied from one ISA country to another and also according to the products supplied.

Sterling Balances

The immense ISA sterling holdings, largely accumulated during the war and representing a British debt for goods and services received, form the most obvious if not the strongest tie between each ISA country and the sterling area since the war. The total sterling holdings of the ISA at the end of 1945 were just over £2 billion, or roughly two-thirds of the United Kingdom's total sterling liabilities to the rest of the world. The big holders have focused their postwar financial policy on the utilization of their balances and by the end 1954 the independent countries as a group had managed to reduce them by about £200 million. The fact that these holdings had to be used largely within the sterling area and Western Europe must have been an important influence in the growth of sterling channels of trade and the continued use of sterling to finance trade.

Available information is limited and somewhat arbitrary. The United Kingdom publishes regularly, though from time to time with unexplained sizable revisions, the total balances held by governments and banks in some form in London. (Table 21) This information is not broken down by country, so British statistics are not helpful in appraising the behavior of the individual members in relationship to the sterling area's credit structure. Some of the members publish their own figures for sterling holdings, but these are not on a comparable basis. Almost always the holdings of private individuals, in contrast to banks and governments, are excluded, although these holdings are known to be significant. As is usually the case with statistics, what they reveal reflects the state of information at hand and the policies governing publication rather than precisely what we want to know. Nevertheless, the available information is suggestive.

Table 21

ISA STERLING BALANCES

As of:	£ millions	
Dec. 31, 1945	2008	
Dec. 31, 1946	1924	− 74
Dec. 31, 1947	1787	−137
Dec. 31, 1948	1809	+ 22
June 30, 1949	1704	−105
Dec. 31, 1949	1771	+ 67
June 30, 1950	1926	+155
Dec. 31, 1950	1980	+ 54
June 30, 1951	2195	+215
Dec. 31, 1951	1825	−370
June 30, 1952	1532	−293
Dec. 31, 1952	1606	+ 74
June 30, 1953	1758	+154
Dec. 31, 1953	1758	+ 16
Change since 1945		−234

Source: Cmd. 8976 and 9119.

Two basic characteristics of the ISA holdings seem clear. The trend has been one of substantial spending by some countries. The up-and-down fluctuations (about 30 per cent either way) can be very large in short periods. India and Pakistan largely account for the heavy spending, and probably Australia for a large part of the fluctuations.

India, Pakistan and Ceylon are spenders. According to their figures they spent over £500 million between 1945 and mid-1952, drawing their balances down from around £1,300 million to about £800 million. Since 1952, the rate of expenditure has been limited by five-year agreements with the United Kingdom. These permit the expenditure of another £202 million by the end of 1957. The parties to the agreements consider that the balances will then be at a "stable" level, i.e., only what is needed for currency reserves and working balances. We have already noted, however, that as a country becomes more developed economically, it is likely to give up its dependence on the promises of a foreign treasury as a basis for the issuance of its own currency. This fact creates a doubt that in the long run there is any such thing as a hard core of sterling that will be held by independent sterling area countries as a reserve for their own currencies. What will be held is the amount needed as working balances in the financing of trade with that part of the world which is willing to accept sterling. On this point, the Reserve Bank of India has noted a significant decline in India's use of sterling to finance its world trade. Egypt, a former sterling area member and still a large holder of sterling, is using sterling less and less in its international transactions.

ISA Reliance on British Capital

According to a familiar argument, a major factor in sterling area cohesion comes from the reliance of sterling countries on the London market as a source of capital. There are formidable problems in analyzing this aspect of sterling area relationships. Although a number of the central banks of the area are studying the matter with increasing interest, at present it is possible only to make very rough observations and guesses about investment trends. Since the United Kingdom has been running a deficit averaging some £40 million a year in its current transactions with the rest of the world, it obviously cannot have been providing *net* funds for investment abroad. Yet the analysis of the United Kingdom's accounts with the rest of the sterling area set forth in the preceding chapter, shows that the United Kingdom apparently made a net investment of some £800 million in the rest of the area, almost certainly—but not demonstrably—in the independent countries, particularly Australia and the Union of South Africa. To meet its dollar deficit, Britain has been able to use special dollar receipts (largely American and Canadian aid) and the dollar surplus earned by the dependent countries. Therefore it is reasonable to suppose that British investment in the ISA has been made possible by funds that flowed into London from these two sources. In short, Britain has not been the original source of funds to finance the immense expansion of British investment in the ISA since the war. The investment has been possibly only because funds, mainly dollar funds, were available from outside in an amount equalling Britain's dollar deficit but exceeding its *over-all* deficit on current account.

The integrity of a monetary area depends, as a distinguished economist remarked to me, on its ability to furnish its own capital. The availability of a huge volume of funds from outside the area cannot in the long run be depended upon to finance the *internal* requirements of the area for development. This is widely recognized in financial circles throughout the sterling area. The problem of generating sufficient funds within the area to cover the cost of developing its resources is persistent and important.

The scarcity of funds for development of the sterling area economies has raised the critical question as to what sort of projects should be preferred, and in what locations. In the communiqué of the 1952 conference of Commonwealth finance ministers in London, a great deal of emphasis was placed on the importance of coordinating Commonwealth development so as to reduce pressures on the sterling area's balance of payments with the rest of the world:

> The Conference agreed that in the Sterling Area countries development should be concentrated on projects which directly or indirectly contribute to the improvement of the area's balance of payments with the rest of the world. Such projects should strengthen the economy of the countries concerned and increase their competitive power in world markets and so, by improving their balance of payments, bring increasing prosperity to their peoples.

Practically speaking this meant that in making loans most members of the area, and certainly London, would give priority to projects which promised dollar earnings or dollar savings. Subsequently some estimates of the possibilities of

Table 22

PROJECTED BALANCE OF PAYMENTS EFFECTS OF DEVELOPMENT PROGRAMS IN INDEPENDENT STERLING COUNTRIES

Country	Commodity to be Developed	Completion of Program	*Projected Balance of Payments Effects for Sterling Area*					
			Improvement in Dollar Position					
			Direct Improvement					
			Dollar Saving	*Dollar Earning*	*Indirect [a] Dollar Saving*	*Total Dollar Improvement*	*Improvement in Non-Dollar Position*	*Total Improvement*
			(Millions of Dollars)					
Australia	*Food Products* Mainly wheat, rice, meat, milk	1957	15	—	260	275	—	275
	Steel	1956	25	—	—	25	25	50
	Lead	1955	—	15	—	15	—	15
	Zinc	1955	—	10	—	10	—	10
	Copper	1954	—	—	3	3	—	3
	Aluminum	1954	—	—	6	6	—	6
	Coal	n.a.	—	—	15	15	15	30
	Petroleum	1956	—	—	—	—	100	100
	Total		40	25	284	349	140	489
Ceylon	*Food,* mainly rice	1952/3	2	—	—	2	—	2
	Vegetable oil	n.a.	—	—	—	—	6	6
	Paper	1953	1	—	—	1	—	1

	Caustic Soda	1953	0.5	—	—	0.5	0.5	1
	Fertilizer	n.a.	3	—	—	3	2	5
	Total		6.5	—	—	6.5	8.5	15
India	*Ammo. Sulphate*	1955/56	10	—	—	10	10	20
	Phosphates	1955/6	2	—	—	2	2	4
	Iron & Steel	1957	40	—	—	40	40	80
	Aluminum	1953	2	—	—	2	—	2
	Total		54	—	—	54	52	106
New Zealand	*Pulp & Paper*	1955	24	—	—	24	—	24
	Meat	1954	—	—	2	2	4	6
	Butter & Cheese	1954	—	—	3	3	7	10
	Total		24	—	5	29	11	40
Pakistan	*Paper*	1954	7	—	—	7	—	7
	Fertilizer	n.a.	1	—	—	1	—	1
	Total		8	—	—	8	—	8
South Africa	*Steel*	n.a.	2	—	—	2	5	7
	Chrome Ore	n.a.	2	—	—	2	2	4
	Gold	1960	—	200	—	200	—	200
	Total		4	200	—	204	7	211
	GRAND TOTAL		136.5	225	289	650.5	218.5	869

Source: British Information Service. Mimeographed press release, 1952.

[a] Indirect dollar savings will occur when the country indicated produces, and exports to another sterling area country, a commodity which now comes from the dollar area. The figures above are the maximum indirect dollar savings which could result from the development programs contemplated, i.e., they are based on the assumption that the entire increase in production will be used to save dollars, and none of it will be used to increase consumption of these commodities in the sterling area. This assumption is merely for the sake of illustration. It probably will be rendered invalid as economic development proceeds.

this sort of development in various of the independent countries were published. These published notes do not amount to a statement of the total development envisaged by the members, but it seems clear that if these projects are as effective as foreseen they will have a pronounced impact on the sterling area's balance of payments with the rest of the world. Some of them have already been carried out but it has not been possible to compare their results with the estimates. Table 22 summarizes the estimated impact of these investment plans.

It is hard to say how earnest or wise may be the expressed intentions to consider projects in the light of the dollars they may earn or save. Such projects might well result in less *production* than rejected projects without dollar aspects, and if that were generally true of the preferred projects, the loss of potential production could be considerable. The Commonwealth policy is carefully phrased to allay fears that it would lead to something in the nature of a closed system. Still, it seems clear that relating economic development to current regional difficulties in the area's balance of payments could conflict with the objective, stated firmly elsewhere in the communiqué, of striving for the widest possible world trade area. It could be a step away from the rest of the world rather than toward it.

The Pooling of Reserves

Another major factor of cohesion in the sterling area, according to traditional arguments, is the practice of pooling reserves. The need to call on reserves, it is argued, is bound to vary for various pool members. By pooling reserves, the members do not have to have reserves which are high enough to cover the maximum likely need of each country separately. Smaller pooled reserves should suffice since at any given time some members' needs will probably be offset by the contribution of others. The resulting economy of reserves seems to have been an established fact of practice before the first World War. Then, sterling held in London was the common form of international reserves and this eased Britain's task of making the reserves available to holders who wanted to spend them elsewhere.

Since the second World War, reserves have meant hard-currency reserves. The inconvertibility of the pound has meant that the traditional sterling reserves are no longer unqualified reserves. The "real" reserves are rather the gold and dollars available to sterling countries from the London pool or elsewhere. Postwar experience has made it clear that the offsetting of needs on which the theory of reserve economy rests cannot be depended on. The temporary dollar needs of members have tended to be cumulative. There has, of course, been a long-run offsetting trend in the tendency of some members (mainly the African dependencies and Malaya) to feed the central reserves and of others (the United Kingdom and most independent members) to draw on them.

Table 23 shows the official and private bank holdings of gold and dollars for most of the larger independent countries.

Table 23

STERLING AREA OFFICIAL AND BANK HOLDINGS OF GOLD AND DOLLARS[a]

($ millions at end of year)

End of:	*1948*	*1949*	*1950*	*1951*	*1952*	*1953*
Sterling Area[b]	2893	2688	4421	3736	3283	4046
UK & DOTs	2221	2027	3677	2943	2431	3117
Australia	110	120	107	150	160	172
New Zealand	28	35	29	37	36	n.a.
India	308	310	303	309	312	346
South Africa	199	134	241	197	194	214
Other ISA[c]	27	61	64	100	150	n.a.
Total ISA	672	660	744	793	852	929

Sources: *Federal Reserve Bulletin* March issues, 1950, 1951, 1952, 1953 and 1954. *International Financial Statistics* February and October 1954. Bank for International Settlements, *Annual Report,* 1953-1954 (Basle, June 1954).

Notes: [a] *Dollar holdings* represent both official and private holdings reported by banks in the United States and include deposits, United States Government securities with maturities up to 20 months, and certain other short-term liabilities to foreigners. *Gold reserves* are given as reported in central bank statements. Where data are incomplete Federal Reserve estimates are used.

[b] Excludes Eire and Iceland.

[c] Residual.

For the ISA as a group, gold and dollars held outside the pool increased by about 20 per cent from 1948 to 1953. In the case of Australia and New Zealand, the increase was 50 per cent, and Australia has declared a policy of building its independent holdings in the interests of fortifying its credit standing in hard-currency countries. The increase in the holdings of other independent countries is noticeable but not large. The trend appears to acknowledge the inadequacy of the central reserves. In turn, the building up of independent reserves probably tends to make the central pool of reserves still more inadequate.

Outlook

This chapter has disclosed several facts about the relation of the ISA to the rest of the sterling area.

Trade was for long a major nexus of the ISA countries. Now the United Kingdom has declined in importance as a market and as a source of supplies for them, but still remains their most important trading partner.

The London capital market has been a second major factor holding the sterling area together. But in recent years the United Kingdom's ability to furnish capital to the ISA appears to have been related to two unusual circumstances. First, there has been a large volume of dollar loans and grants which now have virtually ceased and cannot be expected to be resumed, certainly not in the form of deliberate United States financing of a British dollar deficit in excess of its over-all deficit. Second, there has been a large volume of colonial deposits in London which so far have been pretty well maintained but which may taper off sharply either if the high level of world commodity prices on which colonial earnings are based drops or if the financing of a faster rate of local development keeps the funds at home in the colonies, as is to be expected in the long run.

Finally, there are developments in ISA monetary and fiscal policy indicating a trend toward greater independence from London's guidance and a further weakening of sterling ties. Sterling has become less important as a reserve behind local issues of currency. The independent countries are slowly building up their own gold and dollar reserves outside the pooled central reserves. They are developing monetary and fiscal policies which give greater and greater priority to considerations of the stability and growth of their own national markets rather than to maintaining a balanced budget in international trade alone. (The same trend may be seen in the United Kingdom.) And they have liquidated a fifth of their sterling balances during a period in which the value of their traffic in the world market has been rising rapidly.

Do these trends mean that the independent members of the sterling area are drifting away?

The weaknesses and strains in regional financial relations do not necessarily imply disintegration. The weaknesses and strains are more likely than not to be diagnosed by members of the association as the result of outside factors over which they have no control and against which they want to protect themselves. In any case the question arises whether more satisfactory arrangements could be made by any member on leaving the association. A member, before leaving, would have to ask questions with fairly unpredictable, and therefore politically touchy, answers. Could it broaden or stabilize the market for its products by leaving the sterling world? Would the important sterling markets shrink if it left? Could it get more money for development if it divorced itself from its associates, and particularly from the intense preference, noticeable again in recent years, of British investors to use whatever funds they can lay their hands on to invest in the ISA countries? Going beyond "bread alone," would departure from sterling association tally with the sentiments of the people and with the political and military security of the country?

For most ISA countries the United Kingdom is still by far the most important supplier and customer, though less so for India, Pakistan and Ceylon. For most countries the future use of their present sterling holdings is a primary consideration of their external financial policy, especially for India, Pakistan and Ceylon. In most countries the level and flow of British investment is high, despite the fact that it has been made possible by unusual circumstances. Most countries are embarking on development plans which give priority to projects supporting the expansion of sterling area markets. In varying degrees all countries recognize reasons other than economic for their sterling association—defense, politics, sentiment and inertia.

There are widespread influences working against a member's belief that it could make more satisfactory arrangements if it were outside of the sterling system. In varying degrees, the countries fear what they believe to be the instability of the United States economy and the great potential impact of this instability on countries highly dependent on foreign trade. They believe that their sterling association is some protection against this threat, especially in view of the fact that their independently held gold and dollar reserves, though growing, still range only between 4 and 18 per cent of their annual imports. Finally, they have no assurance that their access to dollar capital would be increased by leaving the sterling area, particularly not unless they should find themselves able to create the freer climate of investment which would attract private funds.

These considerations, all suggesting judgments which the individual countries would find deterrents to any radical change in their international orientation, are undoubtedly more important for some countries than others. India, Pakistan and Ceylon, though still much concerned with their sterling balances, might have little hesitation on non-economic grounds in leaving the sterling area; it is conceivable that United States interest in moving its agricultural surpluses might tally with the food problem of these countries. Australia and New Zealand, though deeply interested in extending their access to dollar capital and though not greatly concerned at the moment with the liquidation of their sterling holdings, would have difficulty in adjusting the exports on which they are most dependent—wool, wheat, meat, dairy products—to dollar markets. Moreover, if they feared the competition of American agricultural surpluses in world markets, these countries might regard their sterling area ties as some degree of assurance that they would have privileged access to traditional outlets, especially in the United Kingdom.

The economic and non-economic considerations which make the independent countries as a whole hesitant to leave the system may not prevent a given country's decision to do so. Conceivably, in the case of countries confronting the United Kingdom with a persistent drain on central reserves or British production, the United Kingdom might even encourage such a decision. But just such a country would be unlikely to want to leave the sterling area, on economic grounds at least, since its draft on the pool indicates that membership permits it to spend more dollars than it earns. Nor can one assume that the United Kingdom would be anxious to throw out of the club even a persistent dollar drainer. Certainly there is no evidence of such a desire. On the contrary, a favorite British line of argument is that as "banker to the sterling area" the United Kingdom must take the bad with the good. According to this view it must tolerate some damage to its own national interests as part of the price of securing the benefits of the sterling system for all its members, including the United Kingdom.

This greater good, for which some people feel Britain has sacrificed some particular or at least temporary advantages, is not conceived only in economic terms. Canada seems living evidence of the sharp distinctions between the economics of belonging to the sterling area and the politics of belonging to the Commonwealth. Yet for the countries that belong to both, it seems hardly possible, at least for an outsider, to isolate the non-economic elements. Perhaps the issue can be summed up by saying that one can hardly conceive of the United Kingdom's pushing a Commonwealth country out of the sterling area, no matter how much of an economic drain it was, while at the same time the United Kingdom could not altogether bar a Commonwealth country's exit from the sterling area if the country thought it would be better off that way.

The historical evidence is that it is exceptional for a country to want to leave the sterling area. But the critical postwar period has been short. As this chapter has shown, there are centrifugal forces in the sterling area as well as centripetal ones. The balance of advantages and disadvantages will differ from one country to another, and for each country will change from time to time. Added to the calculable advantages of membership, there is the strong cohesive force of the habitual way of doing things, of living in a known environment. The governments of the independent countries would find it impossible to predict with certainty the consequences of leaving the sterling area. Therefore they would hesitate to discover them through experience unless continued membership should become critically uncomfortable in a fashion obvious to the voting population. Short of such a situation, it may be less realistic, but it certainly is easier, for a country to believe that present discomforts, such as they may be, are the price of membership in the club, and will disappear in the dreamed-of day when sterling becomes internationally convertible even for the members of the area—a step which so far has not been mentioned in official statements.

Chapter 7

THE DEPENDENT TERRITORIES

Fathers that wear rags
  Do make their children blind;
But fathers that bear bags
  Will see their children kind.

—KING LEAR

ABOUT A QUARTER of the people of the world belong to the Commonwealth of Nations. Of these, about an eighth, or some 75 million, live in British dependencies, officially called Dependent Overseas Territories and conventionally abbreviated DOT or DOTs. The abbreviation is unfortunate. They are by no means "dots" on the map. The lands in which these dependent people dwell are two-thirds the size of the United States, and their resources, which are far from completely inventoried as yet, are rich. Their customs, races and religions are if anything more varied than those of the independent members of the sterling area. Their populations are increasing rapidly and their economies are, they feel, just on the edge of rapid development. All in all, their future role in the sterling area and in the Commonwealth poses questions, both economic and political, that go to the heart of Britain's own future role in the world.

The usual official definition of the dependencies is not very helpful: "those territories for which the Secretary of State for the Colonies is responsible to Parliament." They are scattered over the whole world, and constitute a military, economic and political stake unparalleled by the dependencies of any other country. And yet they are only a small fraction of the Commonwealth.

Few people would describe Britain's colonial problem

primarily in economic terms. Probably no one in the colonies would. But if we may assume—and this is the position taken by the British government—that the end result of modern colonial evolution is inevitably independence, we may inquire with good reason into the economic relationship between the dependencies and the rest of the sterling system. This relationship may or may not prove to be decisive in determining the permanence of colonial ties to sterling or to the Commonwealth. Dependencies which gain economically from membership in the sterling club might, on gaining independence, be impelled to leave it for other reasons if the opportunity arose, and dependencies which apparently could get along very well outside might nonetheless remain in.

These are the present British dependencies, with some United Kingdom and United States figures shown for comparison:

	Area (Thousands of Square Miles)	*Population (millions)*
The United States	3002	160
The United Kingdom	93	50
British Dependencies, *of which*:	2000	75
West Africa (Gambia, Gold Coast, Nigeria, Sierra Leone)	497	38
East and Central Africa (Somaliland, Kenya, Tanganyika, Uganda, Zanzibar, Nyasaland, Northern Rhodesia)	1088	24
Far East (Federation of Malaya, Singapore, Brunei, North Borneo, Sarawak, Hong Kong)	130	10
Caribbean (Bahamas, Barbados, Bermuda, British Guiana, British Honduras, Jamaica, Leeward and Windward Islands, Tobago, Trinidad)	100	3
Others (Fiji, British Solomon Islands, Gilbert and Ellice Islands, New Hebrides, Tonga; Falkland Islands,		

St. Helena, Ascension, Aden, Mauritius; Cyprus, Gibraltar, Malta, Gozo)	150	3

Not included: territories dealt with by the Commonwealth Relations Office, which include Basutoland, Bechuanaland, Swaziland, and the Maldive Islands with a total area of 293,535 square miles and total population of just over one million.

The word "colony" is still used to described any British dependency, but technically a colony is one of several types of dependencies. The dependencies may be actual colonies, like Singapore and the municipality of Lagos in Nigeria. They may be "protected territories," like the rest of the Malayan Federation and the inland areas of Nigeria. They may have been "mandated territories," like Tanganyika in East Africa, taken over after the first World War under League of Nations arrangements and now administered as "trust territories" under United Nations supervision. There are various other shades of difference in the political status of dependencies, but these are the main ones.

British colonials are Britons; they are entitled to British passports, and those passports identify them as British subjects. As British subjects they have the right to move freely within the whole area of Britain and the other colonies. By birth they are entitled to local suffrage rights. The peoples of the protected territories also use British passports identifying them as "British protected persons." Unlike those born in the colonies, British protected persons are entitled to vote locally only after becoming naturalized British subjects. The status of people in the trust territories is very similar.

The typical history of a British colony is one of military or commercial penetration of an alien area followed by at least some degree of permanent settlement by Britons and ultimately political integration with the home country. The colonies all have some sort of local legislature, but the administration of local government is for the most part in the hands of ministers—often from the United Kingdom—who are appointed by governors who represent the Crown. Most large political decisions have to be approved in London and the role of the British government is important in establishing policies on foreign trade and exchange that shape the place of the dependencies in the sterling system.

The official theory of British postwar governments, both Labour and Conservative, is that the proper goal of a dependency is independence. The official hope is that a dependency, on becoming independent, will become a democratic partner of the British Commonwealth (unlike, for example, Egypt), and will remain a member of the sterling area (unlike, for example, Canada).

The hottest proving ground for this theory today is in Africa and the Federation of Malaya, the very parts of the remaining British empire which financially contribute most to the sterling area. In both cases, Britain's theory of independence has a negative and a positive aspect. The negative aspect is that nowadays a metropolitan country really has no choice; the independence of controlled territories is not a policy but an inevitability. The positive aspect is that the mother country can, nonetheless, try to influence the drive of dependent people for independence in such a way that the independence they achieve will be democratic and capable of accommodation within the loose framework of the Commonwealth's political structure. The important economic corollary of this theory is that the achievement of this sort of independence is likely to be consistent with the safeguarding and extension of Britain's large economic interests in the dependencies, and even more, that the friendly encouragement by the metropole of local development toward independence offers the best possible assurance that amicable economic relations will be maintained where they already exist, or achieved where they do not.

Obviously this theory is in the nature of a faith, and it involves a heavy risk. The negative aspect, that independence cannot in any case be blocked, is probably accepted generally by Western students of modern political trends. The gamble lies in gearing policy to the plausibility of the positive aspect, in finding policies that will influence the course of independence in such a way that it will establish a sound permanent basis for the maintenance of all the important aspects of the present relationship between the metropole and the dependency.

There are many people who have such a distrust of Britain's past imperial policies that they hold suspect the sincerity of Britain's present policy of encouraging independence. In my own travels in many of these dependencies, including most of the African ones, I saw no reason whatsoever to doubt the sincerity or firmness of this general policy. As would be expected, it is applied with different degrees of enthusiasm in different places, ranging from an almost complete lack in the case of Cyprus, to complete confidence in the case of the Gold Coast and Nigeria. Far from doubting the earnestness of Britain in its policy of independence, the doubts of on-the-spot observers were rather whether British officials might not be moving too fast, particularly in Africa, so that the hoped-for democratic and Western-tuned character of independence would not have time to form on a solid basis of popular education and a well-trained civil service. Britons find an irony in the fact that people of former colonies, such as the United States, often urge Britain to slow down a bit on the granting of independence to others, in the interests of avoiding a premature rocking of the African boat.

For the study of sterling, the immediate importance of the African dependencies lies in the fact that since the war they have supplied to Britain and the rest of the sterling area a large number of dollars on what is essentially a loan basis. In a time of persistent shortage of dollars and of indigenous savings to finance development in the sterling world, this has been one of the strongest props to the whole sterling system. On the political side, Africa is the greatest remaining dependent area where Western influence is strong and in many places even welcomed—though the welcome, like all welcomes, could easily get worn out. The future lines of the political and economic development of just this one group of British dependencies are, accordingly, of the greatest significance to Britain, to the sterling world, to the British Commonwealth, and to the Western world at large.

Before trying to speculate about what the future relationship of the African and other British dependencies may be to the sterling area and to the Commonwealth, a look at their economic and financial position is in order. As in the case of the independent countries, it needs to be said that if a separate examination of each dependency were made, each would be seen to vary from the picture of the group as a whole. But for the broad problems at hand these discrepancies do not make the group picture invalid.

Colonial Currencies

Colonial currencies today are a hybrid form of sterling. Not quite sterling, not quite something else, they present formidable problems for financial analysis on both internal and external account.

The present colonial monetary system has developed within the historic framework of direct administrative control by the British government. The important benchmarks in its development are the years 1707, 1825, and 1912. In 1707 the rates at which West Indian coins could be exchanged for foreign coins were fixed by an act of Parliament, reaffirming and concretely applying the principle that Britain has the prerogative to maintain a parity between sterling and colonial monies. In 1825 Britain officially inaugurated a policy aimed at making the shilling the standard monetary unit of the empire. This policy did not have immediate success, hampered as it was by the undervaluation of the shilling in terms of other currencies, by the silver standards on which the currencies of the Eastern colonies were based, and by problems of bimetallism. The year 1912 marks the beginning of the present mechanical relationship between colonial currencies and sterling; in that year the West African Currency Board was established and it has become the model for the systems of other British dependencies. The West African system was designed to overcome the chief defects of colonial currencies—currency shortage and the difficulty of conversion into other currencies.

The approach in the currency board system has been regional, and there are now five colonial currency unions in operation:

West African
East African
Southern Rhodesian
Malayan
West Indian.

The African currency boards are, at the time of writing, located in London, and a British official (the Crown Agent) is an ex officio member.

The money of other colonial areas is controlled by currency commissioners whose functions follow the pattern of the currency boards. All currency officials are selected by Britain and their operations are controlled through British legislation.

The function of the currency authorities is to guarantee convertibility between sterling and colonial currencies at a fixed rate. New colonial currency may always be issued against a receipt of sterling; sterling may always be obtained from the authorities against a deposit of local currency. The boards or commissioners usually charge a commission of ½ to 1 per cent for this service, although in the case of Cyprus no commission is charged. This charge enables the boards to accumulate sterling in excess of the colonial issue, and, more importantly, is a cost which would-be exchangers must count along with interest rates in deciding where to hold funds. The theory of the commission charge is that it sets a ceiling on the commission which banks will be able to charge locally, but in practice it leads to difficulties in the effective investment of the large volume of seasonal funds which flow into colonial banks as a result of the marketing of crops.

The currency authorities are permitted to invest their sterling receipts only in British securities, Commonwealth securities, or in such other manner as the Secretary of State for the Colonies may approve. In practice, investments have been confined to British and Commonwealth securities. With the exception of the Southern Rhodesian Currency Board, the authorities have not been permitted to invest in the securities of their own colonial governments. The British government directs that a certain portion of the currency authorities' sterling assets be held in liquid form; beyond that, the distribution of investments by maturities is based on the anticipated demand for sterling against local currency. Theoretically, seasonal surpluses of colonial cash can be invested in London for a yield; actually, the low level of London rates and the commission charge on converting from colonial currency to sterling has discouraged this practice.

Except for the recourse colonies have to British credit, which will be considered below, the mechanics of currency board operations would clearly imply that the only way colonial residents could obtain local currency would be through a prior earning of sterling. This in turn would imply that colonial circulation is the counterpart of colonial investment in the metropole. This pair of implications is the basis for a major familiar criticism of the colonial currency system: the course of investment runs from the poor and undeveloped to the rich and developed.

In the light of the circumstances under which certain colonies have built up their holdings of sterling in the postwar period, there is, I think, reason to suppose that the colonies have been net investors in the United Kingdom and in the rest of the sterling area. Some of these circumstances will be considered later. The point at the moment is to recognize that the mechanics of the currency board system do not make such investment inevitable. Theoretically, colonial currency can be, and no doubt often is, issued to colonial residents—often branches of British firms—against sterling credits obtained in Britain. A colony could "borrow" its entire local issue on the basis of such credits. Whether transactions of this sort lead to a real transfer of resources and in what direction depends on the subsequent chain of events. The initial lending of sterling, which thereupon is immobilized, to a colonial resident in order to obtain colonial currency does not in itself imply any real transfer of resources.

To what extent has the sterling held by colonial currency authorities been "borrowed" from London rather than earned through exports? There is no published information which would make it possible to say. My discussions of the point with bank and government officials both in London and in the dependencies did not lead to a clarification. There seemed general agreement that at least in the case of the colonial currency reserves of sterling, the history was one of *earning,* not *borrowing.* As for other sterling holdings of the dependencies, the process of borrowing may have been important, though the financial policies adopted in colonial administrations are typically designed to minimize calls on London for commercial credit. Known banking practices in the colonies suggest that this is the case. Most banking business is transacted through British banks which operate in many areas. Barclays Bank, for instance, has 93 branches in the colonies. When such banks need local currency, they arrange for a transfer of sterling to the appropriate colonial currency authorities; the customer may be British or colonial. When these banks have an excess of local cash, they are likely to reverse the procedure and buy sterling assets in the metropolitan market—particularly in the usual absence of local opportunities for similarly liquid investment.

Since in the currency board system sterling used for note-cover cannot be spent, the question whether it has been borrowed or earned raises no urgent questions as to who owns the sterling, however urgent a question it may raise as to who is gaining from a transfer of real resources. The question of ownership would, however, be posed if a colony were to achieve sufficient independence to adopt a system of note-cover with a fiduciary element, i.e., the substitution of local obligations for some portion of the sterling now held. The question would probably be handled through political negotiation. When Egypt and Israel left the sterling area, no question was publicly raised as to the ownership of the sterling in their note-covers though both indicated that such sterling would be increasingly "demobilized." When, however, Eritrea was to be federated with Ethiopia and the prospect was for expenditure of part of Eritrea's 100 per cent note-cover, the question became a difficult one ultimately settled by compromise.

The common practice of modern independent countries is to provide for their monetary requirements on the basis of their own national credit structures, which in the last analysis are based on the promises of their national treasuries. The tendency in the colonies, British or other, is to provide for their money needs *via* the earning of other currencies in foreign trade. This means that the simple conversion of a backward economy from a barter basis to a market basis requires giving up to other countries real resources, whereas in other countries only an expansion of internal credit is required. In a dependency there is no effective source of internal credit and the development of such sources tends to be inhibited by the currency system. A great deal can be, and has been, said against the wisdom of the alternative procedure by which a dependency, which as such has no independent credit status in foreign markets, would print money with only its own untried promises behind it. But as a dependency develops, economically and politically, experience clearly indicates that monetary dependence also fades.

Another criticism—and one which is likely to be more serious as colonial development proceeds—is that the colonial monetary system is hardly at all sensitive to the monetary needs of the local economies. It is likely, but not provable, that this is the case. Inasmuch as the local supply of money in a dependency is geared directly to its trade with other areas rather than to its internal trade, it is only partially related to the level of local production and therefore to the total credit requirements of the local market. As long as most of a colony's commerce is with foreign markets, as long as those foreign markets are predominantly sterling, and as long as sterling credits are forthcoming to finance both short-run difficulties and long-run needs, the insensitivity of the present currency system to requirements other than those of sterling trade is not important. It did become important in all the independent Commonwealth countries, and they all now operate currency systems in which domestic economic considerations are primary and in which sterling surpluses or deficits, though still important, are not causes of automatic currency expansion or contraction. The trend of development in most colonies suggests that this insensitivity of the currency board system to local conditions will become more important.

A final criticism of the present colonial currency system is that it tends to impede the development of local money markets. How important this may be is a question of practical judgment rather than banking theory. The colonies have a preferred position in the London market and there are no structural reasons why the London market could not provide all the facilities that a colony would hope for in the development of a local market. The difficulty is that when full reliance is on London, decisions on colonial requirements must be made away from the spot and colonial needs must in any case command fairly low priority among the large and urgent requirements seeking accommodation in London. Colonial habits of saving, investment, production, and marketing are probably all hampered by the rudimentary nature of the local money markets.

Professor J. R. Hicks, who surveyed development possibilities in Jamaica in 1954, concluded that it would be worthwhile to experiment with the introduction of a fiduciary (i.e., independent) element in the local note issue as a means of encouraging the development of a local financial market to provide for the channelling of local savings into new investment. The Gold Coast, which already by 1954 had become virtually independent, has established an embyro central bank which is expected to take over the functions of the present currency board and is studying and experimenting with the problem of marketing its own issues and those of the Gold Coast government. The lack of a local money market is without doubt a barrier to economic progress so opportunities to encourage the growth of such markets should be pursued vigorously. However, the experience of more developed regions strongly suggests that a good local money market, necessarily based on the faith of local residents and foreigners alike, does not precede economic development but rather goes hand in hand with it.

These, then, are the chief criticisms of this mechanical system of colonial currency: that it forces dependencies to "earn" their local issue of currency by a sacrifice of real production to other areas; that it tends to channel investment elsewhere than to the dependencies; that it is not structurally responsive to local currency needs; and that it tends to impede the development of local money markets. Since only partial facts are available, it is not possible to be sure exactly how forceful any of these criticisms are, but they are widely made both in Britain and in the dependencies and have, as the last few pages have indicated, considerable plausibility.

Colonial Trade

What constitutes a colony's *foreign* trade is itself controversial. John Stuart Mill's view was that because of the intimate relationship between a country and its colonies, colonial overseas trade—almost exclusively trade with the mother country—was more like domestic trade than like international trade. Recently this view has been quoted, interpreted, and extended in the economic journals in efforts to show that what the colonies contribute to Britain and Britain to the colonies cannot be inferred from trends in their balances of payments and in their holdings of sterling. Such inferences have been widely drawn in recent years as certain colonies have become major dollar earners and sterling accumulators. Leading British economists have expressed their concern that whether or not these inferences are justified, "the thing simply does not look right and ought to be corrected."

The inference is that the dollar earnings, which have been large and of about the same magnitude as the increase in sterling holdings, have been turned over to the rest of the sterling area, especially the United Kingdom, against sterling IOUs. Against this inference it has been argued that there is no clear line between what the colonies earn and invest on their own, so to speak, and what Britons earn and invest in the guise of being colonials, whether resident in the colonies or not.

Their exports are sent to England and other industrial centers, "not to be exchanged for things exported to the colony and consumed by its inhabitants," but to be sold for the account of the proprietors and corporations who own and control production. It is still external initiative, enterprise, and investment which are eventually reflected in colonial export statistics, and to interpret these in the same way as if they represented the results of wholly internal contributions to production gives a seriously misleading view of the position. . . . For the native inhabitants of a colonial territory, often supported by remote observers who should know better, to claim its exports as "our oil," "our copper," "our rubber," etc., is gratifying chauvinism but inaccurate economics. All that is really theirs is the unproductive land of centuries—arid scrub, unhealthy swamp, uncultivated jungle—remote from the world's commerce. In addition to its niggardliness under primitive methods of explanation, Nature is notoriously deficient in providing capital and technical services, and, without these, "natural resources" would never be converted into economic goods. It is misleading to regard a colony's exports as the product of its own economic system merely because they come from inside its geographical borders.[1]

The notion that an increase in colonial sterling balances amounts to colonial investment in Britain is complicated by more than this ambiguity as to whether the holder of a sterling balance is a Briton or a colonial. It is complicated also by the nature of the currency relation between sterling and colonial currencies, a relation so direct and mechanical that it creates some ambiguity as to how far colonial currencies can or should be distinguished from sterling. Through the mechanics of the currency arrangements, the colonies' currencies are potentially a claim in sterling, and vice versa. Accordingly, the magnitude of claims denominated in sterling and attributed somewhat arbitrarily to the colonies is only a partial reflection of the net debt or credit position of the colonies vis-à-vis the United Kingdom. A final complication is that because the figures for sterling holdings do not include most private holdings they are incomplete.

This line of reasoning has considerable cogency, although its allegedly more direct applicability to the analysis of colonial trade as compared to other trade would seem at most to be a matter of degree. A good bit of the feeling which has attended the reargumentation of the Mill view seems to be in the nature of a British protest against a tendency to discount the role of British enterprise and capital in the foreign trade record of the colonies. The economic activity in a colony is not easily distinguishable from that of the metropole. But it is still of interest to pursue questions of the direction of transfers of real resources. The transfer becomes

[1] Ida Greaves, "The Character of British Colonial Trade," *The Journal of Political Economy,* v. 62, no. 1 (Chicago: University of Chicago Press, February 1954), pp. 5, 7-8.

no less real if one prefers to regard it as a transfer between two British districts (which also would seem to be an exaggeration) rather than as a transfer between areas foreign to each other. Nor does the transfer become less real if one prefers to regard it as typically or partly a transfer of assets owned by Britons in the colonies to their home accounts. The question remains whether economic activity in the colonies, by anyone, is or is not the important prop in the postwar sterling system that it has been widely considered to be.

Colonial Balances of Payments

Unfortunately analysis of the role of the colonies in the sterling area must be based on sketchy statistics. Tables 24, 25, and 26 set out the main facts as presented in official British sources. The note following the tables explains the limitations of the statistics and comments on the significance of some of the figures. A major omission is the lack of figures indicating investment in or by the colonies. More details are available for some colonies, but this is the best that can be done to present an aggregate picture. In spite of the weaknesses of the statistics, they can probably be used to indicate major trends realistically.

Table 26 shows the persistence, but diminishing importance, of colonial surpluses on trade account, and a variable, but fairly steady, deficit on unexplained other accounts. The trade accounts are likely to be more accurate than other accounts; they are derived from records made at the ports as well as at the banks. If the fairly reasonable assumption is made that in a short period of four years the errors or gaps in the figures for one year are likely to be similar to those of the other years, then even incomplete and tentative figures may be considered to indicate trends. Except for dependencies where tourism is important, such as the West Indies, the postwar pattern of trade still takes the traditional colonial form of trade surpluses offset by invisible deficits, but the trend seems to be away from the pattern. One infers that the big colonial earners in the postwar period developed trade surpluses based on a combination of buoyant prices for their exports of primary produce and restrained imports because of the inchoate state of their plans for local development and the use of dollar controls. Basically this situation adds up to an exaggerated earning capacity for the dependencies in world markets and an undeveloped spending capacity.

Changes may be expected as underdeveloped areas import more supplies and equipment for their small but growing local industries and more things which their contact with Western civilization has invited them to prize as comforts of life. Young people in West Africa, for example, leave their quiet and clean villages where they ordinarily enjoy the creature comforts of food and clothes and shelter and the emotional comforts of households embracing three generations of family and faith. They go to the coastal cities and live in makeshift huts where they have a more meager diet and only enough floor space at night to sleep upon. They give up a spacious, if poor, village which sleeps soundly when night falls for a crowded and tawdry city where the new neon lights help them forget the dark as they chat with contemporaries in their doorways or along the muddy streets. Electric lights may be the most potent export of the Western world, no less attractive in unlit lands than to ourselves and to moths.

The wherewithal of light—the bulbs, fixtures, wires, and the dynamos that are the source of power—exemplifies the changes in foreign trade that come from economic development and contact with the West. Capital and consumer goods alike, all these items have to be imported, at least at first. They are new things in the economy and hence new entries in the trading accounts—on the import side.

The foregoing figures show the trend only in the current transactions of the dependencies; good figures on investment in or by the dependencies do not exist. Because of the intimate relationship between the currency structures of the dependencies and Britain, the current accounts of the dependencies do not reflect the total funds available to them from abroad or spent by them abroad. For example, over the years 1952 and 1953, their "savings" (i.e. increased holdings of sterling in Britain as shown in Table 24 and, on a different basis, in Table 29) amounted to some £200 million, and yet on "current" account there appeared a small deficit. On

Table 24

EXTERNAL ACCOUNTS OF THE BRITISH DEPENDENCIES

	1946	*1947*	*1948*	*1949*	*1950*	*1951*	*1952*	*1953*
With Dollar Area ($ millions)								
Imports			310	220	130	210	190	170
Exports & re-exports			495	390	505	645	515	425
Trade surplus			(185)	(170)	(375)	(435)	(325)	(255)
Other (net)			+21	+32	+33	+26	+54	+52
Gold sales to the U.K.	+24	+22	+27	+27	+28	+25	+ 7	+ 1
Dollar surplus	158	62	223	229	436	486	386	308
Dollar surplus in terms of £ millions	39	15	58	66	155	174	137	110
Transactions with O.E.E.C. countries								
(£ millions)				– 8[a]	+51	+12	+16	–1
($ millions)				(–30)	(+143)	(+20)	(+48)	(–3)
Sterling balances (£ millions)								
At end of year	504	510	556	582	754	968	1076	1161
Change	+50	+ 6	+46	+26	+172	+214	+108	+85

Source: Cmd. 8976 and 9119.
[a] The figure for 1949 transactions with OEEC countries is a calculation of the July-December figure at an annual rate.

Table 25

DEPENDENCIES' BALANCES OF PAYMENTS ON CURRENT ACCOUNTS BY AREAS

(£ millions)

	1950	*1951*	*1952*	*1953*	*Total*
West Africa					
with sterling area	+13	+19	+ 5	+10	+ 47
with other areas	+34	+31	+25	+26	+116
Total	+47	+50	+30	+36	+163
East and Central Africa (including Aden)					
with sterling area	— 8	— 6	—33	—72	—119
with other areas	+14	+19	+29	+31	+ 93
Total	+ 6	+13	— 4	—41	— 26
West Indies (including Bermuda and Bahamas)					
with sterling area	— 9	—13	—10	+ 2	— 30
with other areas	+ 7	0	— 5	+ 1	+ 3
Total	— 2	—13	—15	+ 3	— 27
Malayan Area (including North Borneo, Brunei and Sarawak)					
with sterling area	—59	—29	—55	—55	—198
with other areas	+150	+151	+80	+30	+411
Total	+91	+122	+25	—25	+213
Other Territories					
with sterling area	— 2	+ 2	+ 5	+ 6	+ 11
with other areas	0	— 4	— 2	— 6	— 12
Total	— 2	— 2	+ 3	0	— 1
Total (excluding Hong Kong)					
with sterling area	—65	—27	—88	—109	—289
with other areas	+205	+197	+127	+82	+611
Total	+140	+170	+39	—27	+322

Source: Cmd. 8856 and 9169.

Table 26

DEPENDENCIES' BALANCES OF PAYMENTS ON CURRENT ACCOUNT BY TRANSACTIONS

(£ millions)

	1950	*1951*	*1952*	*1953*
West Africa				
Imports (fob)	—103	—138	—160	+160
Exports (fob)	+169	+222	+223	+223
UK grants to colonies	+ 4	+ 2	+ 5	+ 3
Other invisibles (net)	— 28	— 36	— 38	— 30
Balance	+ 42	+ 50	+ 30	+ 36
East and Central Africa (including Aden)				
Imports (fob)	—112	—150	—178	—176
Exports (fob)	+146	+211	+236	+200
UK grants to colonies	+ 5	+ 6	+ 6	+ 4
Other invisibles (net)	— 39	— 54	— 68	— 69
Balance	0	+ 13	— 4	— 41
West Indies (including Bermuda and Bahamas)				
Imports (fob)	— 74	— 94	—106	—101
Exports (fob)	+ 51	+ 59	+ 65	+ 80
UK grants to colonies	+ 4	+ 3	+ 5	+ 4
Other invisibles (net)	+ 16	+ 19	+ 21	+ 20
Balance	— 3	— 13	— 15	+ 3
Malayan Area (including North Borneo, Brunei and Sarawak)				
Imports (fob)	—253	—423	—340	—281
Exports (fob)	+406	+635	+401	+274
UK grants to colonies	+ 4	+ 5	+ 10	+ 9
Other invisibles (net)	— 70	— 95	— 46	— 27
Balance	+ 87	+122	+ 25	— 25
Other Territories				
Imports (fob)	— 48	— 61	— 67	— 67
Exports (fob)	+ 32	+ 44	+ 51	+ 47
UK grants to colonies	+ 1	+ 1	+ 2	+ 2
Other invisibles (net)	+ 12	+ 14	+ 17	+ 18
Balance	— 3	— 2	+ 3	0
Total (excluding Hong Kong)				
Imports (fob)	—590	—866	—842	—778
Exports (fob)	+804	+1171	+967	+817
UK grants to colonies	+ 18	+ 17	+ 28	+ 22
Other invisibles (net)	—109	—152	—114	— 88
Balance	+123	+170	+ 39	— 27

Source: Cmd. 8856 and 9169; Colonial 298.

Note on Tables 24, 25 and 26.

Table 24 is of particular interest because it sets forth colonial accounts on the basis of uniform statistical techniques. The accounts are at least roughly comparable with the similar figures given for the balance of payments of the United Kingdom and the ISA. (Tables 2 and 16) The limitations of these figures are that they do not go back very far, they do not distinguish the separate colonies, and they do not permit a grouping of colonies on the basis of the important distinction between those which contribute to the sterling system and those which draw from it. These are much the same as the limitations noted in the case of the ISA.

In the last several years a remarkable effort has been made to improve the data on colonial transactions. A bi-monthly *Digest of Colonial Statistics* is now published regularly, giving details of the trade account and of the sterling holdings of the major colonial groups. A longer annual report (Cmd. 8856 for 1952-53, and Cmd. 9169 for 1953-54), provides many more details. A separate study of colonial sterling holdings (Colonial No. 298) is also helpful. These sources are used for Tables 25 and 26. Comparison with preceding tables will reveal discrepancies; these are due to differences in definition of accounts in the various sources and to limits on the availability of colonial figures. Colonial gold sales are included in exports but the transactions of British-owned oil companies are not. Intercolonial trade is excluded. These and other limitations and discrepancies are fully noted in the sources. The figures for 1950 in Table 25 have been slightly adjusted for arithmetic consistency.

The figures for the crown colony of Hong Kong are unfortunately but inevitably omitted from Tables 25 and 26. The Hong Kong free dollar market is an anomaly in the sterling area's tight control of dollars; many unrecorded transactions take place through it, and at such prices for dollars as the market establishes. The usual explanation for this free market in dollars is that the dollars come into Hong Kong as gifts from relatives in the United States, and the flow would cease in the event of the imposition of tight controls on the use of the dollars.

The dependencies as a group earn more than they spend in traffic with the rest of the world, but the trend in recent years has been sharply downward. On over-all account their fairly substantial surplus of 1950-51 changed to a deficit in 1953.

the basis of presently available information there is no certain explanation. The figures for current transactions may be subject to a considerable margin of error and omission; the figures for the sterling holdings of the dependencies may include many items (e.g., extensions of credit to the dependencies in London) which do not show up in the trade records of the dependencies. Even though the two sets of figures do not jibe, it is a good guess that the dependencies have managed since the war to contribute substantial sums to the sterling system, that the trend is now the other way, and that unrecorded investment is probably a significant but unknown factor in their over-all financial position.

There is considerable difference in the role of the various dependencies. The big contributors to the sterling system have been the West African dependencies and, until recently, those in the Malayan area. This is due largely to the production of cocoa in the case of West Africa, and rubber and tin in the case of Malaya. So far, postwar cocoa prices have been high and well maintained; this is reflected in the steady surpluses of West Africa. The deterioration in the position of the Malayan area reflects a fall in rubber and tin prices. The Gold Coast and Nigeria are on the verge of independence; Malaya may be not far behind. The recent history of Malaya has been marked by civil disturbance; it lies in an area where the future may well be troubled. The export balance of these colonies rests on world price movements of critical but unpredictable dimensions. All these facts increase the possibility that the postwar role of Malaya and West Africa as contributors to the sterling system may prove to be an ephemeral one.

On dollar accounts, where the attention of sterling authorities has been regularly focused, the dependencies as a group have performed as consistent contributors (see Table 24). Their contribution has come almost entirely from an export surplus with the United States and other dollar countries. Their earning power has reflected growing production of their major primary products and, with the exception of Malayan tin and rubber, relatively favorable world prices. Along with the substantial, though declining, dollar earnings, the British policy of rigid restriction of colonial imports requiring dollar payment has assured a substantial flow of dollars to the central dollar pool. In fact, as Table 27 shows, dollar imports into the colonies fell by more than colonial dollar earnings between 1949 and 1953. This suggests that the colonial dollar contribution to the sterling area has been maintained by tightening colonial quotas on imports from the dollar area.

The colonial dollar quotas occasion considerable controversy. Britons are proud of their administration of the dependencies and of the extent of local control that has been turned over to the residents of them. In my opinion there are many good reasons for this pride. Criticisms of the quotas

Table 27

CHANGES IN COLONIAL DOLLAR POSITION

	Change in Dollar Earnings Compared with Previous Year	*Change in Dollar Imports Compared with Previous Year*
	($ millions)	
1949	− 94	−90
1950	+117	−90
1951	+130	+80
1952	−120	−20
1953	− 98	−20
Total	− 65	−140

Source: Table 24.

by representatives of the United States, commercial and official, are general, frequent, and often heated. Why, it is asked, should American manufactures be arbitrarily ruled out of the countries which are doing such a good business with us? A frequently heard and somewhat resentful British reply is, Well, whose colonies are these, anyway? A less heated form of the criticism is concerned with the apparent dis-economy of ruling more favorably priced or qualified goods out of any market by means of arbitrary quotas. A more sympathetic form of the response is that in a financial association the requirements of the entire group must take precedence over the special, and perhaps temporary, position of individual members.

In all British dependencies, as in most of the independent sterling countries, imports from the dollar world are limited by predetermined annual quotas. Most other dollar payments, such as travel or investments, are subject to official permission and are in fact strictly held down. The procedures for setting import quotas are not uniform. The general procedure is for the local financial authorities to propose to the British authorities a list of what they consider to be their "essential" import requirements from the dollar world in the following year. The British authorities have the power to veto the proposals or revise them as they see fit. Actually, this power is subject to any number of limitations, varying from colony to colony. If a given dependency is near independence, as in the case of the Gold Coast, and is a heavy dollar earner, again as in the case of the Gold Coast, proposed quotas are likely to be dealt with generously. Similarly, if a dependency, for example Northern Rhodesia, has an important element of British settlers who have been there for generations and maintain a sound financial position, they are not likely to be dealt with summarily. Some British officials have stated off the record that they have to act more gingerly in dealing with the chronically sensitive dependencies than they do in negotiations with their independent sterling associates.

Immediately after the war the theory of the dollar quota was a belt-tightening one. Dollar expenditures should be kept down even though it meant an obvious reduction in consumption standards. The current theory is considerably different. It is based on the notion that a proposed import from the dollar area is not essential if some sort of reasonably similar product is available from non-dollar sources. This basis for regulating dollar imports seems on the face of it to be more liberal than the belt-tightening one, but in practice it is far more restrictive. In effect it embodies the principle that however much sterling countries may have to accept competition with dollar goods in the non-sterling world, such competition will be strictly circumscribed in Britain's dependent territories. As Britain's and the other sterling countries' production has grown, and delivery times have become shorter, it has become fairly easy to make a case that there is a reasonable sterling area substitute for proposed dollar imports. In many places throughout the British dependencies, established American traders claim that their business has never been so bad as since the "liberalizing" of the old policies.

For the most part the dependencies accept the "essentiality" theory and its application to the importation of manufactured goods. This seems to be due partly to a recognition that the integrity of the sterling area is basically beneficial to their own economic interests even though it may deprive them of some dollar imports. Partly, the acceptance is due to the fact that the majority of the established trading companies are British-owned or have British connections and are quite willing to go along with restrictions which after all protect them, an attitude not peculiar to British traders. The quota method and its wide application are probably here to stay for some time.

The Pattern of Trade

Since the war, the trend of trade has been toward closer integration of the dependencies and the other sterling countries, as Table 28 illustrates:

Table 28

THE DIRECTION OF COLONIAL TRADE

(per cent of total trade of UK dependencies)

	To				*From*			
	UK	*RSA*	*$ Area*	*W. Europe*	*UK*	*RSA*	*$ Area*	*W. Europe*
1937....	20	12	30	19	27	12	8	9
1950....	23	16	21	13	27	20	9	8
1951....	27	17	17	14	24	18	7	14
1952....	31	15	14	14	29	17	7	12
1953....	32	16	14	30	30	18	7	18

[a] Hong Kong excluded.
Source: *International Financial Statistics,* July 1954, p. 29.

Compared with prewar, the dollar area has declined sharply as a colonial market, and slightly as a colonial supplier. The independent sterling countries have increased in importance. These trends are the reverse of trends already noted in the case of the ISA in the preceding chapter. For the ISA, Britain has declined in importance as a market and as a source of supplies, and the dollar area has gained on both counts. This difference in trade trends in the colonies as compared to the ISA suggests that countries which are in a position to pursue more independent trade policies tend to direct a larger proportion of their trade outside the confines of the sterling area.

The commodity structure of colonial trade remains "colonial" in the sense that exports are largely made up of a limited range of agricultural commodities and raw materials while imports include a variety of manufactured goods. The latter are still predominantly textiles and small consumers items such as cosmetics and personal adornment but machinery for local industrial development is playing a rapidly increasing role.

For the separate groups of dependencies, the trade structure can be rapidly summarized. In *West Africa,* about three-fourths of exports consist of four commodities: cocoa, peanuts, palm kernels, and palm oil. The list of imports is large; however, as is typical of backward economies, by far the largest share of imports, about 30 per cent, is made up of cotton textiles. A similar pattern is found in *East Africa.* Cotton, sisal, and coffee represent by far the preponderant part of exports, while purchases abroad consist chiefly of finished cotton fabrics. As in West Africa, imports of vehicles, machinery, and iron and steel manufactures bear evidence of the concern with economic development.

In *Central Africa,* imports are chiefly food, reflecting the unsuitability of soils and climate for many kinds of crops. About three-fourths of the goods shipped abroad from Nyasaland are tea and tobacco. More than four-fifths of Rhodesia's exports are copper. But as in other colonial areas, here also cotton piece goods are a predominant import, though a wide range of capital goods, including mining equipment, reflects the pace of economic development and mining activity.

In the *Eastern group* of colonies, more than two-fifths of Malaya's exports are rubber and about 15 per cent tin. For the group as a whole, foodstuffs constitute the largest import item, but they import a variety of manufactured goods, including considerable capital equipment.

Sugar is still the mainstay of the *British West Indies.* In recent years about 36 per cent of the region's exports consisted of sugar, though petroleum has greatly increased in importance since before the war. In 1949, Trinidad was the fourth largest producer of petroleum in the sterling area. The islands are highly dependent, however, upon imported foodstuffs, especially rice and wheat.

Colonial Sterling Balances

Colonial finance, like colonial political administration, derives from Britain. There are no local institutions to perform central banking functions such as credit control or, except for a few modest experiments, the holding of colonial debt. The currency authorities have no function as providers of credit to the colonial governments or as fiscal agents. In lieu of local money markets, the colonies use London.

The colonies have recourse to London as both debtors and creditors: they traditionally invest their public revenue and foreign trade surpluses there and approach London for grants or loans to cover budget deficits or special projects. Historically, the debtor aspect of the colonial recourse to London has been the better known; since the war, the accumulation of colonial sterling assets has drawn attention to the creditor aspect.

Colonial sterling holdings are large and have grown rapidly since the war, as Table 29 shows.

Between the end of 1945 and the end of 1953 the sterling holdings of the colonies rose by £800 million, of which about £700 million were obligations of the United Kingdom. Colonial holdings have also grown in importance relative to total United Kingdom obligations to non-residents. At the end of 1945 the colonial holdings were about an eighth of these obligations; by the end of 1953 they were almost a third. Colonial short-term claims against the United Kingdom seem to have risen even more rapidly in proportion to total short-term claims on Britain, but this cannot be demonstrated precisely. During this same period other major groups of sterling holders were reducing their holdings. Those of the non-sterling world fell by about £450 million, and those of the independent sterling area by about £200 million.

The impact of the Korean War on the colonial balance of payments is clearly reflected in the rapid accumulation of sterling assets in 1951 and 1952. Colonial holdings grew at the rate of some £65 million a year from 1946 to 1950. In 1951 the rate rose to £238 million and in 1952 it was £132 million. Even in 1953 the growth was over £100 million.

Table 29
THE STERLING ASSETS OF THE DEPENDENCIES

(£ millions)

End of Year:	*1945*	*1949*	*1950*	*1951*	*1952*	*1953*	*Change During Period*
West Africa	100	200	256	333	362	400	+300
East and Central Africa	100	138	172	217	259	288	+188
Malayan Area	115	107	164	252	283	282	+167
Hong Kong	210 (Hong Kong, West Indies and Others combined)	68	94	116	120	132	+144 (Hong Kong, West Indies and Others combined)
West Indies		67	78	81	91	107	
Others		90	88	91	107	115	
TOTAL	525	670	852	1090	1222	1324	+799
Of which:							
Securities of Dominions and Colonies	71	88	98	122	146	163	+ 92
Obligations of the United Kingdom	454	582	754	968	1076	1161	+707

Source: Col. 298, Cmd. 8976, 9169. For 1945 the estimates have been taken from the Bank for International Settlements, *The Sterling Area,* p. 75.

Note: The area breakdowns are from Col. 298 in which a somewhat different approach was used from that of the other cited command paper. There is, therefore, a slight discrepancy between these figures and earlier tables.

Colonial holdings of the securities of other members of the Commonwealth more than doubled from the end of the war to 1953. The rate of increase was, however, slightly below that for total colonial sterling assets; at the end of 1953, such holdings represented a little over 12 per cent of the total compared with about 14 per cent in December 1945.

The distribution of the sterling assets by individual groups of colonies holding them generally followed a consistent pattern throughout the postwar period. Three areas—West Africa, East and Central Africa, and Malaya—held about two-thirds of the aggregate colonial balances. Moreover, each of the colonial areas shared in the postwar accumulation of balances, though not in equal proportions.

At the end of 1953 West Africa held the largest amount of sterling assets, about £400 million. This represented an increase of 300 per cent over the level at the end of 1945. And in the three years, 1951-53, the accumulation was nearly as large as in the six-year period, 1945-50. These increases must be looked at in the light of West Africa's postwar balance of payments. The consistently favorable over-all balance of payments which made West Africa both a dollar and a sterling earner provided the basis for the expansion in sterling assets. In the period 1950-53, however, surpluses with the dollar area on current account seem to have been of major importance.

The relationship between changes in sterling assets of West Africa and the current account surpluses are given below for the years 1950-53 in millions of pounds sterling:

	1950	*1951*	*1952*	*1953*
Change in sterling assets	+56	+77	+29	+38
Current account	+42	+50	+30	+36
Other capital transactions	+14	+27	− 1	+ 2

Source: Col. 298, Cmd. 9169. Subsequent figures in this section come from the same sources.

The figures suggest that although the current account surplus played a crucial role in the accumulation of sterling assets, other capital transactions—a residual item which includes errors and omissions as well as true capital movements—were significant in 1950 and 1951. In 1952, however, there seems to have been a net outflow of capital of minor magnitude making the current account surplus the chief factor in the increase in sterling assets.

The *Malayan group* of colonies ranked next in importance as a holder of sterling assets during part of the period, but slipped into third place in 1953. At the end of that year these holdings were valued at £282 millions, an increase since 1945 of more than 150 per cent, most of which was registered since the upswing in rubber prices in 1950. In contrast to the case of West Africa, however, Malaya's relative importance as a holder of sterling balances has steadily declined since the end of the war when its assets were the largest of all colonial areas. The decline has been sharp in recent years as the drop in rubber and tin price added to the costly effect of civil disturbances.

In the Malayan case the relationship between changes in sterling assets and the current account surplus is (in millions of pounds):

	1950	*1951*	*1952*	*1953*
Change in sterling assets	+57	+ 88	+31	− 1
Current account	+87	+122	+25	−13
Other capital transactions	−30	− 34	+ 6	+12

Unlike West Africa, the Malayan accumulation of sterling was considerably below the current account surplus, taking the four-year period as a whole. This would suggest that capital transactions contained in the residual item, subject to all the qualifications inherent in it, were negative and thus had to be financed to considerable extent by the current account surplus.

Malaya's accumulation of sterling assets was primarily the consequence of large dollar surpluses, for the area had consistent current deficits with the sterling area. Until 1949, moreover, Malaya probably registered over-all deficits as well, which explains in part the decline in sterling assets during the period from 1945 to 1949.

The *East* and *Central African* dependencies' sterling assets nearly tripled from 1945 to the end of 1953. As in the other groups of colonies, the major part of the increase occurred after 1950. Deficits with the sterling area throughout most of the period made the East and Central African dollar surplus the chief factor, insofar as the current account influenced the accumulation of sterling assets. The relationship between current account surplus and changes in sterling balances is, in millions of pounds:

	1950	*1951*	*1952*	*1953*
Change in sterling assets	+34	+45	+42	+29
Current account	0	+13	− 4	−41
Other capital transactions	+34	+32	+46	+70

The figures suggest there was no close relationship between changes in sterling balances and the position on current account. Net capital inflows must have been the primary factor in the increase in this area's sterling holdings.

The earliest postwar year for which data on sterling assets held by the *West Indies* are available is 1949. In the next four years balances increased about £40 million, to make a total of £107 million at the end of 1953. This has been achieved despite consistent current deficits in most of the postwar period both with the sterling area and with the dollar area. The deficits suggest that the origin of the West Indian sterling balances was similar to that in East Africa, namely an inflow of capital accompanying new settlers.

The figures for the West Indies, in millions of pounds, are:

	1950	*1951*	*1952*	*1953*
Change in sterling assets	+11	+ 3	+10	+16
Current account	− 3	−13	−15	+ 3
Other capital transactions	+14	+16	+25	+13

Taking the dependencies as a whole, the increase in colonial sterling holdings from 1949 to 1953 was almost twice as large as the amount that can be accounted for by the colonial earnings from current trade. What accounts for the remainder? Obviously the United Kingdom's own balance of payments does not suggest investment in the colonies financed out of British savings in anything like this order of magnitude.

The answer probably must be a hybrid one. First, the flows inferred above are fairly refined conclusions from figures admittedly incomplete and tentative. There are no good direct figures on investment flows, although this is a subject of increasing study. Second, the apparent contribution from Britain to the colonies at the end of 1953 may have been largely in the form of undisbursed loans standing to the credit of the colonies in London. Actual capital inflow was probably less than the inferred flow suggests.

Conclusions and Outlook

The facts presented in the last three chapters give an incomplete picture but they strongly suggest that in the postwar period the dependencies have been the main savers and the main net dollar earners of the sterling association.

Special circumstances have contributed to this performance. On the savings side, net earnings have been facilitated by high—sometimes boom—food and raw material prices, especially during the period of build-up in the Western manufacturing countries following the outbreak of the Korean War. It is possible that in the course of the next fifty years the price trend will be favorable for areas producing food and raw materials. At least, many economists foresee a persistently growing demand for such products if the industrialization of the world proceeds in accordance with present trends. But whether such a trend will result in continued surpluses on over-all or dollar account in the colonies depends on how far they may continue to specialize in production for export rather than adapting their agriculture to meet the rising consumption needs of their own rapidly growing populations and in broadening the range of their production. The economic movement seems to be in harmony with the political movement toward independence, and, accordingly, a fracturing of the colonial pattern.

The accumulation of colonial surpluses has been partly the result of British administrative control. Financially, the effect of this control has been to encourage extreme fiscal conservatism, far more conservative than is practiced by the British government, even under the Conservative Party. A budget surplus, which is usual in the more productive colonies except in periods of internal strife, is something to be tucked away for an undefined period and for indefinite future uses, and in London banks. But the explanation of the building up of colonial savings accounts in London lies less in direct British control than in the absence of development plans and opportunities which would afford an attractive alternative use for the money. Colonial funds are now saved for two main purposes: internal price stabilization programs in the event of a drop in world prices for a major export, such as West African cocoa, and the financing of development plans now only in an embryonic stage.

All this may change very soon. The Malayan area has already felt the brunt of a drop in world prices for its major exports. Kenyan savings have been translated into debts to meet the costs of efforts to maintain internal order. The conquest of malaria has resulted in extraordinary increases in population in the colonies, leading to increased consumption and the need to produce more for the home market. African development plans have been stepped up. Reference to these particular areas is made because they have been the main source of "contribution" in the postwar period, and even their contribution does not take account of Britain's own administrative and military expenses. Empire may or may not be worthwhile, but clearly it is not cheap nowadays.

While the outlook for net earnings of the dependencies over the next ten years or so is subject to much doubt, the outlook for expenditures is almost certainly one of constant growth. British estimates place capital formation in the dependencies at £190 million in 1948 and at some £420 million in 1953. This is modest compared to the amount of investment in major industrial countries, but it is large in relation to the London nest-egg of the dependencies and the rate of growth is already fast, potentially faster.

Whether a *general* trend toward colonial independence is to be foreseen or not is almost an imponderable question. For many colonies it is not at all clear what would be gained from independence or how strong or effective the sentiment for it is. It probably is to be foreseen, however, that the trend is and will continue to be toward independence in the very groups that have produced the external surpluses so advantageous in the operation of the postwar sterling system. A weakening in British political authority over these colonies would presumably result in more expensive and less conveniently timed import policies, at least if the behavior of the present independent members of the sterling area is any guide.

As Sir Dennis Robertson wrote:

> But the system meant something more than [the surrender of the proceeds of exports to dollar countries, restriction of the right to import goods costing dollars, abstention from capital investment outside the sterling area]. It meant that each country *as a country* agreed to hand over its surplus dollar earnings to Mother in exchange for sterling, and to go to Mother

when it wanted extra dollars to spend. Naturally the degree of confidence with which it exercised or presented claims on the dollar pool depended partly on its political status; the little black children, who were often the best earners, could be smacked on the head if they showed too great a propensity to spend dollars, while the grown-up white daughters, who were often pretty extravagant, could only be quietly reasoned with.[1]

Also to be foreseen as probable is a gradual change in the mechanical nature of the colonial currency system which, given British control over import policy and development, tends to create sterling savings out of colonial external and internal savings. Such savings are probably more the result than the cause of colonial poverty. To the extent that an increase in colonial currency is in practice earned, rather than borrowed, abroad, it is needlessly costly in real resources compared to currency expansion not directly covered by foreign-exchange surpluses. The economies of most colonies, and particularly the good earners and savers, are undergoing a shift from barter to market, and this shift almost certainly will continue. Again if the experience of the once colonial and now independent members of the sterling system is any guide, it is to be expected that the continued development of colonial economies will lead to the evolution of more independent monetary systems.

The uncertainty that the colonies will continue to play a major role in providing the savings which the system needs and in contributing importantly to easing the system's balance with other areas rests on three important considerations. First, the recent surpluses have been due to special circumstances which swelled the exports of certain colonies. Next, special circumstances have kept the colonies' import expenditures modest. And finally, the monetary system of the colonies has made for a direct translation of these export-import developments into sterling savings.

It is not possible to be at all certain that any of these conditions will pertain in the future, and there is some ground for believing that none of them will. The outlook for continued dollar help from the colonies to the rest of the ster-

[1] Sir Dennis H. Robertson, *Britain in the World Economy,* (London: George Allen & Unwin Ltd., 1954), pp. 38-39.

ling area, even in the absence of over-all colonial surpluses, may be brighter. If the colonies continue to be important dollar earners, even though they are not in a position to maintain over-all surpluses, then the question of the availability of such dollars to the system will turn on whether the other members of the system can meet colonial needs for imported food and developmental goods.

Chapter 8

DEPRESSION, DOLLAR SHORTAGE, AND DISCRIMINATION

> The elephant has joints, but none for courtesy; his legs are legs for necessity, not for flexure.
>
> TROILUS AND CRESSIDA

IN EARLIER CHAPTERS attention has been directed mainly at the way various members of the sterling area function and how the system operates to distribute resources—its own and those available from outside—among the members. The present chapter is concerned with part of the rationale of the system's behavior. In the postwar period so far, this behavior seems to be motivated largely by the conviction that dollars tend to be chronically scarce, that unpredictable ups and downs in economic activity in the non-sterling world (especially the United States) are the source of severe economic disturbances in the sterling world, and that the most effective or least risky way of coping with these problems is by way of controlling the volume of trade with the non-sterling world. The meaning of the events of 1954—when the sterling area proved to be almost immune to an American recession—and of 1955—when Britain had exchange difficulties in the face of rising American activity—has yet to be fully assimilated into the rationale of the sterling area.

The problem of "dollar shortage" symbolizes the fit or misfit of the sterling area in the world economy, and the term "dollar shortage" itself has become imprecise, or multimeaningful at least, as it has been variously defined with reference to complex judgments of the degree of fit or misfit. In the first couple of years after the war, "dollar shortage" was pretty generally understood as a shorthand way of referring to the obvious physical need of countries which, in the awkward posture of war-lameness, needed goods and services they could not pay for out of current earnings and which only the western hemisphere could immediately supply. Gradually, after this initial period, these war-disrupted economies exceeded the hopes of their governments and ours in restoring their output and adapting it to the world's limbo between war and peace; still the shortage of dollars was felt, though the dollar world's temporary virtual monopoly of output had ended. The question inevitably arose, was there a shortage because there were too few dollars or too much other currency? Was it the demand for or supply of dollars which was out of kilter?

Official opinion in the sterling world and much of the rest of the non-dollar world is that the trouble was—and is—a scarcity of dollars, and that hence the supply should be rationed by means of special techniques, notably discrimination. The dollar world's official opinion gradually formed along the line that there was a surfeit of other currencies, not a shortage of dollars. In the last several years a combination of circumstances has demoted the feeling of dollar shortage to a lower level of anxiety in the non-dollar world: the supply of dollars has been sustained by the United States military expenditures abroad and a high level of United States imports, while the demand for them has been cut by more conservative internal financial practices abroad. But while at present the sharper dollar pains have subsided, the relief has been to an unknown but maybe large degree fortuitous and dread of the next attack remains. Meanwhile, the apparatus of discrimination is maintained virtually intact even if some of the practices have been relaxed.

The key question, which in the somewhat easier atmosphere presently prevailing can be more harmoniously debated, is to what extent sterling countries can reasonably regard their relations with the dollar world as subject to external hazards which they can and should resist, and to what extent the difficulties in these relations are due to their own behavior, including a penchant to resist reasonable as well as unreasonable pressures for changing their ways.

The reasonableness of a country's or an area's adjustment to outside pressure is the heart of the matter. From the standpoint of the sterling area's economic and financial policy the question is whether the changes required by the vicissitudes of relations with the dollar world could be resisted with less loss of real income than would be lost in the course of making the changes. And, as with so many questions touching the reasonableness of policy, the evidence is inconclusive.

The rationale of defense against the United States economy has become a very refined structure with numerous highly polished facets, but the basis for the structure is fairly simple. The United States economy, it is argued, is so dynamic and mercurial that it is not just the life of the party but rather an inveterate disturber of the economic peace. The nature of the offense is both chronic and intermittent: chronic in the sense that the rapid rate of productivity in the United States continually displaces foreign sellers in the United States market, and intermittent in the sense that United States demand for foreign products is either manic or depressive, never just normal. If other countries cannot persuade the United States to quiet down, they can at least close a few doors and windows against the noise and draft.

The Usual Charge: United States Productivity

Sir Dennis Roberston describes the disturbing effect of technological advance in the United States by this analogy:

> The simple fellow who, to the advantage of both, has been earning a living by cooking the dinner for a busy and prosperous scientist wakes up one day to find that his master has invented a completely automatic cooker, and that if he wants to remain a member of the household he must turn shoeblack. He acquires a kit and learns the technique, only to find that his master has invented a dust-repelling shoe, but would nevertheless be graciously willing for him to remain on and empty the trash-bins. Would he not do better to remove himself from the orbit of the great man, and cultivate his own back garden? And if he can find some other simple fellows in the same case with whom to gang up and practise the division of labour on a less bewildering basis, so much the better for him.[1]

[1] Sir Dennis H. Robertson, *Britain in the World Economy*, p. 58.

Less light-handedly, Honor Croome in a provocative article writes:

> Let a large group or area A for any reason establish a considerable absolute lead in production per head, giving rise to a correspondingly considerable superiority in its margin available for investment, which will mean a progressive widening of the absolute lead and so *da capo;* then, the reduction in costs in that area, when translated into lower export prices, will exert an unremitting deflationary pressure on the rest of the world, which can benefit from A's low-priced exports only at the cost, first, of continuous downward adjustment of its own price levels (inimical to full employment), and, secondly, of structural unemployment during the adaptations forced by concurrent changes in comparative advantage.[2]

And Professor Balogh says:

> There is the periodic recurrence of the dollar shortage due to the basic, structural unbalance, between rates of dynamic growth, whenever the discrepancy in productivity has become too great to be managed by minor manipulations.[3]

Dissenting, we have Professor Haberler:

> Even in the land of Adam Smith, Ricardo, Marshall, and Keynes it is necessary to point out again and again that trade is governed by comparative not by absolute costs! [4]

And Professor Ellis objects to the proposition that differential productivity rates cause imbalance between areas:

> This is a *non-sequitur.* In so far as trade is governed by productivity, it is governed by comparative, not absolute, differences in productivity.[5]

These scholars probably are not talking about quite the same thing and probably all of them would agree that while trade is classically established as profitable between rich areas

[2] Honor Croome, "The Dollar Siege," *Lloyds Bank Review* (July 1950), p. 30 ff.

[3] Thomas Balogh, *The Dollar Crisis, Causes and Cure* (Oxford: Blackwell Press, 1949), pp. 149-50.

[4] Gottfried Haberler, "Dollar Shortage," in S. Harris, ed., *Foreign Economic Policy of the United States* (Cambridge: Harvard University Press, 1948), p. 436.

[5] Howard S. Ellis, *The Economics of Freedom* (New York: Harper and Bros. for the Council on Foreign Relations, 1950), p. 71.

and poor areas, nevertheless, serious temporary displacements could be occasioned by technological advance in *either* the richer or poorer area. Sir Dennis would probably agree that if his simple fellow were to have an unexpected flash of wit it might disrupt the scientist.

It may be that the more usual situation is for the rich to get richer and in so doing to displace the poor from their markets, but direct examples are hard to come by. What can be offered here has a bearing, I think, on the plausibility of Sir Dennis' analogy, but does not substantiate it or undermine it. On the other hand, it is fairly easy to find evidence suggesting that the cooks learn to displace the services of the scientists; localized production of textiles, for example, undermined the dominant trade influence established by Britain on the basis of the burst of advance summarized as the industrial revolution.

Bearing on the plausibility of the chronically disruptive effect of a productivity differential is first the fact that *in the last 75 years United States productivity has grown rapidly.* The accuracy of international comparisons of labor productivity is notoriously limited. It is hard to find products sufficiently homogeneous for comparison, and cultural differences suggest that what is included in output in one area may be irrelevant to another area's concept of output. And there are the usual problems of evaluating output over a period of time. So, after making this conventional protest that what follows may be true if at all only by coincidence, the usual procedure of going right ahead with the questionable evidence can be followed. Since 1880 American productivity has increased at an average rate of 3 per cent per annum; in Britain the rate has been 1.5 per cent. The implication is that if British and American output per worker were about the same 50 years ago, the American worker now puts out anywhere from 2 to 5 times as much, depending on the industry. Between 1950 and 1951 the mere *increase* in American output was more than the *total* output of Britain.

The reasons for the superiority of American production are many, and there is no need to go into them in detail. But judging from Graham Hutton's analysis of the reports of the Anglo-American productivity teams, the following factors stand out.[6] Higher United States productivity has been achieved not by different methods, but by differences in their application. There is greater standardization, simplification, and specialization in the United States. This has been the result of better management and a greater consciousness of costs. The result has been the accumulation of larger stocks of capital in the United States which are better organized and more intensively used. The last factor is especially important, for it has led to the frequent replacement of machines by new and better ones, thus increasing efficiency and lowering unit costs.

Whether the United States is a little or a lot ahead of Britain in technological creativeness is a question that can only be approached impressionistically. Prevailing impressions frequently skip over the evidence of Britain's current inventiveness. To give just a few examples: Britain established the first public television service in 1936 and has pioneered underwater television for marine salvage. Britain plays a leading part in the production of new synthetic fibers, e.g., Ardil and Terylene. In the field of chemistry, British scientists have been leaders in the discovery of vitamins and penicillin products. In 1941, Britain put the first jet-propelled aircraft in the air. In 1950, the world's first gas-turbine car was produced by a British company. Radar is another British first, and in 1932, at Cavendish Laboratories, Cambridge, the first disintegration of the atom was achieved. These advances have also been applied industrially, as the conspicuous growth in the export of such items as turbo-jet and turbo-propelled aircraft indicates. Britain is also the world's largest exporter of radioactive isotopes used in research. Production of synthetic fibers has also expanded and earnings of foreign exchange increased through such licensing agreements as were made for the production of Terylene in the United States under the name Dacron.

The second fact bearing on the plausibility of the scientist-cook analogy is a negative one: *there seems to be no evidence of American technology advancing by spurts and displacing*

[6] Graham Hutton, *We Too Can Prosper* (New York: Macmillan, 1953), p. 16 ff.

imports suddenly. Even where technology has suddenly struck upon a new product, synthetics for instance, the application to industry and markets has been gradual. Despite the fact that synthetic fibers were discovered before the war, cotton textiles—though shrinking—still account for the preponderant share of world textile commerce.[7] There is little to suggest that changes in the composition of world trade resulting from the application of new technology are in any sense revolutionary. What seem to be of more importance are the gradual technological changes which are the outcome of frequent replacement and perfection of machinery over time. These small changes in technology are of an evolutionary nature, yet their effects are significant. In this connection, Graham Hutton is led to the conclusion that "the spurt of American production and productivity has never been sudden. It has gone on steadily, cumulatively, for over a century, and it has gone on even when there was slack in the rope."[8] The evidence suggests that technological changes have not altered United States import and export patterns so quickly that foreign adjustment was impossible, or obsolete, before it could be completed.

The third fact, illustrated in Tables 30 and 31, is that the *composition of British exports has changed very greatly since 1913, even since 1938, and the change seems to have been toward higher-technology products.*

Table 30

COMPOSITION OF UNITED KINGDOM EXPORTS 1913-1952

(Per cent of Total Value)

	1913	*1929*	*1938*	*1950*	*1952*
Coal	10	7	8	2	2
Textiles	38	33	21	19	15
Metal & Engineering	26	28	37	49	52
Other Manufactures	14	17	19	18	21
Other goods	12	15	15	12	10

Source: *Labor and Industry in Britain,* v. 11, no. 4 (December 1953), p. 155.

[7] G. Lovasy, "Rise in U.S. Share of World Textile Trade," *International Monetary Fund Staff Papers,* v. 3, no. 1 (April 1953).

[8] Hutton, cited, p. 19.

Table 31

VOLUME OF UNITED KINGDOM EXPORTS, 1938-1952

(1935 = 100)

	1938	*1947*	*1950*	*1951*	*1st Q 1952*
All Exports	99	107	173	178	185
Raw materials & semi-manufactures	90	22	48	33	39
Manufactures	99	121	196	204	213
Declining:					
Cotton yarns and manufactures	75	32	50	53	47
Stable:					
Woolen yarns and manufactures	77	68	117	104	82
Apparel	90	123	114	123	105
Iron & steel manufactures	88	94	148	132	136
Expanding:					
Non-ferrous metals mfgrs.	85	147	196	145	169
Chemicals, drugs, dyes	97	135	199	257	254
Cutlery, hardware, and instruments	104	190	247	276	313
Electrical goods	128	209	304	306	352
Machinery and parts	123	195	294	312	359
Vehicles	141	260	551	572	616

Source: Ely Devons, "Some Aspects of United Kingdom Export Trade," *Lloyds Bank Review* (July 1952), p. 29.

Oddly enough, however, output per worker apparently increased most markedly in those industries which exhibited a declining postwar trend, notably mining and textiles. The value of output per worker in major British industries showed the following percentage increase between 1935 and 1948.[9]

[9] Calculated from *Labor and Industry in Britain,* v. 10, no. 2 (June 1952), p. 63. Differences in price rises among the industries would, of course, be reflected in these figures.

Textiles	243
Mining & Quarrying	203
Metal Manufactures	150
Engineering	134
Vehicles	131
Chemicals	79

The relatively smaller increase in output per worker occurred in the industries which underwent a postwar expansion. One cannot conclude from this that productivity played no part in the expansion of exports because no account has been taken of the changes in productivity in the competitor countries. Also, we do not know to what extent changes in productivity are reflected in changes in costs and prices to foreign importers. Nevertheless, the comparison does suggest that the role of productivity may not be as obvious as it is often thought to be. It also serves to direct attention to other factors, such as shortages and reduced demand, and their role in influencing the direction and composition of exports.

The fourth fact is a very general one, namely that *as United States output has grown, imports have declined in relative importance*. Table 32 shows this proportional decline of total imports over three decades and also indicates that United States imports from the sterling area have declined more than other imports. Until 1953 this was apparently due entirely to a relative decline in Britain's exports while those from the rest of the sterling area maintained their share in total American imports. The decline in imports from the RSA in 1953 and 1954 is due almost entirely to the fall in the value of United States purchases of raw materials, notably rubber and wool. A drop in prices as well as in the quantities bought after the boom connected with the Korean War reduced United States imports from the outer sterling area from $1.7 billion in 1951 to $1.0 billion in 1954.

Leaving aside the rather special circumstances of the last few years, Table 33 shows that, as might be expected, the relative shares of Britain and the RSA in United States imports have been connected with changes in the commodity composition of American purchases from the sterling area. Finished manufactures have declined in importance, food has risen, and raw materials have retained their relative importance. In this last category, the figures hide an interesting difference in the performance of the United Kingdom and the rest of the sterling area. The long-term trends of United States imports of crude and semi-finished materials from the

Table 32

UNITED STATES PRODUCTION AND IMPORTS

Years	*Gross National Product* ($ billions)	*Total Imports* ($ billions)	*Imports as per cent of GNP*	*Imports from Sterling Area as per cent of Total Imports*	*RSA Imports as per cent of Total Imports*
1923-29 average	94.0	4.1	4.4	22	13
1929	103.8	4.4	4.2	20	13
1930-39 average	76.6	2.1	2.8	20	12
1938	84.7	2.0	2.4	20	12
1940-45 average	168.7	3.5	2.0	20	17
1946-50 average	249.2	6.5	2.6	19	15
1946	211.1	4.8	2.3	20	17
1947	233.3	5.6	2.4	20	17
1948	259.1	7.0	2.7	20	16
1949	257.3	6.6	2.6	17	14
1950	285.1	8.7	3.1	18	14
1951	328.2	11.0	3.4	20	15
1952	346.1	10.7	3.1	17	13
1953	364.9	10.9	3.0	16	10
1954	360.5	10.2	2.8	15	10

Source: Trade figures through 1950 are calculated from J. H. Adler, E. R. Schlesinger and E. Van Westerborg, *The Pattern of United States Import Trade Since 1923*. Federal Reserve Bank of New York, May 1952. Subsequent trade figures as well as GNP data come from Department of Commerce sources.

Note: Through 1950 trade figures refer to imports for consumption, thereafter to general imports. Figures for 1954 are preliminary.

United Kingdom and from the rest of the sterling area are in opposite directions. Between 1923 and 1950 those from the United Kingdom dropped by about two-thirds, and those from the rest of the sterling area about doubled. While imports of finished manufactures into the United States have not kept pace with the expansion of American production, Britain's share in the volume imported from the sterling area has not fallen.

Table 33

STERLING AREA SHARE IN UNITED STATES MERCHANDISE IMPORTS

Years	*Crude & Semi-finished Materials*		*Finished Manufactures*		*Crude Foodstuffs*		*Mfg'd Foodstuffs*	
	All Imports	*S.A.*	*All Imports*	*S.A.*	*All Imports*	*S.A.*	*All Imports*	*S.A.*
	(Per cent of Total Value)							
1923-1929	55	73	22	18	12	6	12	2
1930-1939	51	70	21	13	14	8	14	7
1946-1950	53	72	18	12	19	11	10	4

Source: Calculated from J. H. Adler and others, cited, p. 12.

Taking into account all the factors that have been mentioned in this section, the evidence is not conclusive as to the precise effect of American gains in productivity on the position of the United Kingdom in the United States market or in third markets. Such evidence as there is suggests that the important changes which have occurred must be explained by reasons other than that the spurts of United States inventiveness have seriously qualified the principle of comparative advantage.

About Recessions

An important tie binding sterling countries together is the fear of the effects of American recessions. The association of sterling countries in the thirties—an association which was to be formalized later through exchange controls—was born partly of the effort to be free of the downward pull of American depression. The downturns of 1938 and 1949 seemed to sterling countries to justify their fears and confirm the wisdom of their cooperating in resistance.

Whether or not the fear is reasonable, its existence and the probability of its continued existence constitute important determinants of policy. The illustrative material which is set forth briefly below suggests the fear is by no means trumped up. Far less clear is whether available means of resisting American recessions cause more trouble than they prevent. For example, C. P. Kindleberger concludes that vigorous foreign action to resist the effects of United States depression may intensify the depression.[10] The importance of the level of United States economic activity is due to the preponderant influence of the United States economy on world trade. Some countries are very vulnerable to changes in the volume or price of American imports. In 1951 about half of the imports into the United States came from countries where they amounted to more than half the total exports; only about a fifth of United States imports came from countries which sold less than a tenth of their total exports to the United States. In "normal" times this country's imports account for three-fourths or more of foreign dollar earnings and thus largely determine the volume of goods and services foreign countries can buy here.

The influence of the American economy on the income of the sterling area is not immediately obvious in the foregoing sense. In recent years the sterling area's exports to this country have represented only about 10 per cent of its total exports; these goods amounted to some 18 per cent of total United States imports. This would suggest that the American market does not dominate sterling area exports and income.

In fact, however, the influence seems to be great because of indirect effects. The reduction in income resulting from a decrease in exports to the United States as business shifts into a lower gear here affects the trade of sterling countries with third countries. For example, in the interwar period the United Kingdom's total exports very closely followed changes

[10] Charles P. Kindleberger, *The Dollar Shortage* (New York: Technology Press of Massachusetts Institute of Technology, and Wiley, 1950), pp. 111-114 and throughout.

in United States economic activity, even though exports to the United States amounted to only 5 per cent of total British exports.

Table 34 illustrates how far various countries slashed their purchases from the United Kingdom when their earnings from the United States dropped in the course of two prewar business downturns. In the first two years of the Great Depression the indirect effects, measured in this fashion, were of about the same order of magnitude as the loss of direct sales to the United States. In the 1938 drop the indirect effects shown in the table were milder. This may be partly a statistical illusion, concealing a lag that would appear in figures for a longer period. But it is also likely that the effects were milder because the recession was largely confined to the United States whereas in the earlier instance the whole world had felt the effect of depression by 1931.

Table 34

COMPARISON OF VARIOUS COUNTRIES' SALES TO THE UNITED STATES AND PURCHASES FROM THE UNITED KINGDOM

Country	*Exports to United States % Change in Value*		*Imports from United Kingdom % Change in Value*	
	1929 to 31	*1937 to 38*	*1929 to 31*	*1937 to 38*
Canada	−47	−35	−41	−19
Malaya	−65	−54	−60	− 4
Japan	−52	−39	−54	−58
Argentina	−69	−71	−49	− 4
Brazil	−47	−19	−69	−26
China	−60	−54	−44	−31
India/Burma	−61	−39	−59	− 7
Germany	−50	−30	−50	− 5
France	−54	−29	−29	−30
Belgium	−54	−45	−49	−26
Sweden	−35	−23	−27	−10
Italy	−46	−15	−38	+16
Australia	−61	−80	−73	+ 2
Netherlands	−58	−41	−37	−13

Source: *Britain and World Trade* (London: Political and Economic Planning, June 1947), p. 152.

A number of factors influence the effect of economic fluctuations on United States imports from the sterling area. Many of the things bought from the United Kingdom are highly finished consumer goods, often regarded as luxuries. The demand for this sort of product is apt to contract sharply when incomes fall. About 70 per cent of the imports from the sterling area are raw materials or semi-finished products that are used for further manufacture. Demand for these depends largely on the level of industrial production which may be more variable than national income. A decline in demand for raw materials is apt to lead to a drop in prices as well as to the purchasing of smaller quantities, so that the impact of the decline on the producer is increased. As Table 35 shows, prices of imports from the sterling area have, on the whole, varied more than the quantity of imports and have usually intensified the effect of fluctuations.

Table 35

PERCENTAGE CHANGES IN PRICE AND QUANTITY OF UNITED STATES IMPORTS FROM THE STERLING AREA

	PRICES			*QUANTITY*		
Years	*Rubber*	*Others*	*Total*	*Rubber*	*Others*	*Total*
1924-1927	+54	+15	+27	+39	− 4	0
1927-1929	−47	− 8	−19	+56	+11	+15
1929-1933	−75	−49	−56	−26	−38	−33
1933-1937	+282	+37	+84	+24	+61	+39
1937-1946	+48	+17	+37	−47	+35	+ 1
1946-1947	−28	+40	+11	+175	−26	+ 7
1947-1948	− 4	+20	+16	−17	+13	+ 5
1948-1949	−13	− 6	− 6	−31	− 8	−13

Source: Adler and others, cited, p. 19.

At the lowest point of the depression, the price index of United States imports from the overseas sterling area was little more than one-fifth what it had been at the high point in the twenties. No other area showed so great a spread and for raw material imports as a whole the index at the low point was more than one-third what it had been at the high point.[11]

[11] Adler and others, cited, p. 23.

There is some other evidence suggesting that the sterling area is more sensitive than other large regions to fluctuations in the American economy. Table 36 shows the reduction of United States imports in each of four years in which domestic economic activity declined. In every case, imports from the sterling area suffered more than total imports.

By comparing the decline in imports with the drop in the gross national product of the United States for the same years, the table calls attention to two other points. First, imports dropped more sharply than national activity. Second, until the recession of 1954, the impact of a downturn in the United States on imports from the sterling area was growing rather than abating. The meaning of the 1954 experience is

Table 36

FLUCTUATIONS OF VALUE OF UNITED STATES IMPORTS

	Percentage decline in:				*Relation of Import Decline to Decline in GNP:*	
	Total Imports	*Imports from UK*	*Imports from RSA*	*Gross National Product*	*Col. 2 / Col. 4*	*Col. 3 / Col. 4*
1929-30	−30	−36	−35	−12	3.0	2.9
1937-38	−35	−41	−50	− 6	6.8	8.3
1948-49	− 6	−19	−16	− 1	19	16
1953-54	− 6.5	− 8	−12	− 1	8	12

Source: 1929-49 calculated from Adler and others, cited. 1953-54 calculated from Department of Commerce publications.

Note: Figures for 1953-54 are general imports; others are imports for consumption.

discussed elsewhere. In terms of the rationale of sterling area policy the rather dramatic figures of earlier years are more relevant.

The fear of economic changes in the United States would seem then to have special justification in sterling countries. The significance of it has recently been put as follows by two British writers:

If the necessary stability in the American economy should not be attained, it has to be borne in mind that the opening up of larger sales opportunities in the U.S. markets would not be an unmixed blessing. It is not at all improbable that the current social philosophy of the U.K. would prefer a rather lower but assured external income to a higher but variable one with the probable consequence of periodical unemployment.[12]

If . . . [the United States] by reason of the large proportion borne by savings and investment to national income, is more subject than the rest of the world to fluctuations of economic activity, this effect will be periodically enhanced by "exports of unemployment" from [the United States]. In sum, it is possible that the gains to be derived from [America's] increasing productivity . . . may be . . . wiped out through the wastages of unemployment both of men and of other resources.[13]

Discrimination and Fluctuations

The general rationale in support of trade discrimination as a continuing policy, as I understand it, is that for one reason or another the countries which trade with the United States are faced frequently if not continually with the problem of making substantial changes in their economic activity simply to adjust themselves to temporary swings of mood in the United States, *unless* those countries take measures to place their relations with the United States on a special basis. If a group of countries—like the sterling area or the members of the European Payments Union—establish common policies in a joint effort to seal off some of the destabilizing pressures from the dollar market while adopting as tolerant an attitude as possible toward the assumed lesser pressures coming from inside the group, then the result in terms of net losses of potential real income may or may not amount to a sacrifice. Insulation from America implies such losses as are associated with an interruption of the processes of international specialization; it implies such gains as are associated with the continued use, though on less specialized a basis, of resources which would otherwise be temporarily idle in the course of adjustment. The net result of these gains and losses is likely to be more on the plus side for all concerned

[12] Sir Sidney Caine, "Some Doubts About Sterling Area Policy," *Lloyds Bank Review* (April 1954), p. 14.

[13] Honor Croome, cited, p. 30.

(including, it is argued, America) if the economic relationship of the countries in the bloc is a complementary one. It is argued that complementarity minimizes the dangers of inefficiency which insulation against dollar competition invites.

The estimation of the probable gains and losses for a given period of time and for a given group of countries seems to me to be complex almost to the point of being imponderable as far as practical politics are concerned. I doubt that the discrimination of the sterling area or of the EPU was, or could be, based on careful calculations, let alone supportable ones, of these gains and losses. During much of the first postwar decade, trade discrimination against American goods seemed necessary as a means of rationing scarce dollars, and the United States largely acquiesced in this view. It is quite a different matter to argue that discrimination must be continued as a basic element in policy in order to guard against the effects of chronic dollar shortages expected to result either from bursts of American productivity or from American recessions. Such arguments are open to question on grounds of, first, their assumptions about the United States economy, second, the appropriateness of trade discrimination as a method of insulation, and, third, the effectiveness of these methods in cushioning the impact of American fluctuations.

A full examination of these issues goes beyond what is feasible in this book. All that can be done is to raise some questions about the soundness of the rationale that says that the sterling area needs to protect itself against American fluctuations by a discriminatory trade policy.

The evidence of the impact of American fluctuations on sterling area exports is almost always taken as an indication that the main cause of the difficulty is in the United States and that the severe repercussion is inevitable. But even this seems to me to be open to doubt. The American economy is bound to fluctuate somewhat and these shifts are bound to affect imports. Therefore any country deeply involved in world trade is bound to feel some repercussions. It is far from clear that discriminatory trade policies actually provide very effective insulation unless they are carried to autarkic extremes. Is not the real need for margins that will make temporary disturbances tolerable and for flexibility that will make each national economy responsive to the continuous process of change in the world economy?

To what extent is the severity of the repercussions related to the efforts of the sterling area to avoid them? It is fairly widely recognized that an irony of discriminatory policy is a tendency to become less discriminating; walls keep out the good as well as the bad. Adjustments that should be welcomed become hard to distinguish and, if distinguished, hard to carry out.

Foreign-exchange reserves provide a margin. They can be used to tide a country over temporary difficulties. A "reserve crisis" occurs when the settlement of external deficits is draining the reserves at a fast rate. At what point the rate of drain can be regarded as critical certainly cannot be defined precisely. To someone who correctly foresees mounting difficulties in foreign transactions, the loss of a very small amount of official reserve would probably appear critical in the sense of calling for action. No doubt everyone agreed that the loss of $50 million to $75 million a week in the course of the 1951 crisis was an intolerable drain on reserves; at that rate, reserves would have been exhausted within a year. The menace was clear, and its popular recognition gave the government a firm basis for decreeing another round of grim slashes in import quotas.

The recognition of a reserve crisis permits the government to take politically unpleasant but, at last, politically tolerable steps to bring expenditures abroad down closer to the level of earnings from abroad. The sterling area, in opting against continuous small adjustments to world market conditions, may in effect merely be choosing larger adjustments at discrete intervals between which the use of reserves provides a respite. Is the reserve crisis really anything but the signal for decisive slashes of expenditures in a system which has ruled out day-to-day adjustments?

The data of recent years suggest that the common assumptions of the past need to be reexamined. The sterling area did not suffer much from the United States recession of 1953-54, which was deeper than that of 1949. Britain's balance of payments, and that of the sterling area, was generally encouraging. Then, Britain ran into difficulties in 1955 at a time when United States production achieved a new peak. The implication seems to be that the ups and downs of the British economy, augmented in a cumulative way by the activities of the rest of the sterling area, present as troublesome a problem as any caused by shifts in the prosperity of the dollar world.

For several years sterling area financial policy has been more flexible and more tolerant of market pressures than it was before 1950. The events of the last five years suggest but do not prove that a more flexible domestic economy and moderation in dollar defenses may better suit the nature of the menace than the policy of controlling trade within a discriminatory system.

Chapter 9

THE FUTURE OF STERLING

—O that a man might know
The end of this day's business ere it come!
But it sufficeth that the day will end,
And then the end is known.

JULIUS CAESAR

IT HAS BEEN the argument of this book that the future of sterling can best be guessed at by looking carefully at the broad contours of sterling operations and policies in the past and at present. Before raising the direct question of what is in store for sterling, let us see where we stand so far.

The burden of the preceding chapters is that the sterling monetary system has certain fundamentally regional characteristics. Probably the most important of these characteristics is that although sterling is not freely convertible into gold or dollars, it nonetheless is accepted by traders in a defined geographical area in settlement of debts. Next, the members of the sterling area regard sterling as their basic reserve, both for their internal currency structures and for their international transactions. Third, their credit structures are closely linked by habit and law. Finally, the members regard their relations with other monetary areas as largely a common problem, to be coped with on a group basis rather than individually. These characteristics express and reinforce traditional trends; members cooperate in making trade and investment within the area easier than with non-members.

In the earlier discussion of the roles of the various types of members—the metropole, the independent countries, and the dependencies—a number of key elements in postwar operations were noted. The metropole's hope of functioning as an effective independent money market depends directly on its ability to generate surpluses in its foreign transactions, and such surpluses, over anything but short periods of time, are related to the success with which domestic consumption is held below domestic production. Except for 1953 and 1954 there seems to have been a clear lack of success in keeping domestic consumption sufficiently in check to achieve a volume of savings consistent with a continuing and significant balance of payments surplus. The dollar accounts, with their critical bearing on the sterling area's reserves, have swung widely, but the general picture has been one of persistent large deficits. Britain's own efforts, then, have failed to provide net resources for projects in the less developed rest of the sterling area. At the same time Britain's dollar deficits have been the most significant factor in the incessant pressure on central reserves. Loans and grants from abroad have permitted Britain to play a broader role as the money center of the sterling system than it could have afforded on the basis of its own domestic and external savings. Developments in recent years, however, give at least tentative encouragement to the belief that a satisfactory metropolitan position can be established.

The independent members of the area as a group have run fairly consistent large deficits in current transactions with the rest of the world as a whole and even more troublesome deficits with the dollar world. South Africa, Australia, Ireland, India, and the Federation of Rhodesia and Nyasaland have accounted for the largest part of the deficits. In each case except Ireland, the deficits reflect extensive British investment, which in turn was made possible only because the flow of dollars into London from the dependencies and more importantly from sources outside the sterling area (the United States, Canada, and the International Monetary Fund) have exceeded Britain's *over-all* deficit on current account. In effect, Britain's dollar deficit was financed through dollars available from outside, leaving Britain with sterling funds that could be invested in the rest of the sterling area, particularly in the independent countries. The external accounts of the independent countries, especially Australia, have been very volatile and have caused considerable pressure on both British production and central reserves in relatively brief periods of time. But the flow of British investment to the rest of the sterling area has consolidated and extended the already broad commercial ties which make trade inside the area easier than trade with other areas. Meanwhile, the United Kingdom has remained the most important market and source of supply for the independent countries, though to a significantly smaller degree than in the earlier years of this century. As former dependencies became independent of direct British political control, Britain's role in their trade lessened.

Unlike the independent members the sterling dependencies have earned consistent over-all and dollar surpluses in their transactions with other countries. Development has not proceeded as rapidly as the surpluses would permit, and the result has been that the colonies accumulated funds in London—in effect, a poorer area invested in a richer one. This process has been reinforced by the mechanical relation between colonial curriencies and sterling, and also by policies under which a substantial portion of increased earnings due to favorable world prices for colonial agricultural products have been invested in London against the day when they may be needed to offset downward swings in world prices. The colonial contribution to central gold and dollar reserves since the war has been large and well sustained. In effect, colonial postwar savings in foreign transactions have been an important indirect source of financing British investment in the independent sterling area. Trade with the rest of the sterling area, especially with Britain, has dominated colonial exports and imports. Its commodity structure has followed the traditional colonial pattern: exports of a limited range of raw materials and agricultural products, and imports of a variety of manufactured goods, which were typically retailed through British commercial establishments in the colonies.

Much of this postwar picture is new. In the past, sterling was the currency of a nation which outstripped competing nations in the struggle for world supremacy. In the eighteenth and nineteenth centuries success bred further success; Britain's world power was solidly based on industrial leadership and maritime strength in a trading world whose communications were primarily over water and whose trade was primarily the swap of manufactures for food and raw materials. After many trials and errors in the financing of this maritime trade, Britain worked out a system of maintaining its international equilibrium by means of changes in interest rates, rather than by means of direct interference with trade, gold movements, or international exchange markets. Free trade, free exchanges, and variable interest rates were the props of a system geared to Britain's industrial lead and a pattern of trade that brought together a developed country and many undeveloped areas. The operation of the system often involved deflationary hardships for agricultural and industrial workers who were neither organized nor articulate enough to make their objections effective.

The system started to deteriorate when the conditions to which it was geared changed. Formidable industrial rivals appeared in the late nineteenth century as the United States and Germany, for example, became more important in the world market and as their domestic economies grew. Two world wars helped disrupt the old system and threw heavy burdens of adjustment on Britain. The conditions of trade were fundamentally altered as domestic markets became more important than international markets, and as democratic political evolution forced governments to give more attention to maintaining comfortable home markets than to keeping exchange rates stable. Although Britain's production and trade continued to grow, its relative economic position in the world shrank and its control of world finance was gradually lost. Britain's changes of interest rates could not smooth out a world market in which both demand and supply were critically influenced by production and consumption over which Britain had no control.

In the twentieth century the sterling system has been changed from a system of free trade and exchanges to one of inconvertibility and discrimination. Speculation about the future of the sterling system should rest on an appraisal of the strengths and weaknesses it has shown in the postwar period. This is not a simple process because the standards for judging strengths and weaknesses are not clear. Does survival in itself prove strength? Does the maintenance of an established pattern show the strength of durability or the weakness of a failure to adapt to changing circumstances? Are controls on imports an element of weakness or strength? Does a susceptibility to large shifts in the level of reserves reflect resilience or rigidity? Is a fixed exchange rate a liability or an asset to an international currency? Do the responsibilities of sterling countries to one another lead to an enlargement of instabilities or to a moderation of drains? The answer in each case depends on how high a value one sets on certain results and on what the realistic alternatives seem to be. Moreover, measures which may appear as an element of strength from the standpoint of a country's or region's stability of production (for example, discriminatory import controls), may appear as an element of weakness from the standpoint of the country's or region's orientation to the rest of the world. Similarly, inconvertibility may be seen as a reflection of strength or weakness, depending on what economic objective is seen as the more important aim of policy. The conflict which the political authorities of a country or region face, or feel they face, between avoiding uncomfortable national or regional adjustments and avoiding uncomfortable international adjustments must be borne in mind in any appraisal of weaknesses and strengths in a monetary structure.

The appraisal below is based on the assumption that the makers of sterling policy must try to operate a system which will permit a continuing development of the economies of both rich and poor members and that this development in turn will be translated into at least modest continuing increases in the standard of living without incurring serious interruptions of production and employment. Such interruptions could be forced by overspending at home or abroad. The two are familiarly regarded as related. I do not assume that policy makers, in their necessary deference to the people, always aim or must aim at the greatest possible volume of production, or at the greatest possible gains from trade with other communities. Nor do they have to be able to demonstrate that such achievements have been the result of their policies, any more than their critics could demonstrate that things would have been better had alternative policies been followed. Policy is vindicated if things are generally on the upgrade and if unpopular risks have been avoided. Popular fear of a theoretically correct policy is likely to make it unworkable, just as public confidence in a questionable policy may permit it to work pretty well.

The Weaknesses of the Sterling Area

The chief weaknesses, or continuing problems, of the sterling area shown by the postwar experience seem to me to be the following.

1. There has been a tendency, particularly in the first six postwar years, to underestimate the relationship between internal and external financial balance. It was no doubt natural enough that after the bitter privation of war years people would want to spend the funds they had accumulated in the form of liquid war savings, and would look to foreign help to permit a little loosening of the belt. Some years from now it may well be the judgment of economic historians that the postwar crises in the balance of payments were very slight readjustments when compared with the magnitudes of war finance. But it was an awkward way of running things. Britain scarcely knew from one day to the next how the grocery bill for imported food could be paid. An island which had commanded the admiration of the Western world in its thorough commitment of resources, human and material, in defense of democratic principles, had lots of money (Treasury promises) but, for the time being, not much in the way of production to satisfy the monetary claims. As a temporizing measure direct controls were applied—to imports, to domestic consumption, to travel abroad, to the purposes for which banks would be permitted to cash the checks drawn against them. These controls were in the nature of an emergency levee against a continuing flood of money. They did not by themselves create the conditions for continuing balance.

2. The second weakness has been a tendency to overestimate the speed and effectiveness of direct controls as a means of reestablishing balance in external accounts. A system which depends for balance on the tightening of import controls necessarily is subject to the delay leading up to the ad-

ministrative decision that a cut is necessary, and then the subsequent delay before the decision brings about an actual cut in expenditures. The total delay is usually estimated at three or four months. In a period of heavy reserve drain this delay is likely to be enough to weaken foreign confidence in the currency.

3. A third weakness has been the low state of the system's reserves available for settling deficits with the non-sterling world. Fundamentally the purpose of internationally usable reserves in any monetary system is to assure that commitments to the rest of the world can be promptly covered, or, in short, to keep the system liquid. Some facets of the complicated question of how large a reserve is needed will be considered below. For the moment, the point is simply that reserves have been consistently strained in the effort to meet the obligations arising in the course of sterling operations. Ironically, the policy of limiting the scope of conversion of sterling into gold and dollars through the maintenance of direct controls has increased the need for large reserves. This is because a system which depends on administrative review of spending and paying rates is subject to delays before the two rates are made to jibe. Meanwhile, the only means of tiding over current deficits is to use reserves. Since 1951 the major objective of financial policy has been a more flexible and sensitive system in which small and prompt adjustments of deficits can be made more comfortably than large and delayed ones.

4. There has been a heavy dependence on resources outside the system for emergency difficulties, general development, and defense. The availability of such resources from the United States and Canada constitutes a practical testimonial to the importance of the sterling system to the Western world in general. But the fact that help on such a large scale was needed—it amounted to almost the total sterling debts Britain accumulated during the war—suggests that the sterling financial system remained far short of independent operation.

5. This extent to which the postwar operation of the sterling area has depended on the contribution of the DOTs is a potential weakness of considerable importance. The DOTs

have run a trade surplus, supplied many of the area's dollars, and, in effect, financed much of the United Kingdom's investment in the ISA. But as economic development in the DOTs proceeds their imports will increase. Even if the prices of their raw material exports remain favorable, the DOTs are likely to reduce their relative contribution to the dollar pool. As they become independent the DOTs may well come to behave more like the ISA in the postwar years. Whether the problems that result will be serious remains to be seen. There is certainly the possibility that their development will require further adjustments in the area and an alteration in methods of operation.

6. Finally, the system has from time to time exhibited a worrisome lack of coordination. Financial policies of the members have not been dovetailed. If one member spends more than it earns on imports, the usual case has been that a number of other members are doing the same thing. External deficits in general and dollar deficits in particular have tended to be cumulative rather than offsetting, so that the counterbalances on which a credit system must depend have not come into effect. In their absence, difficulties have been met by tardy conferences to deal with emergencies. A regional system, whether international like the sterling system or national like the Federal Reserve System, requires either automatic or at least speedy methods of coordination. In shying away from formal methods, the sterling countries developed methods of coordination designed to reduce their difficulties with one another and their difficulties as a group in transactions with the rest of the world.

The American "Case" Against the Sterling Area

Before turning to the pleasanter task of listing some of the strengths of the sterling system, there should be a statement of the objections which American critics have made to the way the sterling system has operated in the postwar period. Often the case has been overstated, and concentration on the criticisms does not reflect the importance which United States opinion assigns to the efforts of sterling countries to operate a sound international currency. In approaching the capsulated form of the argument immediately below, it should be remembered that neither official nor unofficial opinion in America has been agreed on what sort of sterling policy was best suited to the interests of sterling area members and the rest of the world. Nor has it been agreed at all times how far the United States should go in urging sterling countries, and particularly Britain in its key role, to make major changes in international financial policy. While the prevalent view has probably been that the sterling system should move toward convertibility and the elimination of discrimination, there has been no serious disposition to use American influence to damage or break up the sterling area mechanisms. There has probably been a general belief that until Britain is ready to take its place in a multilateral system, the sterling area—with its imperfections from the point of view of most Americans—is preferable to the likely alternatives. Reinforcing this last view has been the opinion that support for the sterling area is warranted because it is in many respects a source of strength for Britain and a factor of political and economic cohesion and integrity in the free world.

However one analyzes the course of American opinion, postwar United States policy certainly has proceeded along these lines. Apart from doubts as to how much change in British policy would be desirable, there was—and is—the serious question as to how much money the United States would have to be prepared to stake to help the sterling area undertake major changes. The Anglo-American Financial Agreement embodied a major and formal effort to re-design sterling policy in international transactions. It failed of its particular objectives in financial policy, although many, including the present writer, would count it a success in the more basic sense of bringing resources from an area from which they could be spared to an area in which they were badly needed.

During the war it was widely agreed on both sides of the Atlantic that postwar international money markets should not be allowed to fall into the chaotic circumstances of the twenties and thirties. The character of the order that was to be introduced into the chaos is broadly set forth in the Articles of Agreement of the International Monetary Fund. Instead of "exporting unemployment" through "competitive depreciation of currencies,"—in the familiar phrases of the day—countries subscribing to the Fund would agree on solid rates of exchange for their currencies, and would maintain them within close margins by the use of reserves or by such other measures as might be needed. The joining nations also looked to an ever increasing freedom in commercial policy. This was thought of as an international attitude of making trade between nations easier. As financial and commercial barriers to international trade would be withdrawn, trade would grow, production would grow, the stability of recognized rules would be reflected in a more stable commerce, and all nations would gain from recognizing that the prosperity—or adversity—of one affects all the others. The political grounding of these aspirations is somewhat more persuasive than their economic rationale, and this difference has much to do with the continuing debate over what the rules of international finance should be.

The two broadest American criticisms of postwar sterling operations have turned on *inconvertibility* and *discrimination*. The two problems are closely related. Sterling has remained inconvertible into dollars except on such terms as sterling monetary authorities decide from time to time are appropriate. In deciding what terms are appropriate, the authorities consider the nature of the purpose for which a holder of sterling is asking to exchange it for dollars and they consider where the person lives. American critics argue that this governmental control over exchange transactions and imports in general has obviously led to the establishment of priorities which are at odds with the economic gains possible under a free-market system. More specifically it is argued that the priorities have worked to the serious disadvantage of American producers by excluding them arbitrarily from lines of commerce in which they have a genuine competitive advantage over their preferred rivals.

From the standpoint of American traders, the most familiar instances of how sterling area discrimination hurts them are in the field of durable consumer goods, which are continuously kept at a low priority. For instance, most Australian consumers consider American cars as lower priced and better adapted to the roads and spaces of the country than cars obtainable from Britain or elsewhere in the sterling area. Before the war, import policies were freer and American cars predominated in the Australian market. Since the war they have been virtually excluded in accordance with the standard sterling area principle that scarce dollars should be reserved for *essentials* and that any item obtainable in the area, even though costlier or less suitable or subject to delivery delays, could not be regarded as essential. Similarly with refrigerators, laundry conveniences, radios, kitchen gadgets, and the long list of cheaply priced, mass-produced articles with which the American standard of living is identified all over the world.

Another cause for familiar protests from the western side of the Atlantic has been the barriers erected in the sterling area against transferring funds previously invested, earned or inherited there. The use of scarce dollars to permit such transfers has been regarded in the area as far less important than, say, the furthering of new trade and investment. Since the United States imposed no comparable barrier to the transfer of funds or to the importation of goods from the sterling area, these discriminations against the dollar area had the appearance in the dollar world of being obviously flagrant abuses of principles of reciprocity.

But beyond the private commercial and financial difficulties which Americans could—and did—point to, there have been broadly based criticisms of sterling area practices as detrimental to the development of a multilateral and free system of world finance. Countries of the Western world are agreed that ideally the freest possible foreign-exchange and trade policies by the international community would best suit the long-term interests of all countries participating in it. This proposition, though demonstrably true only in the context of numerous and carefully defined assumptions, has a kind of offhand charm when it is set against its opposite. No one would argue with much heart that the greatest possible restriction of international exchange and trade policies could do anything but ruin the interests of the community's would-be traders, with serious prejudice to the standard of living. The United States does not follow as free a trade policy as Britain did when it was, as the United States now is, the manufacturing center of the world. Britain and its sterling associates do not follow now as free a trade policy as the United States does. The sterling-dollar debate goes on in the course of efforts to appraise whose defective degree of freedom of trade is the more important in the general international market. There is also the effort to appraise who should move first and how far. In the pronouncements following the 1952 conference of Commonwealth finance ministers, it was made clear that the question of greater freedom in sterling area rules was regarded as tied to the question of greater freedom in United States trade policy and the building up of much larger reserves in the sterling area.

In short, the range of American criticism has two points of emphasis. First, that the sterling policy of imposing limits on transfers between the sterling and dollar worlds is unfair to United States traders and in all probability denies to members of the sterling area some of the gains that have been traditionally envisaged as the prize of being able to buy in the cheapest markets and sell in the dearest. All markets must be accessible on uniform terms if policy makers are to feel sure that commerce is yielding maximum reciprocal gains. Second, the sluggishness of a system dependent on administrative decisions rather than on the quick interplay of the market is crisis-prone and inflation-prone, and therefore set in a mold of crisis-breeding inflation, and inflation-concealing restrictions.

These are sweeping propositions and, as bluntly stated here, probably overstate the difference between the actual policies of the sterling area and the United States. Sterling trends since the 1951-52 crisis have been generally directed against the "unfairness" and "sluggishness" of a system based on extensive controls. This seems apparent, even though there remains a question of whether the improving productive position of the sterling world made possible the greater flexibility in financial policy, or vice versa. It also leaves open the question of whether sterling countries should not have taken advantage of their prosperity to go even further in making the sterling elephant's joints more flexible. On this latter question, most American critics would answer Yes, and on the former many if not most would do the same.

My own view, suggested in preceding chapters and stated more explicitly in the last sections of this chapter, is that the policy debate between sterling countries and dollar countries has involved a conception of convertibility and import quotas that pictures only part of the problem of how sterling fits into the structure of world finance.

What Sort of Convertibility?

"Convertibility" and "inconvertibility" are widely used terms in discussions of international money difficulties. The need to use them comes up with such frequency that many students are likely to call them simply CV and ICV, like initials for daily associates in an office. Broadly the terms are merely convenient means of tagging the ease or difficulty of exchanging a given money for that of another country, and there is little agreement on when difficulties are small enough to warrant designation of a currency as CV rather than ICV. No currency can be completely inconvertible and still be called a *currency*. In fact, given enough indirection, ingenuity, or infraction of law, every currency in the world is convertible into every other currency on some terms. There is universal convertibility in this literal sense. But the ease and regularity with which a currency, say the dollar, can be changed into other currencies is so much greater than in the case of another currency, like the pound, that the notion of convertibility as commonly used makes a difference of kind out of a difference of degree. Anyone who decides that a given currency is convertible or inconvertible makes an implied judgment as to what *ought* to be a country's rules for international currency exchanges and how strictly such rules should be enforced.

This implied judgment involves a vision of a complete system of international finance. For such a vision to become a reality there is a ticklish question as to how much international credit or gold is available to support the operation of the "rules of the game." The basic postwar vision of the Western world is expressed in the Articles of Agreement of the International Monetary Fund. There were many controversies among participants, both during negotiations and during later debates, on how the rules should be applied but the general lines of operation are clear. Members would define the value of their currencies in gold, or in dollars at their gold equivalence at the beginning of the Fund's operations. Members would maintain the market value of their currencies on international exchanges within narrow limits of this defined gold/dollar parity. Members would resist devaluation, avoid exchange controls and trade restrictions, and strive for the rising levels of production associated with common prosperity. The Fund system of convertibility is a system of fixed and stable exchange rates, non-interference in international exchanges except to support the defined values of currencies, and limited assistance out of the Fund's pool of subscribed funds to tide members over temporary derangements in their balances of payments.

The exchange system embodied in the Fund agreement has not been achieved. Members have dealt with their balance of payments difficulties primarily through sweeping restrictions on current transactions. The expected regime in which exchange and import controls would not be an important factor in current trade has not been realized. Similarly, members have in fact had little recourse to the Fund's pool of currencies in their efforts to ride out "temporary" deficits. Currency devaluation and discriminatory import quotas have been the standard techniques in coping with difficulties in balances of payments. The Fund conception that such difficulties would be met mainly by a tightening, as needed, of internal financial policy has been exceptional. The currencies of Fund members are still not interconvertible on the basis of Fund rules.

This account of the failure of the Fund's system of convertibility is not intended to rule out its practicability under circumstances less distorted than in this period of postwar adjustment. While restrictions on trade and exchange have been eased by Fund members and other countries in the recent years of general prosperity, the fact that such restrictions persist suggests that the Fund's rules are too uniform and its resources too limited to suit the varying needs of the members. Perhaps the less convertible sort of convertibility now practiced by members is about as much as the level of international reserves and the international policies to achieve stability in production will permit.

Since the collapse of the all-out convertibility experiment in 1947 under the Anglo-American Financial Agreement, the sterling area has aimed at a more modest type of convertibility, namely non-resident convertibility for limited but nonetheless broad purposes. In international discussions after the 1952 Commonwealth communiqué it became clear that the gist of the effort to make sterling convertible into dollars would be to allow all persons living outside the sterling area to trade their sterling for dollars at official rates for current purposes. No similar privilege would be extended by the members to themselves; sterling held by residents of the area would remain convertible into dollars only in such amounts and for such purposes as might be agreed by the governments from time to time. The theory has been that sterling countries would gain more from the indirect benefits of non-resident convertibility than they could from allowing themselves freer access to the central gold and dollar reserves. This procedure left open the possibility that in the event of a drain on central reserves arising from the behavior of the non-residents who were newly enjoying dollar-conversion facilities, residents would have to tighten discriminatory restrictions on their own dollar spending. In such an event, the new "internationalization" of sterling would be effected by a further consolidation of regional sterling policy. The difference would be a reduction of important international monetary areas to two—sterling and dollar.

At first, the 1952 proposals for convertibility were widely regarded as bold, new, and perhaps even within early grasp. But as discussions proceeded in varying degrees of formality in Europe and the United States as well as in the sterling area many ifs and doubts arose. Would it not be better to proceed cautiously, avoiding definite pronouncements on wider convertibility until the success of a freer regime appeared more certain? The dismal experience of the experiment in 1947 was well remembered. Reserves should be higher, in view of the likely ups and downs of the sterling area's accounts with the rest of the world and in view of past experience with the volatile behavior of non-sterling countries when once given greater conversion facilities. There should be some assurance of adequate support from the dollar world in the case of unexpected drains. European countries should undertake similar conversion policies to minimize foreseeable pressures on sterling reserves. The earning capacity of sterling countries in the rest of the world should be supported by the assurance of liberal import policies. And perhaps the step should not be taken before it became more certain that the sterling area's prosperity was not just a short reprieve from further crises. Since 1952 experience on this last point has been encouraging but not so much so as to dispel all fears. On the other points there has been only partial encouragement. Consequently, the dramatic step of announcing broad convertibility for all non-residents of the sterling area has not been taken, and has been in fact abandoned in favor of a policy of gradual steps. When enough of these steps have been taken, it is argued, full convertibility will exist and meanwhile there will be as much convertibility as is feasible. It has been noted that in 1954-55 virtual non-resident convertibility was achieved at rates very close to official rates. Perhaps more important is the fact that it has been achieved without giving assurances of its continuation—assurances which might have to be withdrawn in adverse circumstances at a great cost to the hard-won strengthening of sterling's prestige.

In deciding on a gradual approach to convertibility rather than the faster approach usually called "a dash," the British authorities have liberalized import quotas, including dollar quotas. In effect, this trend has reduced slightly the sharpness of the distinction between conversion facilities accorded to residents of the sterling area and those accorded to non-residents, but there still is a sharp distinction. It has been made even more apparent now that *de facto* convertibility exists in the officially supported markets for all "transferable sterling."

The Strengths of the Sterling System

As of now, the sterling system has more strengths than weaknesses. This is implicit in the fact that it is still a going concern. But our interest in this chapter is in the future of sterling, and the question is whether its present strong points give promise of its continuation in more or less its present form. Like the list of the system's weaknesses, the following list of strengths is riddled with personal judgments. What strikes me as a strength might occur to another as a fatal flaw, depending heavily on one's view of the whole present system of international finance.

The strengths of the sterling system, as I see them, are:

1. Production has steadily risen throughout the area and trade within the area as well as with the rest of the world has steadily grown. This has encouraged members to believe that the regional financial arrangements in which they participate are, at the very least, not inimical to economic progress. Many members have already seen the effects of this economic growth translated into improved standards of living. The poorer and more populous members have confidence that their plans for economic development will shortly be reflected in higher living standards. Their confidence is an element of strength in the sterling area, even though there are grave reasons to doubt that it is warranted. In any case, their large sterling holdings constitute a heavy commitment to the affairs of the area; they would scarcely choose to leave a "bank" in which they have so large a deposit.

2. A second factor of strength is in the complementarity of the members' economies. The degree of complementarity is not demonstrable and has in fact been the cause of heated controversy. In earlier chapters it has been noted that the simple complementarity implicit in an association which brings together a specialized center of manufacturing and a series of raw material producing areas has been dwindling for some time. As the less-developed "raw material" areas become economically more mature, this simple complementarity is bound to weaken even more. But this evolutionary course does not mean that sterling associates will fail to complement one another in a less simple way. For example, a

very large portion of world trade—perhaps three-fourths, according to United Nations studies—is accounted for by less than a dozen large manufacturing countries. In the complicated matrix of world trade, there seems to be little reason to suppose that trade must be only between the developed economies and the undeveloped ones, or only between manufacturing centers and raw material producers, or only between the rich and the poor. As earlier chapters have shown, the sterling area has also had a *financial* complementarity in the availability of gold and dollar surpluses of some members to offset the deficits of others, giving at least a temporary practicability to the operation of the area's current accounts with the rest of the world.

3. The force of a habit of association is probably the most important strength of the sterling area. For most members the habit has been friendlier than an institution, more like a club, or from the standpoint of finance, "home." Members may quarrel with one another; it is a privilege of membership. For example, Australia, which is seriously dependent on the central reserves of gold and dollars, is a formidable advocate of automatic convertibility for the area. The Union of South Africa, in the happy position of being a gold and dollar contributor, is equally vociferous. Yet both countries are heavily dependent on traditional British sources of capital to maintain their investment programs and would not lightly put aside the access to capital available in London, even though not originating there. Beyond that, the sterling countries are used to conducting their trade on the basis of London facilities—banks, brokers, insurance houses, shipping, and commercial agents. They are familiar with the personalities of their British counterparts, they find the London rates favorable compared to New York, and they consider the service good. In spite of reserve crises, they feel that they have not been let down or exposed to great risks—their stake in sterling has functioned fairly well as a buffer in the changes they have experienced in accounts with the rest of the world as well as with one another. Lacking independent credit status in other markets, they are drawn to the sterling markets they know.

4. Often in the non-sterling world it is argued that the

very informality of sterling arrangements is a weakness of the association. From a financial standpoint, relatively little is spelled out. There are no articles of agreement to specify the obligations of the members. But the members regard this informality as a strength, and make a clear point of it to visitors from outside. Potentially it may be a weakness, true. Who knows exactly what is supposed to be done in a given set of circumstances? The members argue, rightly I am persuaded, that in continually unpredictable circumstances it is better to get together and work out the answers than to have tailor-made solutions originally designed for earlier problems but without much style for present ones. This looseness of organization is not always a point of strength at a given moment, but over the longer haul it gives members a sense of room in which to knock around rather than be cramped. Regionally restricted though the area is, its members are not claustrophobes.

5. Finally, and closely related to foregoing points of strength, is the notion of members that they belong together. One member's reasons for this feeling differ greatly from another's. A partial rationale is that many members have sterling to spend and therefore must abide by the rules; others have dollars to gain from the operation of the dollar pool. These are immediate and powerful reasons for some members. If one has large holdings of sterling which can be spent on better terms if one remains in the club, then remain; if one can get more dollars as a member, then continue to pay the dues. But these reasons of immediate financial gain do not adequately account for the reluctance of members to leave the club. Egypt left, and was still able to get as favorable terms for spending its large sterling holdings as those who remained in. As for access to the area's dollars, we have seen the growing amount made available to non-members, particularly through the European Payments Union. It may be that the stronger rationale for hanging together is that, though the channels are not specified in advance, one member of the sterling area can expect help from the others.

Liquidity and Flexibility

There are two reasons for believing that the position of the sterling area is improving. First, the weaknesses listed above have for the most part become less worrisome in the course of the postwar period, and the strengths have become stronger. Second, there has been steady improvement in the relationship between the amount of sterling outstanding and the volume of production, against which the money supply represents a claim. This second line of improvement requires further spelling out, and this is the concern of this section.

There is no magic ratio to cite as the proper one at a given moment between the volume of money and the volume of production, and such a ratio is not in fact needed to trace the trend of a monetary system's liquidity. Fundamentally the role of Britain in the sterling area is to assure its "liquidity," used here to mean a balance between the monetary claims presented and the resources available for the claimants. In the course of the war, as we have seen, both sides of the balance were adversely affected. Sterling claims against the British Treasury grew rapidly as Britain obligated itself wherever possible to pay later for what it could obtain at the moment, thus maximizing the volume of resources it could marshal for war. Similarly, the marshalling for war of Britain's own resources, both old (investments and reserves) and new (production), reduced what was available for the claimants.

Britain's production at current prices in 1946 was about half again as much in 1938, against almost a fourfold increase of money supply. In comparison, the value of production in the United States just after the war was some two and a half times larger than prewar, against an increase in money supply of just under three and a half times.

The change in the relationship between claims (money supply) and availabilities (production and reserves) gives a crude indication of the liquidity, or solvency, of an economy and its monetary system. It is also a crude indication of the readiness of a monetary system to maintain the convertibility of its money at stable rates for current transactions. A comparison of the broad trends in the two countries suggests that immediately after the war the liquidity of the sterling system was less than half of what it was before the war; in the case of the United States, about three-fourths. By 1954 the United States had gone beyond the point of its prewar liquidity while Britain had not reached it.[1]

Other broad indicators of liquidity also show a considerable improvement. Sterling claims held outside the United Kingdom have been diminishing steadily in relation to total money supply, official reserves, national income, and exports, although the proportions are still much higher in each case than the corresponding ones for the United States.

In circumstances when liquidity deteriorates a great deal, as it did during the war in the sterling system, insolvency can be averted only by reducing in one manner or another the pressure of claims until the resources to meet them can be expanded. The means of doing this, in what has probably been the order of importance in the postwar practices of the sterling world, are: arbitrarily reducing the pressure of domestic claims through import controls; writing down claims through devaluation; freezing claims through blocking balances and scheduling releases over a period of time (basically, funding); and inhibiting the further growth of claims through tighter credit policies, in the hope that liquidity will be improved by a relatively faster growth of production and an inflow of capital.

Since the war, the short-term swings in the earning and spending habits of sterling area members have been large in relation to the resources of the center of the system. In the first six postwar years—the crisis years—policy was directed mainly at a reduction of the rate at which claims could be presented. Import controls, rationing, and devaluation all countered the pressure which the swollen flow of sterling claims exerted against British production and central reserves. But these were the policy instruments of a lethargic

[1] These are crude calculations based on International Monetary Fund figures for money supply and production. There are many limitations on comparing accurately either the money supply or the production of two countries, but the broad trends within single countries are indicative.

system. To quote Professor Robbins' Stamp Memorial Lecture again:

> Undoubtedly the external difficulties have been severe. But this does not explain our failure to meet them. We might well expect that they would affect our standard of living. But there is nothing in the nature of things which should lead us to expect that they should cause a persistent shortage of foreign exchange. It is surely a very poor view of the limits of policy and organization to assume that we can only keep going when nothing untoward occurs. If a car fails to reach its destination, if it is continually running into the side, or if it is continually having to solicit hauls from passing lorries, we should not regard it as a sufficient explanation that the roads are not level and straight, that there are hills to ascend and corners to turn. And, indeed, when one examines this assumption in detail, it is sometimes a little difficult to conceive any circumstances in which, in present moods, we could be expected to prosper.

The policies of the present Conservative government have been directed more to the problem of increasing the responsiveness of the British economy than to restricting credit. True, interest rates have been raised from time to time, and the increases have made London a more attractive place for foreign funds at times when foreign funds were desired to bolster reserves. Some observers question how far or how directly the increases have affected the volume of domestic credit. But most are agreed that the return to a policy of flexible interest rates has made the credit market itself more flexible.

Other significant steps have been taken to place more reliance on the guidance of market forces than on administrative plans. Most of these are familiar. Rationing of consumer supplies has ended, and domestic subsidies stopped. Relatively free private markets in the handling of major world commodities have been restored. The volume of government purchasing has been reduced. A free exchange market, both spot and forward, has been reestablished in Europe as a result of British arrangements with continental countries.

These changes have in fact been accompanied by a distinct improvement in Britain's current external accounts, although it is difficult to appraise the possible causal relationship between the measures and the favorable situation. The 1951 crisis was not arrested until the spring of 1952. At that time the terms of trade started shifting markedly in the United Kingdom's favor; Britain achieved an external surplus in the second half of 1952 and the first half of 1953. And during the first half of 1953 dollar accounts were brought into balance. These favorable developments were of about the same magnitude as the change in the terms of trade.

In 1954-55, despite the new policies, the balance of payments again deteriorated. So to determine whether the freeing of the British economy has been an effective structural change that will make it respond more quickly to adverse external developments and hence be less likely to run into another crisis remains to be seen. The economy has not been faced with deeply adverse developments in the first years of the new policy of flexibility.

The Future of Sterling

To inquire into the future of sterling involves speculation about the future shape of the United Kingdom, of the sterling area, and of the structure of international finance. The more precise the lines of inquiry become, the less certain are the answers; the more the lines of inquiry are broadened, the less meaningful the answers. Much of what remains to be said here is speculation based on the hints afforded by past operations and by statements of intention made by our contemporaries in the sterling world.

My view is that the sterling area is basically viable and not inimical to the valid hopes of the United States for a free system of international trade and finance. This speculation cannot be proved, nor could a contrary one. Judged by the record of action, the policy of the United States has been to give heavy support to the system even while criticizing its regionality and restrictiveness. The tendency of the sharper critics, who for the most part have accepted the need to support the system, has been to exaggerate the deepness of postwar difficulties and to minimize the extent to which restrictive sterling practices have been the least risky response to a world trade that has grown far more rapidly than have orderly means of financing it. For instance, there are no international banking arrangements that can do what the Federal Reserve System does in the United States to promote the stability and growth of internal trade. This is not surprising; "international" implies a divided house, just as "national" implies a united one. And there is no united view about the future of sterling.

Of the various views, there are two extremes, one a theory of decline and fall, the other a theory of rebirth. Both are worth noting. The theory of decline is that the United Kingdom is a dwindling star in the constellation of world power; as the British sun sets in the world of the West, so too must sterling's. The theory of rebirth is that Britain has had to concentrate on two major wars in recent years and that the financial effect of discommoding sterling in world markets is temporary. Both theories can be argued with a wealth of facts. Neither is really plausible according to the argument of this book.

Take the decline theory first. The premise is that British power is no longer emphatic in the design of national powers in the world. Britons themselves are likely to state this premise, at least in the context of discussions of the military and economic power of the various nations. The theory of decline takes many forms. A familiar one is that there are simply too many people living in the British isles to extract a "modern" standard of living out of seriously depleted natural resources, notably coal. The spinning jenny was a great thing, a corollary of the argument goes, but after all the world has gone a little beyond that. Other versions of the argument are even darker. The whole West (whatever a "west" which is flung all around the world can possibly mean as identified in this way) is in a decline, and the British decline is only a dismal sideshow in the affair.

> It is a well known fact that in general, centers of commerce and industry rise through some definite advantage which stimulates their growth, that they flourish for a time and then decline in power. . . . Sometimes they disappear altogether as did Troy, Mycenae, Carthage, and numerous others. Sometimes they become second-rate market towns serving only a restricted area. . . . The conditions which make it possible for any city or coun-

try to attain great preeminence in industry and commerce and to support a large part of its population by trading with other areas are necessarily uncertain and temporary because, as a rule, they arise out of the exercise of some monopoly of skill in production, or experience in trade, or in the possession of certain natural resources which make for low production costs. These advantages can seldom, if ever, be long maintained in the face of competition from other peoples and other areas.[2]

Or better perhaps as Coleridge put it:

> Down the river did glide, with wind and with tide,
> A pig with vast celerity;
> And the Devil look'd wise as he saw how the while
> It cut its own throat. "There!" quoth he, with a smile,
> "Goes England's commercial prosperity."

The second theory—the rebirth of sterling—has a long list of adherents. Tennyson found words for it:

> What shock has fool'd her since, that she should speak
> So feebly? Wealthier—wealthier—hour by hour!
> The voice of Britain, or a sinking land,
> Some third-rate isle half-lost among her seas?

The belief of the adherents to this view, if no better grounded than that of their opponents, is at least less melancholy. It is still an important and maybe the central prop of British financial policy. The argument runs that there is still concentrated in London a tremendous amount of international "know how" and that if Britain manages to tidy up the oppressive debts which arose out of the war effort and postwar reconstruction there is no reason why London should not again play its classic nineteenth-century role as the world center of finance.

In short, the decline theory is that Britain must give in to its obvious senility in the younger-paced "dynamics" of the current world markets. The rebirth theory is that there is nothing wrong with sterling apart from the heavy volume of obligations that a country gets into in the course of two closely spaced all-out wars. In the old days the sterling sys-

[2] Warren S. Thompson, *Population Problems,* 4th ed., (New York: McGraw-Hill, 1953), pp. 329-331.

tem seems to have been primarily a means of financing a worldwide security system. Today it appears as a system of extended obligations and diminished resources. The British defense obligation—a voluntary one—continues in spite of the very great relative impairment of Britain's economic power in the world.

The complex of sterling has never been and cannot be more than the financial reflection of Britain's power in the world. Before this power is discounted, politically or economically, people who live in the United States must ask themselves two searching questions. First, is the dollar, which is now prized as the international currency par excellence, really on a basis that makes it internationally usable? The second is primarily a political question. Does the United States, with its overwhelming internal market, intend, at some possible cost to itself in short-run terms, to provide the credit basis for world commerce which it alone is now in a position to provide, whether through international institutions or through its own money market?

Neither a "collapse" of the sterling area by means of complete non-resident convertibility, nor a reappearance of sterling as again *the* international money of the world seems likely. Collapse of a currency is hard to imagine in the case of an orderly and economically growing nation. Restoration of international financial primacy for the currency of a nation no longer wielding primary economic power is equally hard to imagine. Britain's economy is strong and it is growing, but in relation to the world economy it is no longer large enough to spare from its own consumption sufficient output to form the real basis for meeting the calls which world traders, in their greatly enlarged market, must make from time to time. But there is no reason that it should not meet the calls of a more closely defined region. Between financial decline and rebirth, there is the intermediate position of regionality. That is the position of sterling now.

One operating aspect of this structure has made its regionality definite. The members adopt common, although not always uniform, policies of limiting through direct controls the imports of all members from non-sterling areas and particularly from the dollar area. So important is this one operating aspect of the system that many observers, both inside and outside the geographic sterling area, consider that the lifting of these import restrictions would amount to a complete dissolution of the regional character of the system, or at least that what regional bonds would be left after the removal of import restrictions would be so loose that the regional character would no longer be distinguishable.

From the standpoint of those who give first importance to this one operating aspect, namely discriminatory quantitative restrictions, the main question about the future of the sterling system is whether sterling countries will give up the use of import quotas, thereby deleting the *regional* clearing aspects of the system, or whether they will continue them and thus maintain the explicitly regional character of sterling.

"Discrimination" is described here as an *operating* feature of the sterling system rather than a *structural* one, in the belief that the regionality of the system does not turn primarily on the use of discriminatory quotas. Discriminatory quotas are more the result than the cause of the regionality of the sterling system. Once given the traditional pattern of members' behavior in accepting sterling in settlement of their debts among themselves, and given circumstances under which non-members are disinclined to do so, there is the essence of a regional monetary system, and discrimination becomes simply one possible method of handling the region's payments with other areas. Even without practicing discrimination, which one notable economist has described as merely the opposite of promiscuity, the region might handle its deficits with the rest of the world by concerted exchange-rate depreciation, or by concerted intraregional deflation, or by coordinated tariff policy, or by concerted borrowing (or begging) policies abroad. The adoption of such measures would not render the system less regional even though it abolished direct controls on imports coming from outside.

The real question before the sterling countries is whether any, most, or all of them, prefer to face their payments problems with each other and with the non-sterling world on an individual basis rather than on a group basis. If enough members should opt for independent orientation, that would be the end of a regional sterling system, because sterling would no longer be regarded as acceptable in final payments even among former colleagues of the system. The important change from the standpoint of the operating practice of import controls would be in the abandonment of regional concert, not in the abandonment of quantitative restrictions which might and probably would be even more intensively applied by at least some of the divorcees from the system.

There is no apparent reason why relations between regional groupings of countries should not develop along the lines of the American philosophy of stable exchange rates. Theoretically the possibilities should be no different between regions than between countries; a national market area may be more arbitrary than a regional one. However, with the tremendous national expansion of the markets of big countries—the United States market, for example, is about four times the size of the entire market of the sterling area—world trade has come to be dominated by big national markets. With the tremendous expansion of the markets of big countries and of their trade together, the problem of international credit has been aggravated, probably to the extent of becoming a new problem and one to be distinguished from the problem of restoring systematic monetary relations which in earlier days were worked out for a much smaller volume of trade.

Even apart from "the dollar problem," which since the war has persuaded sterling countries to restrict their imports from the dollar world, the trade problems within the area would have called for considerable changes in the almost automatic gold standard as it operated in the late nineteenth century, or even in the modified gold standard as it operated before the last war. Even in the absence of preoccupation with the dollar supply, serious problems would have remained: wartime sterling balances and how they might be used inside the area; the quick wartime accumulations of sterling, especially by the African colonies and Malaya; the terms of recourse of one sterling member to credit in the market of another, and especially the recourse of all members to the metropole; the means of dealing with the large deficits which one member, for example Australia, runs from time to time with other members; the scope and direction of economic development of the members of the area; the stabilization of prices among members; the maintenance of full employment and the stimulation of production; and so on.

Within the sterling area sterling is almost automatically convertible. But the automaticity is subject to the sterling area's machinery of constant negotiation of each member with the United Kingdom and the consolidation, though informal, of the area's machinery for central bank cooperation. This means that the sterling area has had to face on a somewhat smaller scale the very problems which continue to impede the achievement of an equally high degree of convertibility among all the currencies of the world, and that the answer reached so far for these problems within the area has necessarily differed from the techniques pursued by the United Kingdom in the days when the convertibility of sterling into dollars was maintained as a matter of course.

This new machinery—the machinery of international agreement on adjustment by *other than market disciplines*—is difficult to interpret. How permanent is it? How much is it likely to be extended or withdrawn? We are still too close to the problems which gave rise to it to have any certainty in answering these questions. Obviously, if the problems are transient ones, the machinery ought to be dismantled as the problems pass. A good case can be made out that between 1952 and 1955 the problems were passing and the machinery was being dismantled. Commodity markets were reopened in London, and have tended to replace government trading in basic commodities at negotiated prices. With the broad consolidation of transferable account sterling, and certain liberalizing measures in the handling of capital and invisible transactions, a large segment of exchange control has been eliminated.

Clearly, this trend reflects greater economic stability in international relations. Yet the argument that the basic problems have been overcome is not quite convincing. The period of improvement may be as transient as the preceding period of crisis. Was it produced by factors any less fortuitous than the factors producing six years of crisis? Perhaps we may look forward to a period of greater international economic stability *without anything particular being done to achieve it*. This would be the logical counterpart of the belief that the postwar difficulties up to now were born of the last world war, the Korean War, and some aspects of the cold war. But if the difficulties went beyond these important disturbing factors and included basic, even structural, imperfections in international monetary policy, then it is hard to see that the relative international equilibrium since 1952 has been achieved because of basic changes.

Advance toward sterling convertibility has been regarded by many as likely to reduce and eventually eliminate many of the bonds of the sterling area as we have known it. Yet many of the steps of the last few years may really be signs of a further reinforcement of the area's regionalism. First, though major London commodity markets have been reopened, only three (copper, lead and raw sugar) involved any lowering of the barrier between the sterling world and the rest of the world. Second, import programing in sterling countries followed the familiar previous priorities of preferring sterling sources first, other non-dollar sources next, and dollar sources last. Indeed, as sterling sources of supply continued to ease, the general trend was toward less resort to dollar sources. In the important field of consumer durable goods, the wall against dollar goods became more solid than ever. Third, the planning of economic development continued to be attuned to the objective of improving regional balance with the rest of the world.

This somewhat paradoxical situation in which the relaxation of controls on the international use of sterling may be interpreted either as an extension or a loosening of regionalism arises, at least in part, because of the difference between the concept of sterling as an international currency and the concept of sterling as the money of the Commonwealth, a political grouping of countries. This difference is often assumed not to exist, and, as mentioned before, under favorable circumstances perhaps need not be important—is not the strength of sterling in its regional role a support to its strength internationally, and is not its international strength a support to its regional usefulness? But in fact, policy makers have found it necessary to choose constantly between the two roles in deciding points of emphasis and priority. Granted that sterling's regional and international positions are interrelated, and even more that sterling's position as the national currency of the United Kingdom is embraced in that relationship, the practical question has arisen intermittently since the war and almost continuously since 1952 as to the order of steps which could and should be taken to reinforce the prestige of sterling in any context. The general problem in deliberations of policy has been whether to make sterling more like what it was in the gold standard days or to move along lines that would bolster the economic aspect of Commonwealth political relations. The position of Canada, a dollar country in the Commonwealth, is a constant source of difficulty in generalizing about the sterling-Commonwealth relationship. In financial matters, the Canadian position had been roughly similar to that of the United States. At the same time, Canada is one of the major pillars of the Commonwealth. A fuller study of the special features of this relationship would throw light on the political significance of the sterling area and the nature of the choice between global and regional aims. All we can do here, and in the analysis that follows, is to bear in mind that Canada's position as a Commonwealth dollar country is an anomalous one.

The issue of global or regional emphasis is always there in the familiar arguments about sterling policy, though often only implicitly. Sometimes the implicit decisions on this issue and two other vital related ones have not been recognized at all. For instance, the historic Commonwealth communiqué of 1952 reenshrined the objective of an internationally convertible sterling in a world of multilateral trade, but perhaps the most significant step envisaged in gaining this objective was to coordinate Commonwealth investment policies so as to make the sterling area less dependent on the rest of the world, especially the dollar world. Whether putting economic development on a Commonwealth basis would lead to an internationally convertible sterling was seen partly, perhaps largely, as a problem for the rest of the world, especially the United States. The "Sterling

Commonwealth"—a term used in the 1952 communiqué—would make its currency regionally solid; the rest of the world could de-regionalize sterling if it were willing to take the necessary steps.

The Lack of Credit

Credit means faith. Webster defines it as "reliance on the truth or reality of something; belief; faith; trust." By way of illustration it adds the biblical passage: "When Jonathan and the people heard these words, they gave no credit unto them, nor received them."

A striking but little noted feature of the New York money market—the world's largest—is that it accommodates only a small fraction of world trade. The volume of world trade and services is now about $100 billion; foreign short-term claims reported by United States banks and traders in 1954 amounted to less than $2 billion.

It has been long argued in the sterling world that the price of gold should be raised in the United States, as one means of providing a greater amount of credit. Since this step would have direct effects on the internal monetary structure of the United States, it has been consistently resisted. But no alternative means of expanding credit have as yet been devised. When the International Monetary Fund began work just after the war, the value of world trade was roughly $20 billion and the assets of the Fund were some $8 billion. These assets were to be seen later as grossly inadequate for the task of postwar monetary stabilization, but at the time they appeared large. The growth of postwar world trade has made it clear that a fund of $8 billion could hardly scratch the surface of the credit requirements of world trade. This lack of credit for the finance of international trade probably accounts more than any other single factor for the arbitrary measures which most of the major trading nations have taken in handling their balance of payments.

The official policy of the United States, and for that matter of the International Monetary Fund, has been to oppose import restrictions and to support the convertibility of currencies at fixed exchange rates. The available funds for the financing of world trade, let alone for reconstruction and development, have fallen far short of the needs. United States foreign aid has filled part of the gap. The volume of aid to the whole world has been more than six times the resources of the International Monetary Fund and a still greater multiple of the Fund's resources that were actually used. But American aid has been only an *ad hoc* substitute for credit and has not created a lasting pool of financial fluidity that is the essence of a credit structure.

Major international financial markets have not been geared to the needs of world trade. The international credit output of the United States (apart from government aid) is probably the most striking example of the present dearth of credit. With by far the largest financial market in the world, it provides only a small fraction of the financing required for international trade. Almost the same comment would be true of London, although London has traditionally been oriented to an international market. Since the war London's credit facilities have not notably expanded. The sterling holdings of all countries at the end of 1945 were £3.7 billion; at the end of 1954 the figure was £3.9 billion. Balances had changed hands, of course, and credit flowed in and out, but the ceiling was rather low. And there was no appreciable addition to the funds available.

The presumption can be made that most world trade is financed either in dollars or sterling. The inference from the limited activity of British and American credit agencies is that an increasingly growing portion of world trade is financed in ways other than through the banks of these two major centers. There also seems to be the strong implication that the lack of credit availabilities in the free markets has a strong bearing on the postwar tendency in the Western world for countries to adopt administrative rather than market measures in their attempts to establish a tolerable balance in their transactions in the international market.

It seems clear that the volume of world trade has grown far beyond the amount which the United Kingdom and its sterling associates could support at the present level of their economic development. World trade is a little larger than the entire production of the sterling area. It also seems clear that the United States, whose own production is about four times the size of world trade, is far more preoccupied with domestic finance than with international finance. The blunt conclusion seems to be that Britain, though pervasively implicated in world trade both in fact and in tradition, is not in a position to provide for more than a sector of its finance, and that the United States, though financially capable of it, understandably concentrates on the concerns of its own huge domestic market.

The United States and the Commonwealth

Most students of international finance regard the sterling-dollar relationship as the central problem. Throughout this century it has dominated the thinking of the Western world on matters of international finance. More specifically it has dominated official and scholarly thinking in the United States as to what would be the most satisfactory structure of world financial relations. The unprecedented international negotiations which culminated in the Bretton Woods agreements turned on this relationship, and the crucial question in Congressional debates, involving a United States decision to put several billion dollars into this untried enterprise, was whether it would bring about a livable and productive relationship between dollars and sterling. Some of the most astute scholars and politicians felt at the time that the fundamental importance of the sterling-dollar problem had to be faced directly and solved *before* the broader structure aimed at in the Fund arrangements could succeed. The entire program of United States aid to the war-torn allies, in its financial aspects, was focused on this problem. The loan to Britain, which preceded the Marshall Plan, showed the priority of the dollar-sterling problem in American policy. In the arrangements which the United States sponsored for European economic unity, a central and recurrent question was the role of sterling. Sterling has been the major worry of the American businesses, both large and small, operating abroad since the war, and most of the larger ones have on their staffs financial experts to advise them on the state of sterling-dollar relationships.

The immediate basis for this interest of the dollar world in the sterling world is the importance of the commerce between them, but the underlying basis is more complex and involves not only these important commercial interests but also the political, social, and cultural aspects of a very large part of the world. Sterling is only one facet, though an important one, of that world. The fact that sterling can be exchanged into dollars only in accordance with the discretionary regulations of sterling area governments has, in the postwar period, underlined the importance of the financial facet. But it still is only one facet of the deeper relationship between the dollar and sterling worlds. And these "worlds" embrace a large part of the people living on this planet.

* * * *

We have been made aware of the continuous slow changes of the contours of the earth's seas and shores. The swifter changes in the contours of its peoples as they vie in efforts to secure their living is less familiar. Just as Rachel Carson in *The Sea Around Us* shows her great gift for making the geophysical drifts of the planet less obscure, so Dudley Stamp, the British geographer, shows a similar ability to make the complicated drifts of its peoples more understandable in his remarkable book *Our Undeveloped World.*

Population statistics of the world are not credible before 1650. Since then and in contrast to prevalent notions, Stamp calls attention to the fact that the white population of the world has increased about four times as fast as the average rate of increase of the world's population. The implication seems to be that the higher standard of living achieved in this white world provides a far better basis for expanding families than the low—or even marginal—standards of most of the world.

This picture may be changed, and in a way that will strongly influence the nature of the relations between the United States and the Commonwealth of Nations. In Nigeria and Ceylon, for example, the medical achievement of getting rid of the anopheles mosquito has almost eradicated malaria, and in so doing has dramatically lowered death rates. The result has been a large increase in the rate of population growth in the so-called populous areas which in the West were regarded as backward and most in need of help.

The long-range relevance of these developments to the international position of sterling may not be easy to see, but in my judgment it is decisive. Britain's present problem as leader of the Commonwealth is one of almost unaccountable complexity. The future of sterling lies primarily in the future of the Commonwealth. This is the opposite of the familiar theme that the future of sterling will determine the future of the Commonwealth. International monetary arrangements are the result rather than the cause of international associations. An association without a satisfactory world money might find commerce with the rest of the world uncomfortable, and this to a large extent has been the postwar experience of the sterling area. But an international money, without a strong association to support it, would be an anomaly. The main interest of the United States in "sterling" is not a technical monetary interest. It is rather in "sterling" as it reflects the financial aspect of an important, and at present the most effective, worldwide association.

Appendix

COMMONWEALTH ECONOMIC CONFERENCE COMMUNIQUE

The following communique was issued in London on December 11, 1952, at the conclusion of the Commonwealth Economic Conference.[1]

1. The Commonwealth Economic Conference which ended today was covened with the aim of concerting measures for increasing the economic strength of the Commonwealth countries, including the Colonial Territories, and creating conditions in which their peoples can play their part in securing prosperity and contentment for themselves and for the world.

2. In recent years the Sterling Area has been faced with recurrent economic crises which have forced its members to take emergency measures of trade and exchange restriction. These measures were necessary but they have inevitably tended to frustrate long-term economic expansion on which our hopes and opportunities for the future are founded. This was recognized at the January meeting of the Commonwealth Finance Ministers. Measures taken in accordance with the conclusions of that meeting have, however, enabled the present Conference to decide that a more positive policy can now be adopted, both by the Commonwealth countries themselves and in concert with other friendly countries, to promote expansion of world production and trade.

3. The Conference agreed that the Commonwealth countries would work together to achieve certain broad common objectives. They have no intention of seeking the creation of a discriminatory economic bloc, rather their object is by strengthening themselves to benefit the world economy generally.

Accordingly, the following principles were agreed upon as governing the approach to a whole range of subjects under discussion:—

[1] Official text released in mimeographed form, December 13, 1952.

(a) Internal economic policies designed to curb inflation and rises in the cost of living should be steadily followed.
(b) Sound economic development should be encouraged with the object of increasing productive strength and competitive power, providing employment and raising standards of life.
(c) A multilateral trade and payment system should be extended over the widest possible area.

4. Application of these principles will require individual action by the Commonwealth Governments, cooperation among them and international action with other trading nations and existing international organizations.

Internal Measures

5. All Commonwealth Governments have agreed to persevere in their efforts to curb inflation. Inflationary conditions frustrate the progress of sound development both by increasing its cost and by destroying savings necessary to finance it. Moreover, they damage the external balance by stimulating excessive imports and by diverting to internal use goods which would otherwise be available for export.

6. An adequate and stable external balance must be a first objective for all Governments. Failure to achieve this means repeated crises, a continuously rising cost of living, a constant threat to employment and failure to develop resources effectively. The Conference welcomed the improvement which had taken place in the balance of payments both of the individual Sterling Area countries and of the Sterling Area as a whole, following upon the conclusions reached by the Commonwealth Finance Ministers at their meeting in January, 1952. It noted with satisfaction that the Sterling Area would achieve balance with the rest of the world in the second half of this year. It was agreed, however, that the achievement, while reassuring, was only the first step towards a stable balance for the Sterling Area. Policies were agreed upon for 1953 which it is hoped will lead to further improvement in reserves during that year. Nevertheless, while there has been steady improvement, the level of reserves is as yet too low to warrant any substantial relaxation of restrictions on imports from outside the Sterling Area.

7. The Conference considered the extensive restrictions which some countries of the sterling Commonwealth have needed to impose upon imports from the United Kingdom and other Com-

monwealth sources. There was agreement that the restrictions imposed because of the balance of payments problems should be relaxed as the external financial position of the countries improved. In considering the whole problem the Governments concerned would have clearly in mind the difficulties which restrictions have raised for export industries affected.

8. The economic and social objectives of the Commonwealth countries, individually and in association, depend upon their ability to produce and supply under competitive conditions an expanding flow of exports. There was, therefore, general agreement in the Conference on the vital need to expand the earning power of all the Sterling countries.

Development Policy

9. Throughout the Commonwealth there is wide scope for expanding production of essential supplies which the whole world needs—food and agricultural products, minerals and engineering products—and improving the means for transporting them. This development of the basic essentials has on occasion been impeded by other development of a less sound and permanent kind, which has overtaxed the countries' resources and has failed to contribute to the building of economic strength. The Conference agreed that in the Sterling Area countries development should be concentrated on projects which directly or indirectly contribute to the improvement of the area's balance of payments with the rest of the world. Such projects should strengthen the economy of the countries concerned and increase their competitive power in world markets and so, by improving their balance of payments, bring increasing prosperity to their peoples. In some countries of the area, however, development plans have been or are being made to provide for some basic improvement in standards of living which is a necessary foundation for further economic development. Some social investment is also urgently needed in the more developed countries, certain of which have rapidly increasing populations. The Conference recognized the need in such cases for these types of investment.

10. To enable development to go forward, a sufficient flow of savings must be provided in the countries undertaking the development and also in other countries which are ready to invest their savings there. The amount of savings which will be available from external sources will at best be small in relation to the size of the development programmes of countries of the Sterling

Commonwealth and it is therefore essential that these countries should themselves adopt policies which increase the flow of savings. Although this is inevitably a slow process for countries with low incomes and little margin above the basic needs for existence, the process of development will itself increase income and increase the flow of savings.

11. The United Kingdom is the traditional source of external capital for Commonwealth investment and has special responsibilities in the Colonial territories. The United Kingdom Government are determined that the flow of capital from London for sound development throughout the Commonwealth shall be maintained and increased. This will only be possible if the United Kingdom can sustain the necessary level of internal savings and can achieve a surplus on overseas account additional to that required to meet its heavy existing commitments.

12. The United Kingdom Government have however undertaken to make a special effort to provide additional capital for Commonwealth development by facilitating the financing of schemes in other Commonwealth countries which will contribute to the improvement of the Sterling area's balance of payments. The Conference took note that the United Kingdom Government would wish before making any of this additional finance available for Commonwealth development to be sure that the country concerned was itself devoting an adequate part of its resources to investment designed to improve the Sterling area's balance of payments, and was ready to make a sufficient contribution towards the particular scheme in question to ensure that both countries had an interest in seeing that it was carried through as efficiently and economically as possible.

13. The Conference welcomed the proposal by a group of important financial, industrial and commercial concerns in the United Kingdom to form a company to further development in other countries of the Commonwealth and the colonial empire. It was pleased to note that an announcement by this group is being issued today. The Conference also welcomed a statement by the United Kingdom representatives that the United Kingdom Government intend to discuss with the International Bank for Reconstruction and Development arrangements to give effect to their decision to make sterling available for lending by the Bank, for projects designed to improve the sterling area's balance of payments.

14. The Conference recognized the important contribution which investors outside the sterling area, particularly in the United States, can make to economic development in the sterling area and agreed that every effort should be made to create conditions which would encourage such investment. It further agreed that all sterling area Governments should strive to attain this by reducing such obstacles as controls over the movements of capital across the exchanges. The United Kingdom Government have reviewed the right which is now enjoyed by residents outside the sterling area who have invested capital in approved projects in the United Kingdom and colonial empire since 1st January 1950 to transfer their capital across the exchanges. At present this right only extends to the sterling equivalent of the initial investment. The United Kingdom Government informed the Conference that they have decided that henceforth it shall extend also to capital profits.

Commodity policy

15. The Conference recognized that there was no one universal remedy for the problem of instability of prices for primary commodities. Each commodity must be considered on its merits in the light of the conditions prevailing at the time, and the circumstances must determine what form of arrangements would be appropriate. The Conference agreed that violent fluctuations and an uneconomic level of prices for primary commodities were against the interest of consumers as well as producers. All Commonwealth Governments are therefore ready to cooperate in considering, commodity by commodity, international schemes designed to ensure stability of demand and prices at an economic level. They also recognize the need for an agreed procedure for calling together the Governments concerned to consider emergency action in the event of rapidly developing conditions of surplus or shortage of commodities entering into international trade.

Imperial Preference

16. There was general recognition at the Conference of the value of existing preferences. On the initiative of the United Kingdom a discussion took place on a proposal that all Commonwealth countries should join in seeking release from the "No new preference" rule in the General Agreement on Tariffs and Trade (G.A.T.T.), and this United Kingdom proposal was supported by the representatives of some countries. The representatives of

other countries felt that such an approach would not advance the agreed objective of restoring multilateral world trade and the Conference was therefore unable to support it. All Commonwealth Governments agreed, however, to cooperate with the United Kingdom Government in an approach to the other contracting parties to the G.A.T.T. to meet particular difficulties arising on the United Kingdom tariff. The object would be to enable the United Kingdom, consistently with the basic provisions of the G.A.T.T., to continue the duty-free entry for Commonwealth goods notwithstanding any increases that might from time to time become necessary in duties designed to protect domestic industry and agriculture in the United Kingdom. The Commonwealth Governments also agreed to consider sympathetically certain special tariff problems affecting the Colonies.

International Action

17. Resolute action in accordance with the conclusions recorded above will in itself do much to strengthen the economies of the sterling Commonwealth countries, but this is not enough. Action in a wider sphere is also necessary. The Conference therefore agreed to seek the cooperation of other countries in a plan to create the conditions for expanding world production and trade. The aim is to secure international agreement on the adoption of policies by creditor and debtor countries which will restore balance in the world economy on the lines of "Trade, not aid" and will by progressive stages and within reasonable time create an effective multilateral trade and payments system covering the widest possible area.

Trade

18. The plan envisages positive international action for the progressive removal, as circumstances permit, of import restrictions imposed for the purpose of bringing a country's external accounts into balance. Action will be required by both creditor and debtor countries. The rate of progress in removing discrimination will depend upon the advance towards equilibrium between the United States and the rest of the world.

19. The sterling Commonwealth countries will not all be able to remove restrictions at the same time. In particular the representatives of some countries have emphasized that they must continue to use their exchange resources in the manner which enables them to carry out their planned development pro-

grammes most effectively, and that they are likely to continue to need import restrictions for this purpose.

Finance

20. The Conference agreed that it is important not only for the United Kingdom and the sterling area but also for the world that sterling should resume its full role as a medium of world trade and exchange. An integral part of any effective multilateral system is the restoration of the convertibility of sterling but it can only be reached by progressive stages. The achievement of convertibility will depend fundamentally upon three conditions:

(a) the continuing success of the action by sterling Commonwealth countries themselves, as outlined above;
(b) the prospect that trading nations will adopt trade policies which are conducive to the expansion of world trade, and
(c) the availability of adequate financial support through the International Monetary Fund or otherwise.

Procedure

21. It is proposed to seek acceptance of this plan by the Governments of the United States and of European countries whose cooperation is essential, and to work as far as possible through existing international institutions dealing with finance and trade.

22. The timing of the successive stages of this plan cannot be decided at present. This can only be judged as the necessary conditions are satisfactorily fulfilled.

Conclusion

23. The Conference is happy to be able to present this account of the confident understanding which exists between members of the Commonwealth, and the wide measure of agreement which they have been able to achieve over the whole range of economic policy. The aims of their cooperation are entirely consistent with their close ties with the United States and the members of the Organization for European Economic Cooperation. The Commonwealth countries look outward to similar cooperation with other countries, not inward to a closed association. It is their common purpose by their own efforts and together with others to increase world trade for the mutual benefit of all peoples.

BIBLIOGRAPHY: AN ACCOUNT OF HELP FROM OTHER WORKS

Literature about sterling is voluminous and rapidly growing, reflecting the breadth of interest throughout the world in sterling problems. Almost every issue of a scholarly journal or a financial periodical presents an essay of interest. A comprehensive catalog would be close to an encyclopedia of finance and would fill many pages. Here the notes on the works of others must be confined to essays which proved particularly helpful in the span of this project. I hope the notes will serve to express thanks to these authors, and offer an invitation to readers of this book to pursue their interest in sterling through studies they may have missed.

For the Broad Setting

The hardest part of studying the meaning of sterling in world finance is to get a sense of the worldwide arrangement of which it is a part. The context is a broad one. I derived much help from the following books:

WILLIAMS, JOHN H. *Post-War Monetary Plans.* Oxford: Blackwell, 1949. 395 p.

This book brings together in an English edition a number of Professor Williams' major essays written between 1929 and 1948. They are still fresh.

VINER, JACOB. *The Customs Union Issue.* New York: Carnegie Endowment for International Peace, 1950. 221 p.

This is an exceptionally lucid treatment of the complicated arguments for and against countries' getting together to establish freer trade with one another than with the rest of the world.

MEADE, J. E. *Problems of Economic Union.* Chicago: University of Chicago Press, 1953. 102 p.

A provocative account of the problems posed by the practices of economic unions.

TOYNBEE, ARNOLD. *The World and the West.* New York: Oxford University Press, 1953. 99 p.

Professor Toynbee's short volume of lectures given over the British Broadcasting System offers, in capsulated form, an account of the broad impact of the "Western" world on the civilization of the whole world.

FRANKEL, S. HERBERT. *The Economic Impact on Underdeveloped Societies.* Cambridge: Harvard University Press, 1953. 179 p.

This is a thoughtful essay which poses some of the hard economic problems of "development" as a process of material growth against the harder cultural problems of development "for what?"

STAMP, L. DUDLEY. *Our Underdeveloped World.* London: Faber, 1953. 186 p.

This short book is an extraordinary exposition of the world's demographic and agricultural trends and was helpful to me in the effort to interpret the influence of the Commonwealth and the United States in the world.

THOMPSON, WARREN S. *Population Problems.* 4th ed. New York: McGraw-Hill, 1953. 488 p.

This standard book takes a gloomy view of Britain's future, but presents the facts for differing judgments.

The Sterling Area as a Whole

As noted a number of times in the text, a difficulty in studying the sterling area is that there are few works which treat the area as an entity. But there are exceptions:

ROBERTSON, DENNIS H. *Britain in the World Economy.* London: Allen and Unwin, 1954. 92 p.

These graceful essays set forth the troubles and strengths of the sterling association as seen by an economist who has grappled with sterling problems for a long time.

BANK FOR INTERNATIONAL SETTLEMENTS (Monetary and Economic Department). *The Sterling Area,* Basle, 1953. 92 p.

This critique of sterling arrangements brings together prewar and postwar trends effectively.

U.S. ECONOMIC COOPERATION ADMINISTRATION (Special Mission to the United Kingdom). *The Sterling Area: An American Analysis.* John M. Cassels, director. London, 1951. 672 p.

This study is a careful exposition of the history and operations of the sterling countries as financial associates.

CONAN, A. R. *The Sterling Area.* New York: St. Martin's Press, 1952. 192 p.

A provocative treatment of sterling area trade trends.

CRICK, W. F. *Origin and Development of the Sterling Area.* London: Institute of Bankers, 1948. 19 p.

——. *The Sterling Area During and After the War.* London: Institute of Bankers, 1948. 19 p.

These pamphlets are particularly effective in presenting an exposition of the cohesive effects of sterling area traditions.

There are a number of good brief accounts of how the sterling area operates *as an area:*

HEATHERINGTON, DONALD F. "The Sterling Area (A Study of Monetary and Exchange Policy)." *International Reference Service,* (United States Department of Commerce), v. 2, no. 32 (November 1945).

PEP (Political and Economic Planning). "The Sterling Area." *Planning,* nos. 331 and 332 (July 23 and August 12, 1951).

SPEARMAN, DIANA. *The Sterling Area.* London: Conservative Political Centre, 1953. 48 p.

A number of doctoral theses and conversations with their authors were helpful:

BELL, PHILIP W. *The Sterling Area in the Postwar World: Internal Mechanism and Cohesion 1946-1952.* New York: Oxford University Press, 1956. Originally submitted to Princeton University.

GARDNER, RICHARD. *Sterling-Dollar Diplomacy: Anglo-American Collaboration in the Reconstruction of Multilateral Trade.* New York: Oxford University Press, 1956. Originally submitted to Oxford University.

I had the privilege of examining both the Bell and Gardner books in their original unpublished versions.

WHITELAW, R. J. *The Sterling Area as a Changing Mechanism of Financing International Transactions.* Unpublished. Submitted to the University of London, 1952.

WRIGHT, KENNETH M. *The Sterling Area Dollar Pool.* Unpublished. Submitted to Columbia University, 1954. A resumé of this study was published under the title "Dollar Pooling in the Sterling Area, 1939-1952," *American Economic Review,* v. 44 (September 1954), pp. 559-576.

ZUPNICK, ELLIOT. *Britain's Postwar Dollar Problem, 1946-1951: A Study in International Disequilibrium.* Unpublished. Submitted to Columbia University, 1954. A resumé of this study was published under the title, "The Sterling Area's Central Pooling System Re-examined" in the *Quarterly Journal of Economics,* v. 69 (February 1955), pp. 71-84. This is to be published by Columbia University Press, probably in the Fall of 1956.

History

In striving for some degree of historical perspective in this project, Walter J. Sedwitz, my assistant, and I found the following works of help:

ANDREADES, A. *History of the Bank of England.* London: King, 1935. 455 p.

A detailed account of the development of central banking in Britain, drawn against the background of trade and financial crises.

BEER, M. *Early British Economics.* London: Allen and Unwin, 1938. 250 p.

An analysis of the development of economic thought in the pre-mercantilist period.

CHALMERS, GEORGE. *An Estimate of the Comparative Strength of Great Britain.* London, 1810.

An early statistical effort to analyze British trade by geographic areas.

CLAPHAM, JOHN. *A Concise Economic History of Britain.* Cambridge: Cambridge University Press, 1949. 324 p.

A factual and analytical account of British development from medieval to modern times.

CLARK, G. N. *The Wealth of England from 1496 to 1760.* London: Oxford University Press, 1946. 199 p.

An analysis, with statistics, of the industrial revolution in Britain and the growth of international trade in the nineteenth century.

DACEY, W. MANNING. *The British Banking Mechanism.* London: Hutchinson House, 1951. 203 p.

A description of the British banking mechanism, with a discussion of the historical antecedents.

DE VEGH, IMRE. *The Pound Sterling: A Study of the Sterling Area.* New York: Scudder, Stevens and Clark, 1939. 130 p.

DIETZ, FREDERICK C. *An Economic History of England.* New York: Holt, 1942. 616 p.

This work traces the development of the British economy from its early Anglo-Saxon beginnings to the twentieth century. There is a thorough discussion of the impact of commercial and technological changes in the sixteenth and seventeenth centuries.

FEAVEARYEAR, A. E. *The Pound Sterling.* London: Oxford University Press, 1931. 367 p.

This study, rich in facts, traces the history of British finance from the cycle of debasement in the thirteenth century to the abandonment of the gold standard in 1931. Its focus is on the role of monetary factors in the history of trade cycles.

GAYER, ARTHUR D., and others. *Growth and Fluctuation of the British Economy, 1790-1950.* Oxford: Clarendon Press, 1953. 2 v.

An empirical study of British commercial crises in the first half of the nineteenth century, with copious statistics on industry, agriculture, trade, finance, and prices.

HAWTREY, R. G. *A Century of Bank Rate.* New York: Longmans, 1937. 328 p.

An analysis of the role of Bank rate in British monetary policy, and a critique of nineteenth century monetary debates.

LEAGUE OF NATIONS. Economic, Financial and Transit Department. *International Currency Experience,* (by Ragnar Nurkse). 1944. II. A. 4. (Princeton): League of Nations, 1944. 249 p.

PUMPHREY, LOWELL. *The Exchange Equalisation Account of Great Britain.* Unpublished thesis. Submitted to Princeton University, 1941.

A detailed account of the operation of the flexible sterling rate in the thirties, and the reasons why the rate was not very flexible in practice.

ROSTOW, W. W. *British Economy in the 19th Century.* Oxford: Clarendon Press, 1948. 240 p.

An analysis of British trade cycles, 1799-1914, against the background of long-run trends and with particular attention to the influence of investment.

TREVELYAN, G. M. *English Social History.* New York: Longmans, 1943. 628 p.

This study puts in perspective the social and economic foundations of the British economy from medieval to modern times.

VINER, JACOB. *Studies in the Theory of International Trade.* New York: Harper, 1937. 650 p.

This collection of essays includes a synthesis of economic thought in the Middle Ages and in early modern times. The focus is on the wide differences in economic doctrine during the mercantilist period and on the extent of anticipation of later theories and policies.

WAIGHT, LEONARD. *The History and Mechanism of the Exchange Equalisation Account.* London: Cambridge University Press, 1939. 191 p.

A thorough coverage of the operations of this official institution created to stabilize the sterling exchange rate after the abandonment of the gold standard.

Britain, the Metropole

In this book the account of Britain is based mainly on an inspection of official publications, cited at the end of this bibliographical note, and on personal interviews with British economists, government officials, and financial reporters. Beyond these sources, many books, articles and pamphlets were helpful. This huge literature can be readily discovered through standard reference procedures; an effort to catalog it would be out of place here. But a few notes on works which helped me throughout the project are in order.

HAWTREY, R. G. *The Balance of Payments and the Standard of Living.* London: Oxford University Press, for the Royal Institute of International Affairs, 1950. 158 p.

A good critique of the relationship, constantly troublesome in the internationally committed British economy, between internal and external financial policies.

SAYERS, R. S., ed. *Banking in the British Commonwealth.* Oxford: Clarendon Press, 1952. 486 p.

Revealing essays in Commonwealth financial relations as centered on sterling.

WORSWICK, G. D. N., and P. H. ADY, eds. *The British Economy, 1945-1950.* Oxford: Clarendon Press, 1952. 621 p.

The editors, who have also contributed essays to the volume, have brought together the views of leading contemporary British economists on both the domestic and international aspects of Britain's economic position in the world. An excellent compendium, with an expression of many points of view.

As contributions to the elusive problem of maintaining even keel for an island economy rocked between outside and inside forces, I gained many insights from the following essays:

BILLEWICZ, W. Z. "The Import Content of British Exports," *Economica,* n. s., v. 20 (1953), pp. 162-169.

BLAGBURN, C. H. "Import-replacement by British Agriculture," *Economic Journal,* v. 60 (March 1950), pp. 19-45.

FLEMING, J. MARCUS. "Regional Organization of Trade and Payments," *American Economic Review,* v. 42 (May 1952), Supplement: Papers and Proceedings, pp. 345-358.

HEATHERINGTON, D. F. "Sterling Balances and Britain's External Debt," *Foreign Commerce Weekly,* October 28, November 4, and November 11, 1944.

KATZ, SAMUEL I. "Sterling Instability and the Postwar Sterling System," *The Review of Economics and Statistics,* v. 31 (February 1954), pp. 81-87.

——. "Sterling's Recurring Postwar Payments Crises," *The Journal of Political Economy,* v. 63 (June 1955), pp. 216-226.

MORGAN, E. VICTOR. "The National Debt and Monetary Policy," *Lloyds Bank Review,* n. s., no. 37 (July 1955), pp. 18-33.

PAISH, F. W. "Sources of Finance for British Industry," *Financial Times* (London), July 6, 1953 (Special Issue to Commemorate 20,000th Issue).

——. "The Sterling Area Crisis," *International Affairs,* v. 28 (July 1952), pp. 323-350.

——. "The United Kingdom as a Source of Capital," *District Bank Review,* no. 105 (March 1953), pp. 3-27.

ROBBINS, LIONEL. *The Balance of Payments.* The Stamp Memorial Lecture delivered before the University of London on Nov. 20, 1951. London: Athlone Press, 1951. 32 p.

ROBINSON, E. A. G. "The Changing Structure of the British Economy," *Economic Journal,* v. 64 (September 1954), pp. 443-461.

The Independent Sterling Area

As mentioned in the preceding notes on the metropole, the richest sources of facts and ideas about the independent countries were personal interviews with officials, economists, businessmen, and journalists in the various countries. Much of this information was off the cuff and not citable. Of published books and articles, I found the following very worthwhile and a useful counterbalance to impressions formed in considering sterling area problems from the point of view of the metropole.

BENHAM, FREDERIC. "The Colombo Plan," *Economica,* n. s., v. 21 (May 1954), pp. 93-112.

BUTLIN, S. J. *Foundations of the Australian Monetary System, 1788-1851.* Melbourne: Melbourne University Press, 1953. 727 p.

COPLAND, DOUGLAS. *Problems of the Sterling Area with Special Reference to Australia.* Princeton University, International Finance Section, 1954. 28 p. (Essays in International Finance, 17).

FRANKLIN, N. N. "South Africa's Balance of Payments and the Sterling Area 1939-1950" *Economic Journal,* v. 61 (June 1951), pp. 290-309.

INTERNATIONAL MONETARY FUND. *Economic Development with Stability: A Report to the Government of India.* Washington, 1953. 77 p.

MELVILLE, L. G. "Convertibility of Sterling," *The Australian Quarterly,* v. 26 (September 1954), pp. 12-24.

MERRY, D. H. "Australia as a Factor in the Sterling Area," *Lloyds Bank Review,* n. s., no. 37 (July 1955), pp. 34-46.

PERKINS, J. O. N. "Australia in the Sterling Area," *The Banker,* v. 100 (January 1954), pp. 38-42.

——. "Monetary Policy in the Sterling Dominions," *The Banker,* v. 103 (October 1954), pp. 230-234.

ROWAN, DAVID. "Central Banking in the Commonwealth," *Banca Nazionale del Lavoro Quarterly Review,* no. 25 (April-June 1953), pp. 130-142.

The Dependencies

Here again personal interviews were by far the richest source of information and ideas. In the large volume of printed literature, I found the works listed below helpful in giving thoughtful guidance in my outsider's effort to understand the position of the colonies in the sterling world.

ALPORT, C. J. M. "Kenya's Answer to the Mau Mau Challenge," *African Affairs,* v. 53 (July 1954), pp. 241-247.

THE BANKER. *Monetary Systems of the Colonies.* A revised edition of eight articles appearing in *The Banker,* July 1948-February 1949.

GREAT BRITAIN. BRITISH INFORMATION SERVICES. *Towards Self-Government in the British Colonies.* B. I. S. Reference Division, no. I.D. 598 (revised), January 1950. 59 p.

——. *Britain's Colonial Policy and Record.* B. I. S. Reference Division, no. I.D. 1157, October 1952. 18 p.

GREAT BRITAIN. COLONIAL OFFICE. *The Colonial Territories, 1952-53.* Cmd. 8856. London: HMSO, 1953. 157 p.

——. *The Colonial Territories, 1953-54.* Cmd. 9169. London: HMSO, 1954. 196 p.

GREAVES, IDA. *Colonial Monetary Conditions.* Colonial Research Studies, no. 10. London: HMSO, 1953. 95 p.

——. *The Colonial Sterling Balances.* Princeton University, International Finance Section, 1954. 21 p. (Essays in International Finance, 20).

——. "The Character of British Colonial Trade," *Journal of Political Economy,* v. 62 (February 1954), pp. 1-11.

LEGUM, COLIN. *Must We Lose Africa?* London: W. H. Allen, 1954. 264 p.

MARS, J. "The Monetary and Banking System and the Loan Market of Nigeria," in M. Perham, ed., *Mining, Commerce and Finance in Nigeria,* v. 2 of *The Economics of a Tropical Dependency.* London: Faber, for Nuffield College, 1948. pp. 177-224.

MERIVALE, HERMAN. *Lectures on Colonization and Colonies.* (Delivered before the University of Oxford, 1839-1841.) London: Oxford University Press, 1948. 273 p.

Financial Problems

Almost all writing on international finance touches in some way on the broad problems dealt with in Chapter 8 of this book. A few of these studies have already been indicated in the text, but for convenience will be noted again here. In addition I am listing a few works which I found stimulating and helpful in the labyrinth of convertibility, dollar shortage, depression, discrimination, liquidity, and productivity. Other works cited in the notes and bibliographies of the works mentioned here cover broadly the literature which here must be neglected. I am particularly indebted to the works mentioned of Kindleberger, MacDougall, and Robertson (cited above).

BALOGH, T. *Dollar Crisis, Causes and Cure.* Oxford: Blackwell, 1949. 269 p.

BERNSTEIN, E. M. "American Productivity and the Dollar Payments Problem," *The Review of Economics and Statistics,* v. 37 (May 1955), pp. 101-109.

——. "Scarce Currencies and the International Monetary Fund," *Journal of Political Economy,* v. 53 (March 1945), pp. 1-14.

GAITSKELL, HUGH. "The Sterling Area," *International Affairs,* v. 28 (April 1952), pp. 170-176.

HABERLER, GOTTFRIED. *A Survey of International Trade Theory* Princeton University, International Finance Section, 1955. 68 p. (Special Papers in International Economics, 1).

HARROD, ROY. *The Pound Sterling.* Princeton University, International Finance Section, 1952. 42 p. (Essays in International Finance, 13).

——. *The Dollar.* New York: Harcourt, Brace, 1954. 156 p.

HUTTON, GRAHAM. *We Too Can Prosper.* New York: Macmillan, 1953. 248 p.

KINDLEBERGER, CHARLES P. *The Dollar Shortage.* Cambridge: Technology Press of Massachusetts Institute of Technology, and New York: Wiley, 1950. 276 p.

KNORR, KLAUS. "Market Instability and United States Policy," *Journal of Political Economy,* v. 62 (October 1954), pp. 375-389.

MACDOUGALL, G. D. A. "British and American Exports: A Study Suggested by the Theory of Comparative Costs," *Economic Journal,* v. 61 (1951), pp. 697-724, and v. 62 (1952), pp. 487-522.

——. "A Lecture on the Dollar Problem," *Economica,* n. s., v. 21 (August 1954), pp. 185-200.

PIQUET, HOWARD S. *Aid, Trade and the Tariff,* New York: Crowell, 1953. 358 p.

U. S. COMMISSION ON FOREIGN ECONOMIC POLICY. *Staff Papers.* Washington: GPO, 1954. 531 p.

The Future of Sterling

All of the works already cited bear on a judgment of the future of sterling. In the following section of this bibliographical note I call attention to some of the literature dealing directly and cogently with financial policies of the United States, of Britain, and of the sterling area.

Among British criticisms of sterling area policies, I found the following had arresting conceptions of the limits of future possibilities:

CAINE, SYDNEY. "Some Doubts about Sterling Area Policy," *Lloyds Bank Review,* no. 32 (April 1954), pp. 1-18.

CLAY, HENRY. "Britain's Declining Role in World Trade," *Foreign Affairs,* v. 24 (April 1946), pp. 411-428.

DAY, A. C. L. *The Future of Sterling.* Oxford: Clarendon Press, 1954. 227 p.

HAWTREY, R. G. *Towards the Rescue of Sterling;* London: Longmans, 1954. 159 p.

MAKINS, ROGER. "The World Since the War: The Third Phase," *Foreign Affairs,* v. 33 (October 1954), pp. 1-16.

I found many insights into general financial policy or particular aspects of it in the following works:

ARNDT, H. W., and J. O. N. PERKINS. "The Cost of Convertibility," *The Australian Quarterly,* v. 26 (December 1954), pp. 83-93.

BAREAU, PAUL. "The Future of the Sterling Area," *Lloyds Bank Review,* n. s., no. 23 (January 1952), pp. 1-16.

BEVERIDGE, WILLIAM. "British Exports and the Barometer," *Economic Journal,* v. 30 (1920), pp. 13-25, 209-213.

BLOOMFIELD, ARTHUR I. *Speculative Flight Movements of Capital in Postwar International Finance.* Princeton University, International Finance Section, 1954. 88 p. (Studies in International Finance, 3).

COHEN, JEROME B. "Economic Development in India," *Political Science Quarterly,* v. 68 (September, 1953), pp. 376-395.

DIEBOLD, WILLIAM, JR. *Trade and Payments in Western Europe: A Study in Economic Cooperation, 1947-1951.* New York: Harper for the Council on Foreign Relations, 1952. 488 p.

——. *The End of the I. T. O.* Princeton University, International Finance Section, 1952. 37 p. (Essays in International Finance, 16).

DOUGLAS, LEWIS H. *Report on Sterling.* Mimeographed. Released by White House Press Secretary, August 24, 1953.

ELLIS, HOWARD S. and LLOYD A. METZLER, eds. *Readings in the Theory of International Trade.* Philadelphia: Blakiston, 1949. 637 p.

Among the many useful essays by leading economists in this volume, I found Ragnar Nurkse's "Conditions of International Monetary Equilibrium" particularly helpful.

GRONDONA, L. ST. CLARE. *Commonwealth Stocktaking.* London: Butterworths Publications, 1953. 389 p.

HIRSCHMAN, A. O. "The Commodity Structure of World Trade," *Quarterly Journal of Economics,* v. 57 (1942-1943), pp. 565-595.

INTERNATIONAL CHAMBER OF COMMERCE. *Steps to Convertibility.* Council Statement and Sub-Committee Report, no. 163. Paris, 1953. 27 p.

LEONTIEFF, WASSILY. "Domestic Production and Foreign Trade; The American Capital Position Re-examined," *Proceedings of the American Philosophical Society,* v. 97 (September 1953).

MACDOUGALL, G. D. A. "Flexible Exchange Rates," *Westminster Bank Review,* August 1954, pp. 1-3.

MEADE, J. E. "The Convertibility of Sterling," *Three Banks Review,* no. 19 (September 1953), pp. 3-26.

NEVIN, EDWARD. "Social Priorities and the Flow of Capital," *Three Banks Review,* no. 19 (September 1953), pp. 27-43.

NURKSE, RAGNAR. *Some Aspects of Capital Accumulation in Underdeveloped Countries.* Cairo: National Bank of Egypt, 1952. 65 p.

ROBBINS, LIONEL. "Britain in the World Economy," *Financial Times* (London), July 6, 1953 (Special Issue to Commemorate the 20,000th Issue).

SALTER, ARTHUR. *Foreign Investment.* Princeton University, International Finance Section, 1951. 56 p. (Essays in International Finance, 12).

SARGENT, J. R. "The Background of Sterling Convertibility," *The Political Quarterly,* v. 26 (January-March 1955), pp. 55-65.

SHANNON, H. A. "The Sterling Balances of the Sterling Area, 1939-49," *Economic Journal,* v. 60 (September 1950), pp. 531-551.

TAMAGNA, FRANK M. and STEPHEN H. AXILROD. "United States Banks and Foreign Trade Financing," *Federal Reserve Bulletin,* v. 41 (April 1955), pp. 357-367.

VERNON, RAYMOND. *America's Foreign Trade Policy and the GATT.* Princeton University, International Finance Section, 1954. 25 p. (Essays in International Finance, 21).

VINER, JACOB. "Two Plans for International Monetary Stabilization," *Yale Review,* n. s., v. 33 (September 1943), pp. 77-107.

VINER, JACOB AND OTHERS. *The United States in a Multi-national Economy.* New York: The Council on Foreign Relations, 1945. 174 p.

WALKER, P. C. GORDON. "The Perfected Commonwealth," *New Commonwealth,* v. 28 (September 30, 1954), pp. 335-336.

Most of these titles speak for themselves, but I would like to add a few comments. Beveridge's essay presents a curious meteorological theory, related to the old sun-spot school, of a seventeen-year British export cycle. Diebold's studies give the detailed background of general European soft-currency policies, both commercial and financial. Grondona undertakes a factual examination of the extent to which the Commonwealth is short of self-sufficiency. Douglas' report was one of the first major advices of caution against premature sterling convertibility, offered in a season of over-optimism. Tamagna and Axilrod present some very arresting facts about the limitations of present international credit availabilities.

Finally, mention should be made of the official advisory views on the international economy and on United States policy made in the majority and minority reports of the Randall Commission:

U. S. COMMISSION ON FOREIGN ECONOMIC POLICY. *Report to the President and the Congress.* Washington: GPO, 1954. 94 p.
——. *Minority Report.* Washington: GPO, 1954. 24 p.

The majority report, which was disconcerting to those who hoped for bold recommendations of a free trade policy for the United States as a basis for a free financial policy in the sterling area, is an interesting analysis suggesting why haste in policy must be made slowly to be made at all. This, as I see it, has been the dollar counterpart of sterling area policy.

Statistics

The greater part of the statistical material used to illustrate arguments in this book comes from the series of official "white papers" published by the British Government. Although these are compiled as accounts of the United Kingdom and do not presume to be sterling area accounts, they nonetheless contain much useful information on the operations of the area as a whole.

I have relied on the standard semi-annual series of these papers:

GREAT BRITAIN. TREASURY. *United Kingdom Balance of Payments.* 1946 to 1950 (No. 2), Cmd. 8201; 1948 to 1951 (No. 2), Cmd. 8505; 1949 to 1952 (No. 2), Cmd. 8808; 1946 to 1953, Cmd. 8976; 1946 to 1953 (No. 2), Cmd. 9119; 1946 to 1954, Cmd. 9291; 1946 to 1954 (No. 2), Cmd. 9430. London: HMSO.

These papers are published first in the form of preliminary estimates for the last semester covered, with revised figures for preceding semesters. A succeeding paper does not necessarily replace the previous ones; figures may be given by quarters in earlier ones. The revisions made in preliminary estimates are ordinarily slight, and not of consequence in the interpretation of trends. Therefore, to save extensive arithmetic and delay in publication, some tables still show the preliminary figures from which they were originally calculated even though later revised figures appeared before the book went to press.

Along with this fundamental balance of payments series, there are two related white papers useful in interpreting external accounts of Britain:

GREAT BRITAIN. COLONIAL OFFICE. *Memorandum on the Sterling Assets of the British Colonies.* Colonial no. 298. London: HMSO, 1953. 17 p.

GREAT BRITAIN. TREASURY. *Reserves and Liabilities 1931 to 1945.* Cmd. 8354. London: HMSO, 1951.

The following documents provide important basic data about the British economy.

GREAT BRITAIN. TREASURY. *National Income and Expenditure of the United Kingdom 1938 to 1946.* Cmd. 7099. London: HMSO, 1947.

——. —— *1946 to 1951.* London: HMSO, 1952.

——. —— *1946 to 1952.* London: HMSO, 1953.

——. —— *1946 to 1953.* London: HMSO, 1954.

GREAT BRITAIN. PRIME MINISTER. *Economic Survey 1954.* Cmd. 9108. London: HMSO, 1954.

——. *Economic Survey 1955.* Cmd. 9412. London: HMSO, 1955.

I have also found useful the annual reports of the Bank for International Settlements (Basle, Switzerland) which uniformly give a careful analysis of international financial trends.

The treasuries, ministries of finance, and central banks of independent sterling countries regularly publish reports on their internal and external accounts, and can be easily obtained on request. Comparable information from the dependencies is available from their ministries of finance or their official statisticians.

No bibliographical note on sterling would be complete without a bow of thanks to *The Economist* for its broad and critical weekly reporting of the international scene. I have relied on it, but do not ask its editors to share the responsibility, for many ideas.

LIST OF TABLES

INDEX

This is a brief, analytical index that deals primarily with certain major issues. It is not exhaustive. The names of authors and works cited in the text, footnotes and bibliography are not repeated in this index. Nor does the index cover the tables which are separately listed on pages 282-283.